Praise for *VIVA M*

"With her extensive and illuminating research, Andrea Benoit tells the powerful story of a fearless company with heart. Harnessing the unbridled creativity that ran rampant in Toronto during M·A·C's formative years, 'the Franks' tapped into the pride and psyche of an entire society and inspired it to new artistic heights. Despite AIDS's dark shadow, Benoit paints a compelling portrait of an exhilarating fashion era, illustrating how courage and compassion can exist on a corporate level when hearts and minds are open and passionate."

JEANNE BEKER, journalist, author, and style editor

"This book is highly original, as there is no other sociocultural or business history of M·A·C. Benoit fuses a detailed historical record of M·A·C, AIDS within a setting of entrepreneurship, and the Toronto fashion scene in a readable and enjoyable style that is framed within relevant critical theories that support and explain these histories. This is a work that should be much referenced."

ALEXANDRA PALMER, Nora E. Vaughan senior curator, textiles and costume, Royal Ontario Museum

"This is a story that needs to be told. Today's generation of fashion students has no history of the losses the industry faced in the 1980s and 1990s as the AIDS epidemic was ravishing every level of the fashion and the arts industries. *VIVA M·A·C* gives a thorough account of how we got to where we are today."

SUSAN BAXTER, associate professor of marketing and dean of graduate studies, LIM College

"What happens when a company engages in 'cause marketing' long before that concept is widely known or practised? Benoit tells this fascinating story with panache, analytical rigour, and far-ranging historical investigation."

DANIEL J. ROBINSON, associate professor of media studies, Western University

VIVA M·A·C

AIDS, Fashion, and the Philanthropic Practices of M·A·C Cosmetics

Andrea Benoit

UNIVERSITY OF TORONTO PRESS
Toronto Buffalo London

© University of Toronto Press 2019
Toronto Buffalo London
utorontopress.com
Printed in Canada

ISBN 978-1-4875-0040-5 (cloth)
ISBN 978-1-4875-2028-1 (paper)

∞ Printed on acid-free, 100% post-consumer recycled paper
with vegetable-based inks.

___

Library and Archives Canada Cataloguing in Publication

Title: Viva M·A·C : AIDS, fashion, and the philanthropic practices
of M·A·C Cosmetics / Andrea Benoit.

Names: Benoit, Andrea, 1967–, author.

Description: Includes bibliographical references and index.

Identifiers: Canadiana 2019007065X | ISBN 9781487520281 (paper)
| ISBN 9781487500405 (cloth)

Subjects: LCSH: MAC Cosmetics (Firm) – History. | LCSH: Cosmetics industry –
Social aspects – Ontario – Toronto – Case studies. | LCSH: Fashion – Social
aspects – Ontario – Toronto – Case studies. | LCSH: Corporations – Charitable
contributions – Ontario – Toronto – Case studies. | LCSH: Social responsibility of
business – Ontario – Toronto – Case studies. | LCSH: AIDS (Disease) – Social aspects –
Ontario – Toronto – Case studies.

Classification: LCC HD9970.5.C674 M33 2019 | DDC 338.7/6685509713541 – dc23

___

This book has been published with the help of a grant from the Federation for the
Humanities and Social Sciences, through the Awards to Scholarly Publications
Program, using funds provided by the Social Sciences and Humanities Research
Council of Canada.

University of Toronto Press acknowledges the financial assistance to its publishing
program of the Canada Council for the Arts and the Ontario Arts Council, an agency
of the Government of Ontario.

  Canada Council   Conseil des Arts
for the Arts   du Canada

 ONTARIO ARTS COUNCIL
CONSEIL DES ARTS DE L'ONTARIO
an Ontario government agency
un organisme du gouvernement de l'Ontario

Funded by the   Financé par le
Government   gouvernement
of Canada   du Canada   Canadä

To the underdogs

Contents

Acknowledgments ix

Prologue: Rise Up 3

Introduction: The Rules of Make-up Art Cosmetics 14

Part I: Spaces of Original Possibilities

1 The Kitchen Sink 37

2 Fashion Capital 67

3 Caring Is Never Out of Fashion 105

Part II: Creative Activism

4 Put Your Money Where Your Mouth Is 133

5 Selling Out 160

6 Dragging Theory into Practice 190

Epilogue: The Brightest Jewel in Our Crown 217

Notes 221

Bibliography 245

Index 263

Colour plates follow page 182

Acknowledgments

My thanks first to my editors Mark Thompson and Janice Evans at the University of Toronto Press, for seeing my work through to completion and being so patient with its many ups and downs along the way. Thank you to everyone at the Press who brought the book to life, including the sales and marketing team. Matthew Kudelka meticulously copy edited the manuscript – thank you so much. My thanks and sincere appreciation to the two anonymous reviewers for the time and care they took in reviewing the manuscript and for their incredibly helpful comments and suggestions. The additions and edits that resulted from their thoughtful consideration of the manuscript have undoubtedly made for a stronger narrative. I would also like to acknowledge Siobhan McMenemy, formerly of UTP, who took a chance with my project.

I'd like to thank Daniel Robinson and Susan Knabe in the Faculty of Information and Media Studies at the University of Western Ontario, who were the first readers of the early (very early!) incarnations of this work. Thanks also to Amanda Grzyb, Alison Hearn, Allison Johnson, and Sharon Sliwinski at Western University, and Anne MacLennan at York University, for their input along the way.

Without Alan Miller and Helen Jefferson Lenskyj and the other archivists, scholars, activists, and volunteers at the Canadian Lesbian and Gay Archives in Toronto, who have preserved the stories of LGBTQ folks, there would be no book. I thank them for their steadfast commitment to keeping those stories alive and available to all.

So many thanks go to my pals – Kyle Asquith, Laura Cayen, Nicole Cohen, Richard Davila, Maja Jovanovic, Kara Manovich, and Tiara Sukhan – for their friendship, support, and laughs. Shout-out to my family – Sung, Max, Zoë, Mum, and Dad – for hanging in there with me.

I'm grateful to Syd Beder, Jeanne Beker, Suzanne Boyd, Karen Buglisi Weiler, Victor Casale, John Demsey, Brett Ginty, Frances Hathaway, Phillip Ing, Steven Levy, the late David Livingstone, Valerie MacKenzie, Jane McKay, Bernadette Morra, Rick Mugford, Kim Myers-Robertson, Donald Robertson, and Susie Sheffman for their recollections of M·A·C, Fashion Cares, and the Toronto fashion scene. Their memories brought this book to life. My thanks especially to Shauna Levy, who really got me started with talking to everyone. I would also like to thank Bryan Greenwood for the lengthy discussion about D.Q. and the history of drag in Toronto, including its "forgotten queens," a story that deserves its own book.

I'm grateful to M·A·C Cosmetics and the Estée Lauder Companies Inc. for their permission to reproduce so many of the images, without which this story would be incomplete. My thanks also to RuPaul, k.d. lang and Direct Management Group, Albert Sanchez and DLMUS, David LaChapelle and CXA, Walter Chin and Cerutti + Co., and Floria Sigismondi and Echo Lake Entertainment for allowing me to reproduce their work in the book.

I have Donald Robertson to thank for creating the uniquely Donald artwork that became the book cover. I always had a picture in my head of what I wanted the book to look like, and Donald captured it perfectly. Thanks to Kimberly Glyder for turning the artwork into such an eye-catching cover.

Finally, my thanks to Frank Toskan and the late Frank Angelo. I had originally hoped only that I might get an hour or so of Frank Toskan's time to introduce myself and my project, and that he would be okay with it. I never imagined the many hours of conversation we would eventually have, as he told me his stories, shared with me his mementos and photos, and advocated for my project as he introduced me to the many other people whose stories have also made their way into this book. His trust in me in telling the M·A·C story is immeasurable.

VIVA M·A·C
AIDS, Fashion, and the Philanthropic
Practices of M·A·C Cosmetics

PROLOGUE

Rise Up

On 7 November 2014, on a crisp Friday evening in downtown Toronto that was just cold enough to break out one's new fall coat but not yet snowy enough to ruin designer shoes, a mix of creative types, industry stalwarts, fashionistas, and others just looking for a fun night out gathered at the city's old Stock Exchange building. The Design Exchange, or DX, the hub for Toronto's fashion and design industries, is housed there, and that night it was holding its annual fundraising gala called "Intersection." Inside the historic building, Lorraine Segato, the lead singer of Toronto 80s band The Parachute Club, opened the evening's events with a rousing reprisal of her group's 1983 hit – and the gala's theme – "Rise Up," many in the audience singing along. The song had also been the anthem for World Pride, which Toronto had hosted just a couple of months earlier in June, and it celebrated the diversity that has long characterized Toronto's multicultural composition and accepting world view. Guests on the first floor of the Exchange building were busy making "slogan" buttons and eating exquisite culinary treats while socializing, networking, and awaiting the voguing competition – a highly stylized form of dance that mimicked a supermodel's fashion shoot and was popular in the late 80s and 90s – that would take place shortly.

The DX fundraising gala in Toronto took its inspiration that year from the Design Exchange's concurrent in-house exhibition, Politics of Fashion | Fashion of Politics, which had opened on 18 September 2014 and would run until 25 January 2015. Curator Sara Nickleson and Canadian designer Jeremy Laing, assisted by

Toronto media personality and fashion veteran Jeanne Beker, had collectively assembled the two-hundred-odd fashion designs on display. The exhibition illustrated how fashion has mirrored society by igniting social awareness and contributing to its progress. Taking sixties counterculture and second-wave feminism as its starting points, the exhibition considered how fashion has historically intersected with activism, gender, sexuality, and politics. Visitors alighting from the elevator, which was covered in "protest" signs paying homage to English designer Katharine Hamnett's notorious Autumn/Winter 1985 protest T-shirts, were met at the third-floor entrance to the exhibit by Oliviero Toscani's portrait of three human hearts. This ascetic and disturbing image had been used for an infamous Benetton clothing advertisement in the 1990s, one in a series that ostensibly represented the Italian knitwear company's social conscience. Moving into the first part of the exhibition, "Politics of Fashion," an even more graphic installation displayed PETA's (People for the Ethical Treatment of Animals) anti-fur signs and red-splattered fur coats, with several televisions playing PETA activist footage.

Further in were pieces from Hussein Chalayan's controversial Spring 1998 chador collection, two designs from Alexander McQueen's posthumous 2010 collection, and a series featuring the avant-garde Japanese designers Rei Kawakubo of Comme des Garçons, Yohji Yamamoto, and Issey Miyake. Other pieces by Mary Quant, Vivienne Westwood, and Jean Paul Gaultier – many acquired through Beker's vast connections – rounded out this portion of the exhibition. Each exhibit was labelled with a "zine"-style placard that used a pastiche of irregularly sized and shaped letters, connoting a countercultural, DIY feeling. A collection of slogan T-shirts – including one bearing Barbara Kruger's iconic 1987 image "I Shop Therefore I Am" – hung behind glass, escorting visitors through the exhibition's exit. The T-shirts were set to be offered in the silent fundraising auction that would take place later in the evening. And at the very back of the stark white exhibition space, a red lace-up bustier and matching red thigh-high stiletto boots could be spotted. The American drag performer RuPaul had worn this outfit in an infamous advertisement for M·A·C Cosmetics' VIVA GLAM lipstick in 1995. It was a silhouette hardly done justice by the relatively petite and, ironically, female mannequin, which stood at least one foot shorter than RuPaul's statuesque six foot seven inches (in heels). Despite the minimal fanfare around this particular design, the DX "Rise Up" event that night was inextricably tied to this vivid red ensemble.

Unknown to many of the revellers, a dinner was taking place in a private room on the second floor for a very special guest. Each year, the Design Exchange honours a person who "exemplifies creativity, outstanding talent and innovative vision." In 2014, that person was Frank Toskan, co-founder, along with the late Frank Angelo, of Make-up Art Cosmetics – better known simply as M·A·C. The DX was celebrating Toskan's "creative activism" and fundraising for HIV/AIDS through the M·A·C AIDS Fund. In 1992, Toskan created the VIVA GLAM lipstick as the company's signature fundraising mechanism. Since that time, M·A·C has covered the full cost of producing, distributing, and selling VIVA GLAM, and 100 per cent of VIVA GLAM sales have been donated to the M·A·C AIDS Fund and directed to local AIDS organizations. Twenty-five years after the fund's inception, and many VIVA GLAM lipsticks later, the M·A·C AIDS Fund has raised more than $487 million, and it continues to give funds back to the communities in which they are raised through VIVA GLAM sales. And it all began in Toronto, with a red VIVA GLAM lipstick that asserted "long live glamour." This book, *Viva M·A·C: AIDS, Fashion, and the Philanthropic Practices of M·A·C Cosmetics*, is the first scholarly work to document the history of M·A·C's unusual form of corporate philanthropy and the people who drove it. It explains how M·A·C's attention to HIV/AIDS arose when it did and where it did and why VIVA GLAM and its extraordinary advertising featuring RuPaul and k.d. lang resonated so strongly with the 1990s cultural zeitgeist, setting the stage for M·A·C's long-standing corporate philanthropy in the AIDS arena.

To be sure, M·A·C's AIDS philanthropy has always been known to many Torontonians and to those in the fashion industry. Certainly, many people now of a "certain age" who lived, shopped, and went clubbing in Toronto during the 1980s, who faithfully watched the local broadcaster CityTV each week for the latest trends on *FashionTelevision*, and who obsessively read *Flare* and *Toronto Life Fashion* magazines and the style sections of the *Toronto Star* and the *Globe and Mail* knew about M·A·C. They likely had a M·A·C lipstick stashed away in a purse or pocket, purchased from The Bay on Queen Street or from the M·A·C store on Carlton Street. In the 1980s, M·A·C offered a new kind of cosmetic line: unusual lipsticks with a dry matte finish that were vibrant and seemed indelible and had odd names like "Razzpa" and "Russian Red," and lime-green and neon-yellow eye shadows that looked like candies. *FashionTelevision* host Jeanne Beker remembers M·A·C as the "hip, happening, edgy brand that was catering to drag queens and to theatrical people and people shooting really cutting-edge editorial. These were the guys who were doing colours that we hadn't seen before."[1] Indeed, the M·A·C story – about a guy who mixed lipstick in his kitchen – has become something of an urban legend.

Make-up artist, hairstylist, and photographer Frank Toskan and his life and business partner Frank Angelo created M·A·C in Toronto in the early 1980s. Toskan originally developed his professional line to suit his own artistic needs. He created bold colours and a diverse range of products that suited all skin colours, particularly darker tones, using highly pigmented matte textures that photographed well. By offering a wider range of colour products than was commercially available at the time, M·A·C accommodated and embraced the racially and ethnically diverse consumers found in multicultural Toronto. Toskan and Angelo – everybody knew them as "the Franks" – positioned M·A·C within Toronto's thriving fashion industry, part of the revitalization in Canadian design, retail, and media that began in the late 1970s. M·A·C quickly gained a loyal following in Toronto as its products became highly sought after by make-up artists, models, photographers, and eventually celebrities. M·A·C was contemptuous of traditional cosmetics industry rules, especially conventional beauty advertising, and built its reputation on its products' outstanding performance and the brand's "cool" factor, largely through word-of-mouth within professional insider networks and at trade events like the Festival of Canadian Fashion. By the end of the 1980s, M·A·C had retail counters in The Bay department stores across

Canada, in the upscale store Henri Bendel in New York City, and in Nordstrom in the western United States.

But even while M·A·C's status in the Toronto fashion industry was growing during the 1980s, so was the AIDS epidemic, and AIDS and fashion were closely linked. Supporting AIDS research and people living with AIDS was controversial; the Canadian and US governments avoided directly addressing the epidemic in its early years, and corporations and other organizations steered clear of AIDS and its connotations, creating silence and inaction around the medical disorder.[2] Since AIDS was most common at that time among gay men, AIDS raised uncomfortable questions surrounding gay male sexuality that seemingly threatened the hegemonic ideas about morality and family values that characterized the 1980s. In Toronto, and in other urban centres in North America, AIDS had a devastating impact – personal and professional – on creative industries like fashion. The Toronto fashion industry responded to the health crisis with a trailblazing new event called Fashion Cares, a fundraiser to benefit the AIDS Committee of Toronto, the city's largest AIDS service organization. The first Fashion Cares took place in June 1987 as an underground party geared to Toronto's most fashion-savvy crowd. Fashion Cares evolved into a yearly event and Toronto's most highly anticipated fashion happening. Through Fashion Cares, a formal connection between fashion and AIDS in Toronto was established, one that literally set the stage for M·A·C's own AIDS philanthropy over the following decade. From the start, M·A·C donated the cosmetics for every Fashion Cares show, with M·A·C artists creating the make-up looks, becoming the event's official corporate sponsor in 1994.

The red bustier and matching thigh-high stiletto boots exhibited at the 2014 Politics of Fashion | Fashion of Politics event had figured in M·A·C's very first advertisement, for the first VIVA GLAM lipstick, released in March 1995. That ad had featured the black drag queen RuPaul, who had recently achieved mainstream attention with his dance hit "Supermodel (You Better Work)." Never before had a man been the "face" – let alone the body – of a cosmetics brand. In the VIVA GLAM ad, RuPaul's statuesque, bustier-and-heels-clad body spelled out each of the letters V-I-V-A

G-L-A-M. Many were uncomfortable with the image, especially the "M" that showed RuPaul's legs provocatively spread open. At a time when associating with AIDS was considered a very risky move for a brand or corporation, M·A·C assumed a defiant stance. Furthermore, even while M·A·C commanded attention for its AIDS charity through the ad, it poked fun at female beauty culture as strongly perpetuated by the bland, homogeneous, stereotypical cosmetics advertising of the sort the company had always rejected.

In 1996 the Canadian singer and outspoken animal rights activist k.d. lang joined RuPaul in promoting the M·A·C AIDS Fund. M·A·C produced a second iteration of the lipstick specifically for lang, and a new advertisement appeared in 1997. An out lesbian, lang was portrayed in M·A·C's second ad as a gender-fluid sailor with a quiff hairstyle and tattoos, proudly showing off a distinct pink lipstick print on her cheek, presumably planted by another woman. This ad further made visible issues of gender, sex, sexuality, and female beauty that resonated with media culture, popular culture, and queer culture alike. Together, these two ads proudly advocated for AIDS awareness and fundraising. More importantly, they visually embodied the principles of diversity, individuality, and inclusiveness that M·A·C's founders and employees had long practised, explicitly celebrating LGBTQ folks. In September 2013, M·A·C re-released the 1995 VIVA GLAM ad, now called "VIVA GLAM The Original." The reissued VIVA GLAM ad in 2013, along with Toskan's recognition at the DX Intersection gala in 2014, suggested that a renewed interest in the relationship between M·A·C and AIDS was in the air. In 2017, Canada's sesquicentennial year, #MACProudToBeCanadian appeared in M·A·C's merchandising and promotional communications; on its storefront on Bloor Street in Toronto, the company declared "We Heart Our Homeland," explicitly, if perhaps conveniently, capitalizing on the brand's relatively unknown Canadian heritage. The year 2019 marks the twenty-fifth anniversary of the M·A·C AIDS Fund.

Undoubtedly, M·A·C is one of *the* Canadian business success stories, a completely original and innovative brand that has transformed the global cosmetics industry, particularly by making the "make-up artist" product line an industry standard. The company's unprecedented success in the 1990s, sparked by a global demand for its products, compelled Toskan and Angelo to sell M·A·C to the New York-based cosmetics conglomerate Estée Lauder Companies Inc. Lauder purchased 51 per cent of M·A·C in late 1994, another 19 per cent in early 1997, and the final 30 per cent in 1998. M·A·C's founding partners and Lauder then parted ways. Under Lauder's auspices M·A·C has become one of the most profitable prestige brands in the cosmetics industry and has proudly continued to promote VIVA GLAM and the M·A·C AIDS Fund. Estée Lauder Executive Group President John Demsey declares M·A·C "the greatest fashion success story to ever happen in Canada. To this very day, it remains so."[3] And Demsey isn't wrong.

Yet it seems that the details of this Canadian success story are relatively unfamiliar to most and are generally absent from the scholarly literature. For instance, while M·A·C has been described as "the hippest thing to come out of Canada," there has been no extended history of the brand or its founders.[4] Biographical, business, and cultural histories exist for other twentieth-century cosmetics entrepreneurs-cum-moguls like Max Factor, Charles Revson, Estée Lauder, Elizabeth Arden, Helena Rubinstein, and Madam C.J. Walker, but not for M·A·C.[5] Cultural histories of cosmetics and lipstick often refer to M·A·C, but none of these "historicize" the brand.[6] In business-oriented scholarship on the cosmetics industry, there has been no substantial coverage of M·A·C. Business historian Geoffrey Jones's monumental 2010 history of the cosmetics industry, *Beauty Imagined: A History of the Global Beauty Industry*, includes biographical information about many cosmetics company founders but mentions the M·A·C AIDS Fund only in passing when noting that cosmetics brands began associating with social causes during the 1990s; this completely glosses over M·A·C's history. In his work on branding, advertising, and the media, journalist Mark Tungate does assert that M·A·C stands out as a leader in the cosmetics industry by having introduced a professional make-up artist brand, exceptional service, and unusual counter staff, but he does not consider the brand's philanthropic work and how it might relate to the features he singles out.[7] Branding practitioners are more familiar with M·A·C and praise its unique identity. They are highly attuned to M·A·C's cultural presence, to the "diversity" and "authenticity" of its brand, and to the unconventional ways these have operated to sell M·A·C's products. M·A·C's identity as *the* brand used by make-up artists established an authenticity that could be conferred only through word-of-mouth promotion, not through traditional advertising. M·A·C's strategy was to capitalize on its already existing relationships with other forms of cultural production, including fashion and music. M·A·C established early on what it was *not* – that is, it was neither conventional nor traditional in appearance or values, and it did not conform to cosmetics industry conventions. As such, the overarching quality that initially distinguished M·A·C from its competitors was the company's apparent indifference to the rules of the cosmetics industry, a feature that may partly explain its absence from histories of the beauty industry.[8]

And despite M·A·C's longevity and success, both of these intimately tied to its philanthropy around AIDS and embodied in its innovative advertisements, the brand's history has not been fully examined in any detailed or sustained manner by critical scholars in other disciplines either. Cultural and media studies scholars have either failed to address or only barely acknowledged M·A·C's philanthropic model, let alone its genesis, or studied how its unusual advertising emerged. M·A·C's advertising with VIVA GLAM is particularly intriguing from the standpoint of gender, sexuality, media representations of women, and forms of activism. What has been the nature of Toskan's "creative activism"? Does an exploration of M·A·C's advertising and its corporate philanthropy offer different ways to think about how corporations align with social causes? Since scholarly attention to M·A·C is practically nonexistent, an easy answer to such questions is elusive. The relationship between M·A·C's brand identity and its involvement with the AIDS cause is certainly unlike anything seen with other brands, cosmetic or otherwise. First, this relationship began well before today's (it would seem) ubiquitous cause marketing phenomenon. Second, M·A·C's brand identity is closely linked to its philanthropic ethos and non-traditional promotional processes. The task of *Viva M·A·C: AIDS, Fashion, and the Philanthropic Practices of M·A·C Cosmetics*, then, is to document, for the first time and in a rigorous scholarly manner, how M·A·C's cultural practices – its behaviours, performances, knowledges, discourses, and objects – emerged and developed alongside its brand identity, its corporate activities, and its subsequent commitment to AIDS awareness and fundraising. This examination of M·A·C goes beyond traditional scholarship on cause marketing, which generally examines the "face value" of a campaign's communications, by assuming that M·A·C's evolution and its relationship to a social cause were mutually determining historical processes.

My construction of M·A·C's history in this book has largely entailed traditional historical re-creation guided by discourse analysis and supplemented by interviews and oral histories. I have assembled this story from a variety of archives, resources, and discourses to describe the cultural practices, performances, and narratives surrounding M·A·C and others in the Toronto fashion industry over an almost twenty-year time span. These sources include Canadian and American mainstream media as well as long-forgotten archives stored in dusty basements. This volume relies heavily on contemporaneous accounts of M·A·C and the fashion industry by the very players involved – including fashion, entertainment, and business journalists – as well as on television programs, newscasts, and elements of popular media and culture. The Canadian Lesbian and Gay Archives (CLGA) in Toronto offered rich archival materials, such as meeting minutes, letters, internal memos, annual reports, newspaper articles, interviews, web pages, transcripts, posters, event programs, T-shirts, flyers, invitations, video recordings, films, and music videos. The records of the AIDS Committee of Toronto (ACT) from 1983 to 1991 are housed at the CLGA. York University's Sound and Moving Image Library in Toronto received and catalogued ACT's video archives in 2010, providing another plentiful source of primary material such as footage of Fashion Cares, CityTV's *FashionTelevision*'s coverage of Fashion Cares, and the locally broadcast Rogers Cable television specials on Fashion Cares, which included interviews with Frank Toskan and other members of the Toronto fashion scene. M·A·C's public corporate archives from the 1990s, which include items such as press releases, promotional communications, websites, and advertising, add to this history.[9] Other publicly available materials include media accounts of M·A·C, Fashion Cares, and the VIVA GLAM campaigns from mainstream and alternative newspapers, which were largely first-person accounts.

Thirty-five years on, M·A·C's story is vulnerable to fading from collective memory as a result of rumour mongering, misrepresentation, and a lack of documentation. Memory is tricky, and nostalgia and grief can colour accounts of the past. However, a number of people who were key players on Toronto's fashion scene in the 1980s and 1990s were eager to offer their recollections about this unusual time and place and this innovative brand. As veteran Toronto fashion stylist Susie Sheffman asserts about M·A·C's success, "There's nothing but national pride."[10] Interviews were conducted with past and present journalists, stylists, make-up artists, fashion directors, fashion magazine editors, and fashion retailers in Toronto's fashion and media industries, as well as employees of M·A·C and Estée Lauder, including its executives, along with M·A·C founding partner Victor Casale and co-founder Frank Toskan. With their informative and often quirky memories and insights, this book took on a new life. Spanning the beginning of the 1980s to the end of the 1990s, the pages that follow demonstrate how M·A·C's philanthropy and its remarkable advertisements for VIVA GLAM did not simply appear out of nowhere. Reflected and represented in these ads was the company's ethos, one that nurtured and supported marginalized people and communities, fostered creativity, and celebrated differences, enacted through practices that extended to those affected by HIV and AIDS. Rather than the starting point for a superficial corporate social responsibility initiative based solely on strategic marketing goals, the RuPaul and k.d. lang VIVA GLAM ads were the culmination of a historical trajectory of personal and professional corporate "philanthropic practices."

Viva M·A·C cuts across disciplines such as cultural studies, queer studies, and media studies; it engages with advertising, fashion, and business history. It offers new insights into local Canadian history – specifically, it examines the revitalization of Toronto's fashion industry in the 1980s, of which there has been a paucity of academic work. Since the current scholarly dialogue about cause marketing neglects M·A·C (perhaps because the brand's philanthropy resists easy categorization), *Viva M·A·C* also intervenes in debates about the commodification of social causes by presenting an admittedly anomalous example of corporate philanthropy that emphasizes creativity rather than an instrumental marketing strategy. This volume does not seek to offer directives on how to "do" successful branding or cause marketing. It sits more comfortably within media and communications scholarship, influenced by critical branding theorists such as Adam Arvidsson, Celia Lury, and Liz Moor.[11] While there is some intersection with applied work on branding and marketing, a key difference is that communications work on promotional culture is critical of capitalism *writ large*, a perspective that generally is not found within more applied work. This is not to say that applied work is not useful to thinking through these topics. There are several scholars, such as Detlev Zwick, and especially Douglas B. Holt, who regard marketing as a distinctly cultural, indeed social activity.[12] However, I am not offering a treatise on how to develop a brand identity or nurture brand values (even while acknowledging that many writers do note that M·A·C is exemplary in these areas). Nor is it my intention to outline a new type of management or branding strategy, although I realize that business scholars and practitioners may well regard the M·A·C story as instructive.

Rather, *Viva M·A·C* aims to present a different perspective for contemplating M·A·C, Toronto, the AIDS epidemic, and the power of creative work in corporate philanthropy. Ultimately, the goal is to document a series of practices and events such that featuring a drag queen wearing a red leather bustier and thigh-high stilettos in a cosmetics advertisement was not just something that made sense for M·A·C Cosmetics – in fact, it was almost inevitable.

INTRODUCTION

The Rules of Make-up Art Cosmetics

Aligning with the AIDS cause and developing a successful consumer-based, purchase-triggered arrangement through the VIVA GLAM initiative certainly made M·A·C very different from other cosmetics companies of its time, especially since identifying with HIV and AIDS was practically verboten in the epidemic's early days. At face value, the VIVA GLAM campaign appears to be what is now commonly called "cause marketing."[1] Cause marketing, which describes a partnership between a consumer brand and a social cause or charity, has become a common advertising and marketing tactic. Cause marketing is an important form of corporate social responsibility (CSR). While there are many conceptions of CSR, broadly speaking it is about corporate actions that satisfy social needs, although it also encompasses the corporation's responsibility to stakeholders and its impact on the environment. Various forms of CSR have existed since the 1800s, but a more modern concept of CSR began forming in the 1960s with the idea that corporations have responsibilities that go beyond profit. At the heart of CSR is the relationship between a corporation and society, defined in multiple ways. The belief that philanthropic efforts benefit both the corporation and certain beneficiaries within society legitimizes and rationalizes CSR decision-making. International and cultural differences can substantially influence the types of social responsibility exercised; for instance, laws and government policies can affect some activities through the regulations they impose.[2]

Cause marketing, as a more contemporary subcategory of CSR, is characterized by an overt, explicitly articulated partnership between a brand and a social cause or charity, whereby the parent corporation donates a portion of the sales of a particular product on behalf of that brand to the cause, charity, or not-for-profit organization. The communications surrounding this relationship are especially important and include packaging and, most importantly, advertising. As such, cause marketing has evolved into a common marketing, public relations, and advertising tactic. The goal is to increase consumer loyalty and build brand identity, ostensibly "doing good" while driving profit. Since it is reputation that substantially differentiates a particular brand or product from others within its category, the cause attached to that brand or commodity becomes a distinct selling feature. Additional media coverage can heighten the formal communications around a cause marketing initiative, generating residual brand value.

A number of scholars cite American Express's 1983 campaign to restore the Statue of Liberty as the first major cause marketing initiative; that program generated close to $2 million based solely on AMEX credit card transactions.[3] However, the March of Dimes exhibited a very early example of a for-profit/not-for-profit partnership. The March of Dimes is a not-for-profit organization that brings attention to those with physical disabilities. Its work covers a lot of ground, not just in fundraising and offering various services but also in advocacy, especially for babies and children. In 1976 the Marriott Hotel Corporation was fundraising for its new family theme park called Marriott's Great America, located in Santa Clara, California. Marriott's PR expert, Bruce Burtch, decided to partner with a family-oriented charity as a strategic public relations move and chose the March of Dimes, an effort that was beneficial for both parties. Burtch created a pledge-based contest across the western United States, the winner of which, along with one hundred of her or his friends, won a trip to the opening of the new theme park. For Marriott, the campaign generated huge publicity and record-breaking attendance for a regional park. For the March of Dimes, the pledges raised $2.5 million, 40 per cent more than it had ever raised before.[4] This example does not illustrate the "purchase-triggered" arrangement that largely defines the contemporary cause marketing landscape; even so, it stands as a precursor to for-profit/not-for-profit alliances that are based on the mutual goals of media attention and PR through fundraising.

Breast cancer philanthropy, and indeed breast cancer "culture," is a ubiquitous phenomenon that many will recognize, particularly every October, which has been designated "breast cancer awareness month." As gender and cultural studies scholar Samantha King discusses in her seminal book on the topic, *Pink Ribbons, Inc.: Breast Cancer and the Politics of Philanthropy*, breast cancer was a "hot" charity by 1996, focusing on a topic no longer forbidden in public and polite discourse.[5] King situates her work within a larger body of writing about the breast cancer movement in the United States. Breast cancer activists have a long history, beginning with those who were unable to enter the workforce and were then co-opted by the medical establishment to assist in campaigns. In tandem with feminist movements in the 1960s and the increasing politicization of the "personal," cancer activism became more visible and communities began building around these issues. Missing, however, was an activist organization that challenged the federal research agenda – something that the AIDS movement was successfully doing. In 1992, cosmetics giant Estée Lauder had begun distributing pink ribbons at its counters with information on self-exams, alongside pink-ribbon-embossed cosmetics for sale. For King, the pink ribbon is particularly symbolic of the close tie between corporations and breast cancer campaigns. And by using the word "culture" to describe a new kind of corporate philanthropic activity, King makes the case for considering how cultural signs and symbols such as the pink ribbon have come to represent support for breast cancer research, support that is now deeply embedded in the capitalist landscape.

What *is* new is the practice of incorporating philanthropic efforts as part of a general marketing strategy. This is related to the rise of neoliberalism. King uses the term "neoliberalism" here to "refer to a philosophy and a set of economic and political policies aimed at cutting expenditures on public goods such as education, health care, and income assistance in order to enhance corporate profit rates."[6] Its tactics include deregulation, privatization, and fiscal austerity. King states: "Under this regime, public-private initiatives and individual and corporate giving are promoted as morally and economically viable means through which to respond to societal needs, in lieu of the state's role in mitigating the social effects of capitalism."[7] Underlying this is a spirit of giving, in time or money, as a chief indicator of and vehicle for citizenship, self-responsibility, and political participation. King rejects the idea that the free market is the sole context for such philanthropic action. Instead, she positions this philanthropy in a context of ethical responsibility and community service. Governing thus occurs less through the formal state apparatus and more through private and commercial sites within the social body, in accordance with neoliberalism. These activities can be seen as both threatening and supporting the neoliberal formation and as regulating conduct. Cause marketing dovetails with this focus on market logic and an internalized sense of ethical conduct and individualized responsibility for social progress and change.

Many of the largest and best-known contemporary cause marketing campaigns raise funds for breast cancer research. An example is Yoplait's "Save Lids to Save Lives." Since 1999, consumers have sent Yoplait yogurt lids to parent company General Mills, which donates ten cents for each lid received to the Susan G. Komen Foundation, the world's largest breast cancer organization; this program has raised more than $50 million since its inception. Renamed "Friends in the Fight" in 2014 and using social media and barcodes instead of yogurt lids to indicate participation, Yoplait's cause marketing expanded to include two other charities, Living Beyond Breast Cancer and Bright Pink, and even beyond the Yoplait brand to other General Mills brands. It was terminated in 2016 in favour of broader corporate philanthropic initiatives.[8]

Another noteworthy example of cause marketing is Dove's Campaign for Real Beauty.[9] In 2004, Dove, the Unilever brand of skincare and hair care products, launched a global marketing strategy to reinvigorate its staid soap brand (and its tagline "1/4 moisturizing cream") with a new advertising and branding campaign that questioned and challenged advertising's preoccupation with an unattainable female beauty ideal. The campaign has a cause marketing component whereby a portion of sales from

Dove's new and vast body care range is channelled to the Dove Self-Esteem Fund to subsidize self-esteem workshops for girls. For Dove, cause marketing appears to be a win–win situation for the brand, its charity, the media, and consumers alike. Launched in the UK in 2004 and in North America in 2006, the Dove Campaign for Real Beauty immediately distinguished itself with its frank discussion of unrealistic beauty ideals in the media, distilled into a notorious claim, based on its own global market research, that only 2 per cent of women worldwide considered themselves "beautiful."[10] Its advertisements featured "real" women – code for non-models – depicted in various visual representations of body size, age, race, and facial features that did not conform to the fantastic, unattainable standard of beauty and body size usually seen in beauty advertising. This high-profile advertising campaign challenged the cosmetics and fashion industries' narrow definition of female beauty, particularly the qualities of the typically young, white, slim, flawless-skinned model most prevalent in contemporary advertisements. The campaign's advertisements instead were unretouched, unmediated images of these "real" women. The Dove Campaign's initial "Tick Box" ads were rhetorically clever; for instance, a grey-haired woman was presented and consumers were asked if she was "grey" or "gorgeous." In another ad, consumers were asked of an arguably plus-size woman whether she was "fat" or "fab." Consumers could then "vote" online (and, presumably, with their dollars) for the winning descriptor. Dove also created ads, ostensibly as short "films," to promote the campaign's Self-Esteem Fund, including the widely viewed and controversial "Evolution" (2006), "Little Girls" (2007), and "Onslaught" (2007) ads. The campaign positioned itself as a democratic apparatus (on the cusp of the social media revolution) that empowered consumers to reject "unrealistic" representations of women in the media. Dove attracted global media attention and attained consumer buy-in through the persuasive rhetoric of its launch ads but substantially through a highly participatory media culture, including an instructional website that invited consumer interaction, and especially the widely shared "Evolution" video, which depicted the transformation of an ordinary-looking girl into a cover model through hair, make-up, and digital manipulation.[11] The campaign suggested that advertising messages and images combined with consumer assent have the power to foster vast social change. In doing so, the campaign co-opted media activists' techniques and promoted a corporate image of responsible advertising practices.

Scholarly analysis of all this was slow to arrive but highly critical once it did. For instance, sociologists Josée Johnston and Judith Taylor deployed a variety of theoretical lenses including Foucault and fat studies to challenge the Dove campaign, primarily for its lack of efficacy as truly "activist" because it ultimately served capitalist goals.[12] As Dove released new products – including, inexplicably, a body-firming cream – more critique, both popular and scholarly, emerged. Popular media noted the inconsistencies surrounding a brand that promoted "real" women but sold a cream that purportedly acted to firm the undesirable flabbiness associated with such reality.[13] Johnston and Taylor contended that the arguments contained within the ads' rhetoric and images were inherently contradictory, as no overt challenge to a beauty ideology actually occurred through Dove's version of "feminist consumerism," merely a rearranging of the hierarchy within that beauty system. Dove's project of producing and promoting responsible, diverse physical representations of female "beauty" in its advertising was not enough.

The Dove Self-Esteem Fund is committed to supporting initiatives that foster positive body image in young girls, particularly as related to individual perceptions of "beauty." Many girls and women are fraught with self-esteem and body image issues that negatively impact all aspects of their relationships with themselves and others. Through responsible advertising and the Self-Esteem Fund's initiatives, Dove strives to enable women to create stronger selves. The campaign's website provides numerous activities and resources for young girls, their mothers, and educators on issues such as body image, friendship, family influence, female health, and, of course, the media. A portion of the proceeds of the sale of each Dove product is donated to the Self-Esteem Fund; this constitutes the cause marketing element of the Campaign for Real Beauty. Dove, in the process, has become a leader in the field. As the campaign has evolved, new representations of female bodies and faces have emerged describing "real" and inclusive "beauty," with varying degrees of relevancy and success, however that may be evaluated. In any case, the Dove Campaign continues to be an influential force in contemporary cause marketing and advertising to women, generating discussion in the popular media and in academic circles about its unconventional directions and experimental promotional initiatives.[14] Dove is an interesting and relevant example to consider alongside M·A·C's VIVA GLAM advertising, both because of its cause marketing element and because its advertising campaign explicitly seeks to change, or at least challenge, definitions of female beauty, albeit in vastly different ways than M·A·C.

For many scholars, the entry point to understanding how cause marketing operates and evaluating its pros and cons is through Product (RED), the cause marketing campaign *par excellence* that, like M·A·C, targets the global HIV/AIDS pandemic.[15] In 2006, U2 singer Bono and activist Bobby Shriver launched Product (RED) as a "business model" to raise money for the Global Fund to Fight AIDS, Tuberculosis and Malaria in sub-Saharan Africa.[16] Supported by its many celebrity endorsers, (RED) explicitly encourages consumption as a means for helping people (mostly women and children) living with HIV and AIDS. This business model, an explicitly for-profit marketing campaign, is premised on (RED) licensing its logo for a fee to corporate partners, who then create specially branded (RED) products. The licensing fee paid to (RED) is used to help (RED) stay in business and to generate awareness about HIV/AIDS. Brands that have aligned with (RED) since 2006 include The Gap, Apple, Converse, Nike, Starbucks, Dell, Armani, American Express, and Hallmark. (RED) helps its partner brands direct existing marketing strategies and budgets in ways appropriate to the marketing of (RED) products and HIV/AIDS issues – budgets already earmarked for the partner brand's products, (RED) or otherwise.

Each partner brand provides an exclusive product, such as a T-shirt, iPod, or running shoes. These products are meant to be sold at no additional cost to consumers, and a portion of the profits, sometimes up to 50 per cent, is donated to the Global Fund (RED) Portfolio – not to (RED) itself – which uses most of the funds to purchase antiretroviral medications. (RED) had early promotional relationships with *Vanity Fair* and *Elle* magazines, social media partners including Facebook, Twitter, and YouTube, and charitable "friends" like the Bill & Melinda Gates Foundation, the United Nations Foundation, and UNAIDS. When (RED) launched in the United States in October 2006, Bono appeared on the *Oprah Winfrey Show*, and Winfrey devoted an entire hour to the (RED) campaign. Winfrey and Bono went shopping on Chicago's Michigan Avenue and stopped at the Apple store and The Gap, where Winfrey purchased multiple (RED) products. Besides providing priceless publicity for (RED), Winfrey's endorsement imbued the campaign with her own brand of cultural legitimacy. In July 2007, *Vanity Fair* devoted its entire issue to Africa and featured (RED), producing multiple covers with celebrities and models including Bono, Winfrey, and Brad Pitt. Since 2006, (RED) has donated more than $500 million to the Global Fund. (RED)'s advertising campaigns, most notably for The Gap, are perhaps the initiative's predominant feature. The early ads were clearly run on branding logic and the lure of celebrity culture. These ads featured actors like Jennifer Garner, Penelope Cruz, and Don Cheadle, Mary J. Blige, Chris Rock, and "supermodels" Christy Turlington and Gisele Bündchen. They all wore T-shirts bearing clever semantic configurations of the (RED) logo to convey emotional messages, such as "Inspi(RED)" and "Desi(RED)."

While there are a number of disciplinary approaches to understanding (RED), many scholars have honed in on the fact that (RED)'s cultural resonance relies primarily on its branding logic, and (RED)'s early promotional communications and ads displayed great semiotic creativity. For instance, the colour red indicates emergency. Red is the colour of blood, which is the conduit for the circulation of HIV in the body yet also signifies love. Almost all (RED) products are red (although this is not required under the licensing arrangement), and products bear the (RED) logo in addition to the partner brand's logo. Even though (RED) exists in association with its partner brands, (RED) is also its own brand, signified by a logo that is very rich in connotations. The parentheses suggest all-encompassing arms that touch, enclosing their contents like a hug, signifying (RED)'s emotional or compassionate nature. The various partner brands are represented within parentheses, such as (GAP)^{RED}, signifying that the partner brand is augmented by its (RED)-ness. The partner brand's logo within the parentheses also denotes the exponential nature of (RED), just like a mathematical equation. Parentheses function grammatically to set something aside; they augment or amplify, but their contents are not primary. The variable brand name within the parenthetical space demonstrates how each individual brand is arbitrary, merely one of many within an ever-increasing roster. The partner brand appears to be in the limelight, yet the (RED) logo actually diminishes each partner brand's authority by bestowing each with an overarching (RED)-ness: caring, compassionate, responsible consumption that saves lives from AIDS in Africa. As such, the parentheses unify the diverse lifestyle brands contained within them, reducing the brands to "products" themselves, all defined by the same metanarrative of concern encapsulated by the (RED) brand.

Scholars are highly critical of disingenuous, poorly executed, and inauthentic forms of corporate philanthropy that embed political action within consumerism, making shopping the primary action and mechanism for social change, and they have found much to critique about (RED) and, by extension, cause marketing. For instance, media studies scholar Kathleen M. Kuehn's focus on (RED) examines how the campaign fetishized and thus obscured the material realities of capitalism in general, and of Africa in particular, instead developing affective brand relationships with consumers that conflated being a consumer with being a responsible citizen. Communications scholar Sarah Banet-Weiser and communications specialist Charlotte Lapsansky note that (RED)'s model allows consumers to consume guilt-free – to "do good" while consuming, but without experiencing any sacrifice or change in behaviour, or questioning the capitalist underpinnings of philanthropy. Consumer subjectivities, tastes, needs, and preferences are organized and unified by the brand. Cultural studies scholar Jo Littler's analysis of (RED)'s partnership with AMEX takes a similar position, to which she adds that (RED)'s brand of cause marketing has a "cosmopolitan" quality based on higher-end goods and experiences whereby globalization cultivates consumers as "citizens of the world." Such cosmopolitanism as privilege is related to an implied imperial benevolence and colonialism that looks "fun" and makes this type of caring consumption "sexy" and "glamorous." In this sense, (RED)'s ads, especially the AMEX image that featured Gisele Bündchen and a Maasai warrior laughing and dancing happily, often fetishize buying (RED) products while ignoring the racism and colonialism inherent in the contemporary AIDS pandemic in sub-Saharan Africa. Tactics like these distance consumers from the material reality of AIDS in Africa and from Africans who are living with HIV/AIDS.[17] Cause marketing thus legitimizes capitalism and the way that neoliberal logic has made corporate philanthropy necessary; this generates a self-perpetuating cycle where branding logic comes out on top. Kuehn spotlights (RED) partner brand The Gap and its known history of international labour violations, AMEX's federal and state labour violations, and the link between global capitalism and poverty seen in Africa, the recipient of this "compassionate consumption." Along with Kuehn, others including communications scholar Inger L. Stole have documented how, in its first year, (RED) was reported to have raised only $18 million for (RED). This amount pales in comparison to the combined $100 million spent by The Gap, Motorola, and Apple in marketing and promotions, money directed towards increasing their own brand value at the expense of "saving lives" had it been donated directly to the Global Fund. Exact donation amounts for other (RED) partner brands were not widely available, since partner brands did not report on profits, donations, and expenditures related to (RED) in its early days, rendering (RED) less than transparent.[18]

In their examination of (RED), Lisa Ann Richey and Stefano Ponte combine these approaches with their views on international aid and development and its relationship with corporate social responsibility, specifically as it is linked to the logic of corporate branding. Having done fieldwork in Africa and worked with many AIDS organizations, Richey and Ponte have written a number of empirically informed pieces on (RED), their most ambitious project being *Brand Aid: Shopping Well to Save the World*.[19] Richey and Ponte assert that (RED)'s cause marketing relies on a consumer society and a form of conspicuous consumption that, enhanced by the cult of celebrity, offers legitimacy to consumers. (RED)'s defining feature is its neoliberal brand logic, which explicitly harnesses together capitalism, consumerism, individualism, and celebrity culture with the primary goal of increasing sales and driving profits for its partner brands. For scholars, then, cause marketing, especially as represented by (RED), can induce scepticism, distrust, and even contempt for intentions that are more about profit than philanthropy. Interestingly, Richey and Ponte are the only scholars to suggest – albeit only in passing – that M·A·C was one of (RED)'s precursors in the AIDS cause marketing arena. While it may seem on the surface that similar mechanisms of branding, consumer culture, and capitalism are at work with M·A·C's VIVA GLAM campaign, M·A·C and its philanthropy operate under an entirely different logic than (RED), Dove, or breast cancer initiatives.

M·A·C's current owner and caretaker of the M·A·C AIDS Fund, Estée Lauder, certainly views M·A·C's approach as quite different from other types of corporate philanthropy or corporate social responsibility, including cause marketing. Nancy Mahon, Senior Vice-President, Global Corporate Citizenship and Sustainability at Lauder, and Global Executive Director of the M·A·C AIDS Fund, recognized early in her tenure at M·A·C (which began in 2006):

> I'm not quite sure we're [M·A·C AIDS Fund] part of the cause marketing space. I think part of why VIVA GLAM has worked is that it's part of the conscience of the company. It was voted on by the original employees, many of whom remain. M·A·C remains – even though it's a very large company – a family business, and this is important to the family. I think there's a lot of scepticism about the "portion of the net proceeds" giving model that we see a lot in cause marketing – there needs to be more transparency around the model. We're lucky enough to have that transparency and that clarity.[20]

As Mahon wrote in *Harvard Business Review* in 2010, "what has made the Fund and the brand a commercial success is in many ways our noncommercial approach to sales and charitable giving. Profits are not antithetical to good work; in fact, they can make good work possible."[21] This ethos continues today at M·A·C as a working directive. Karen Buglisi Weiler, one of the first employees hired by M·A·C after the Lauder purchase, eventually becoming Global Brand President of M·A·C, concurs: "There's a fine line between being authentic and doing it for the right reason, or appearing to use it as a marketing ploy. We were more concerned about making sure that we held true to what it [VIVA GLAM] was: a mechanism to raise funds to fight HIV and AIDS around the world."[22] This overtly non-commercial imperative, and, just as importantly, consumers' perception of that imperative, is the first characteristic of M·A·C's philanthropy that stands as a crucial point of difference from other cause marketing initiatives, including the ones discussed earlier.

The perceived authenticity of a cause marketing effort appears to rest substantially upon how consumers understand the brand's motivation and its commitment to the cause it is championing. The effort's success is directly correlated with consumers' sense of the right "fit" between brand and cause and with their sense that the project is not market-driven. Understandably, this fit is of particular interest to marketers contemplating cause marketing's utility. Conceptualizing the congruence or fit between a brand and a social cause as a shared "territory," branding specialists Hamish Pringle and Marjorie Thompson state that "marketing's understanding and interpretation of a brand's 'territory' needs to be extended beyond functional performance and emotional or aspirational imagery into that of 'ethics' and 'beliefs.'"[23] There is no firm consensus on what constitutes a "successful" fit between a brand and a social cause (that is, one that leads to consumer buy-in and thus sales). However, there is general agreement that the cause must be prevalent but not controversial, that there should be some overlap between those affected by the cause or issue and the brand's target market, and that the brand and cause must share similar values.[24] Such directives suggest that a brand/cause pairing must be a conscious marketing decision, one made with careful, instrumental, and strategic attention, though it should not appear so to consumers.

Very few scholars have made the connection between M·A·C's brand identity and its philanthropy, if they pay any attention at all to M·A·C's work around AIDS. Marketing and media scholar Mara Einstein is one exception. In *Compassion, Inc.: How Corporate America Blurs the Line between What We Buy, Who We Are, and Those We Help*, Einstein identifies the M·A·C AIDS Fund as an exemplary contemporary form of what she calls "social innovation," one that exists on a different level from more superficial cause marketing arrangements. Einstein notes that in M·A·C's case, its "cause is related to an industry affected by the product, the campaign is embedded in the corporate culture ... and finally, the source of funding is unambiguous." She asserts that M·A·C's success rests on its brand/cause fit, and she goes so far as to pinpoint the cultural components behind M·A·C's philanthropy around AIDS. For M·A·C, she notes, the AIDS cause is immediately relevant to the people – employees and customers – intimately connected to the brand. Einstein observes how M·A·C's choice to make HIV/AIDS its cause simply makes sense, given the local fashion industry in which the company exists. Einstein's work provides a brief but insightful commentary on M·A·C's corporate philanthropy. Her project does not explore exactly *how* M·A·C's philanthropy makes sense in the context of fashion (that is not her objective), but she is one of the very few scholars to recognize that it does.[25]

Estée Lauder Executive Group President John Demsey, who joined M·A·C in 1998 as its new president, is well-equipped to articulate this connection between M·A·C and its cultural milieu. He recalls: "I came to understand from the first day I was there that the heart and soul of the brand were the make-up artists, the make-up artist community, [and] the idea of community: the idea of the emotional core of the company being the soul of the make-up artists and their connection with the world that they lived in; the profound effect of HIV/AIDS on the make-up artist and fashion community; and the largesse of community spirit that the brand was about."[26] Demsey's statement brings into focus the second point of difference that underpins this history of M·A·C: it is impossible to fully appreciate M·A·C's unique form of corporate philanthropy, culminating in the RuPaul and k.d. lang VIVA GLAM advertisements, without a clearer picture of this community of make-up artists and the cultural context in which M·A·C and its philanthropy arose. This was an environment quite different from, even antithetical to, the more conventional marketing, advertising, and branding worlds in which much of the recent corporate philanthropy is devised, where cause marketing is more likely intended to solve a branding issue first and foremost, not a social problem.

Of course, it is reasonable and prudent to be cautious about these assertions by Mahon, Buglisi Weiler, and Demsey. Are they just corporate-speak, merely promotional language in disguise? Is there any truth to their claims, and if so, how much, and why? This attention to M·A·C's philanthropy in *Viva M·A·C* moves beyond assessing its cause marketing campaign's "success," however that is defined, to attending to the history of the relationship between M·A·C and AIDS and how that relationship influenced the company's philanthropy. Scholarly analysis does not often delve into a brand's history in relation to its cause marketing initiatives. *Viva M·A·C*, however, reveals that M·A·C and the AIDS cause have historically shared a cultural space or territory, making this brand and its cause inherently compatible, even harmonious. M·A·C arose and developed alongside both the renaissance of the fashion industry and the emergence of the AIDS epidemic in Toronto in the 1980s. What makes M·A·C's attention to AIDS awareness and fundraising stand out from other types of cause marketing, as epitomized by (RED) and other examples of corporate philanthropy, is that M·A·C's philanthropy stems from its origins in cultural production, based within the world of Toronto fashion – not marketing or branding.

The Rules of the Game

Considering M·A·C's corporate philanthropy as arising from cultural production within fashion, as an automatic and even unconsciously motivated response to the AIDS crisis, requires a theoretical shift from the usual types of critique levied at (RED), for instance. This means moving away from regarding M·A·C's philanthropy as existing primarily within branding culture or as a marketing enterprise, which scholarly critique tends to assume. This is not to say that M·A·C does not or has never participated in promotional culture. To the contrary, M·A·C established a strong and distinct brand identity early on that has only intensified in the last thirty-odd years as it has achieved commercial dominance within the global cosmetics industry. However, as Nancy Mahon asserted, commercial motives have not historically been the driver of the M·A·C AIDS Fund.

Business historian Per H. Hansen argues that business and the economy are infused with culture; culture shapes and gives meaning to that reality.[27] He suggests that "a cultural and narrative perspective can enrich the business history field."[28] Traditionally, as business historian Kenneth Lipartito explains in his overview of both traditional and cultural approaches to business scholarship, business history adopted the premises of economics, which assigns an instrumental quality to all market operations and activities and minimizes the human experience.[29] The ruling logic of economics views humans as calculating, self-interested, and rational, an assumption that has extended into how business histories are often told. However, the idea that the market is all-powerful is a myth. Lipartito supports the proposition that attention must be directed "away from strategies, structures, and organizations to behaviors, routines, processes, power relations, knowledge, information systems (including means of representation), and personal and social relations within the firm," since, he asserts, "markets operate through particular sets of symbols and meanings."[30] Such a perspective avoids the rationalized version of human agency and social order common to economics and attendant business histories. Lipartito notes that those historians who have been influenced by cultural theory have thus been equipped to explore more fully the "shared symbolic structures and meanings that shaped human wants and desires."[31]

Unearthing this history of M·A·C's "philanthropic practices" similarly requires looking to cultural theory in general and the work of French sociologist Pierre Bourdieu in particular. Such a tactic relates to this larger turn in business history scholarship that incorporates cultural theory as an explanatory framework for organizational behaviour. While Pierre Bourdieu's ideas have been used to study a variety of organizations, Walter A. Friedman and Geoffrey Jones note the prevalence of Bourdieu's ideas in business scholarship on the creative industries such as fashion and cosmetics, where "the opposing pressures of creativity and commerce" must be confronted and balanced.[32] Borrowing from such scholarship yields novel insights into M·A·C's philanthropic practices. It is useful to stress here, though, that *Viva M·A·C* is not a business or organizational history *per se*, but rather a type of hybrid, a culturally infused account of M·A·C's business that is preoccupied with its cultural practices, products, and expressions as the explanatory framework for its philanthropy around AIDS. Bourdieu's conceptual tools lend themselves to an intellectual inquiry about the social world in multiple and flexible ways. It is also important to resist the urge to apply Bourdieu formulaically; this is not to suggest a theoretical free-for-all, but rather that Bourdieu's concepts are used in *Viva M·A·C* not as a strict mechanical framework but rather as explanatory tools and guiding principles for developing new ways of understanding M·A·C's philanthropy.[33] Practice theory did not originate with historians but is instead based on empirical sociological study. An ethnographic study of M·A·C and its philanthropic practices now, more than thirty years after the company's inception, is, of course, impossible; this history of M·A·C is by necessity instead a historical re-creation of those practices, just as Lipartito argues.

Lipartito states that business historians must "attend both to the field of the firm but also the firm's place in a larger set of fields."[34] This foundational concept of *field* and Bourdieu's accompanying ideas about *habitus*, *capital*, and *autonomous production* structure the interpretation of M·A·C's history and Frank Toskan's "creative activism" in *Viva M·A·C*. Bourdieu's concepts are particularly useful in establishing the domain or "field" of fashion in which M·A·C and its founders and employees lived, produced their art, and creatively responded to AIDS. Bourdieu's field is a separate social universe within which its own laws function independently of other fields (including education, politics, art, literature, and journalism, for instance). The field's structure is determined by the relationships between the positions that agents occupy within that field. Bourdieu himself wrote about fashion and considered it a legitimate and socially valuable field of cultural production. In the 1970s, when Bourdieu wrote "Haute Couture and Haute Culture," Paris was *the* fashion centre and French haute couture symbolically dominated the entire fashion field.[35] Haute couture designers set the standard for all fashion, which also, as Bourdieu's title suggests, marked high or legitimate culture. The "field of production of haute couture" that Bourdieu describes is the "game" within which a fashion player or agent is positioned. In his 1975 French version of this article, "Le couturier et sa griffe" ("griffe" means fashion "label"), Bourdieu outlines the 1970s French fashion field by categorizing Christian Dior and Pierre Balmain as the dominant and established figures, or agents, identifying avant-garde, or dominated, agents such as Paco Rabanne and Emanuel Ungaro, and placing Yves Saint Laurent somewhere in between these two opposite sides of the field.[36] Regarding fashion as a field, Bourdieu notes that "[f]ashion is a very prestigious subject in the sociological tradition, at the same time as being apparently rather frivolous."[37] Yet analysing any field of cultural production requires a deep understanding of that field and its complex dynamics through the study of its agents over time, as they enter into and move within the various positions available to them.[38]

Viva M·A·C thus first seeks to outline the field of Toronto fashion and how M·A·C moved within and through it during the 1980s and 1990s to eventually develop its inimitable philanthropy around AIDS. In Part I, "Spaces of Original Possibilities," the first chapter, titled "The Kitchen Sink," documents how Frank Toskan and Frank Angelo met, how M·A·C evolved from, of all things, a laundry service, and the unique ways in which it did business in Toronto in its early days, generally by not following the traditional "rules" of the cosmetics industry. Much of the detail in this chapter has never been captured, based as it is on oral histories. M·A·C's co-founders, but particularly Frank Toskan, were active members of the fashion field in Toronto. Toskan produced a creative cosmetic product with M·A·C, but he was also involved in the cultural production and reproduction of the Toronto fashion scene itself through his photography and editorial work, and, notably, fashion shows such as the Festival of Canadian Fashion and Fashion Cares. The broader perimeters of the fashion community or field are established by identifying many of its players, including fashion designers, hair and make-up artists, models, stylists, retailers, visual presentation artists, fashion editors, and journalists in newspapers, magazines, trade and industry publications, and television, many of whom served as cultural storytellers about M·A·C themselves. This is the theme of Chapter 2, "Fashion Capital."

Bourdieu's related concept of *habitus* is part of this conceptualization of how M·A·C's philanthropic practices evolved over time and space within the fashion field. Bourdieu developed his ideas in numerous works throughout his career, including *Outline of a Theory of Practice*, *The Field of Cultural Production*, and *The Rules of Art*.[39] Agents operate within their field according to their *habitus*. The *habitus* is a way to think about the link between the individual and his or her social context. The *habitus* is composed of the "structuring structures" and the dispositions that incline an agent to act and, importantly, react, in particular ways, which then generate perceptions about, and practices within, his or her social world. Social institutions such as family and education initially influence these dispositions; then professional contacts or networks, for instance, shape them. In the *habitus*, the agent calls upon certain techniques, references, and beliefs that provide the knowledge of the "rules" of that field, allowing him or her to play the "game" of the field along with others who share a similar *habitus* and thus also know the same rules. M·A·C co-founders Frank Toskan and Frank Angelo, the make-up artists who worked at M·A·C, and indeed the entire fashion community, knew the fashion "game" in Toronto and had the abilities, derived from their *habitus*, to operate within this field.

Bourdieu saw change in the field as resulting from struggle among agents, old and new, for more dominant and powerful positions within that field. While movement within the field is centred mainly on routine and the ongoing internal struggles and exhibitions of power by its players, changes can sometimes have external, political, even lifestyle influences and correspondences stemming from particular historical moments and circumstances. For instance, in "Haute Couture and Haute Culture," Bourdieu suggests that André Courrèges, an avant-garde designer, was able to carry out "a specific revolution in a specific field because the logic of the internal distinctions led him to meet up with something that already existed outside." Bourdieu identifies the larger, "outside" force in the 1970s with "modern women" (associated with second-wave feminism), who were "free, uninhibited, sporty, relaxed."[40] Bourdieu notes that such external influences affect the field as a whole. Bourdieu does not discuss the specific nature of these external forces or the shapes they can take, nor does he discuss these as predictable phenomena. He acknowledges that they exist, but he is more interested in how the effects they have on the field's cultural production are translated into cultural artefacts or works of art. As *Viva M·A·C* shows, one of the most influential "outside" forces on the Toronto fashion industry during the 1980s was the AIDS epidemic. The epidemic resonated with struggles already occurring within the Toronto field of fashion, which were then translated into creative output, notably at Fashion Cares, and then with VIVA GLAM and the M·A·C AIDS Fund. The appearance, movement, and disappearance of agents within the field also affect its dynamics. The fact that the disappearance of people in the field occurred because of AIDS is certainly a different type of movement than Bourdieu had envisioned. Chapter 3, "Caring Is Never Out of Fashion," describes how the AIDS epidemic's effects proved devastating to those in the fashion industry in Toronto and New York, and documents the rise of Fashion Cares in Toronto.

Agents in a field share similar interests; they understand everything that is linked to the existence of the field – "what goes without saying"; and they generally agree on what is worth fighting about. This is what Bourdieu called *doxa*, or the attitude towards the rules and how to play according to those rules. Bourdieu describes *doxa* as that which is beyond question, as what is unsaid because it does not need to be said and thus serves to maintain social conventions, positions, and actions. A consciousness of the "feel for the game" must be both recognized and unspoken in a language that only agents in the field can understand. *Doxa* is difficult to identify precisely because it is largely unspoken, and it is different from opinion, which exists within the discursive realm and can thus be openly discussed and challenged. The Toronto fashion industry's and M·A·C's actions around AIDS were part of the *doxa*, a response that was automatic and unquestioned by those within the Toronto field of fashion in the 1980s. Notably, Toronto responded differently than other fashion centres such as New York, or than corporations and even governments.

As Bourdieu explains, there is always a struggle between those who are established, or "consecrated," and those newcomers who often have subversive tendencies compared to those already established. This struggle is the "motor" of the field, instigated by those who have or want power. This power is expressed through *cultural capital*, or knowledge of the field; *symbolic capital*, or prestige within the field; and *social capital*, which can be understood as one's network. *Economic capital* also exists in Bourdieu's model. Frank Toskan and Frank Angelo simultaneously built their own and M·A·C's capital as they tapped into cultural events, figures, and movements in the 1980s and into the 1990s. Toskan's various forms of capital in particular ensured that M·A·C's standing within the field as a fashionable brand was maintained throughout the 1990s, first in Canada and then in the United States. Chapter 4, "Put Your Money Where Your Mouth Is," which marks the beginning of Part II, "Creative Activism," describes how M·A·C emerged as a brand increasingly known for its social conscience, drawing upon the fashion field's creative response to AIDS as well as more personal reactions to the AIDS epidemic. The result was the creation of VIVA GLAM and the M·A·C AIDS Fund.

Frank Toskan consciously sought to keep the availability of M·A·C products restricted, limiting access and avoiding overt commercial practices, particularly advertising. According to Bourdieu, the field is divided into a subfield of small-scale, restricted, or *autonomous* production, opposite the subfield of large-scale, *heteronomous* production, roughly equated with mass production. This heteronomous, mass production is associated with commercial cultural goods. As an agent or work of art moves from the autonomous side to the heteronomous side, economic capital, or profit, increases, but symbolic capital decreases. Bourdieu illustrates how these subfields operated by describing a debate between Pierre Balmain, a "consecrated" or established player, and Jean-Louis Scherrer, an avant-garde player who "spoke like a student leader in May '68." Bourdieu even claims that one could predict the aesthetic decisions a fashion agent would make depending on his position in the field. For instance, those at the dominated, avant-garde pole would show more trousers, or "sales-girls in miniskirts," both signifiers of cutting-edge fashion sense and progressive thinking at that historical moment.[41] According to Bourdieu, there is artistic legitimacy in staying on the autonomous side of the field. Even within this subfield of small-scale production, there is a division into further poles. Those with very high levels of symbolic capital represent the avant-garde. This kind of autonomous small-scale production can be considered "pure" art, or art for art's sake, including art for other artists.[42] In M·A·C's early days, Toskan designed his products as artistic creations; once the brand became an unexpectedly successful commercial enterprise, despite Toskan's commitment to his artistic vision, M·A·C landed squarely in the middle of the struggle between art and the economy. Furthermore, M·A·C's advocacy around AIDS was complicated by the rising phenomenon of corporate philanthropy in the form of cause marketing–type schemes and the contradictions these presented. This struggle is encapsulated in the title of Chapter 5, "Selling Out." Yet Toskan's and M·A·C's "fashion capital" imbued the AIDS cause with greater legitimacy as M·A·C continued to publicly endorse awareness and fundraising through VIVA GLAM and Fashion Cares into the 1990s, leading to the eventual corporate acceptance of AIDS as a valid, rather than stigmatizing, social cause to endorse.

Chapter 6, "Dragging Theory into Practice," closely analyses the 1995 RuPaul ad and the 1997 k.d. lang ad for VIVA GLAM. Together, these ads represented the culmination of the philanthropic practices of M·A·C Cosmetics and the people behind the company. This chapter relies on the seminal work of queer scholar and philosopher Judith Butler to augment Bourdieu's practice theory. These two VIVA GLAM ads cemented M·A·C's corporate ethos within cultural practices instead of marketing logic and thereby effectively challenged critics' claims that M·A·C had "sold out." M·A·C's cultural authority over its AIDS philanthropy rested on how the ads co-opted and captured a number of significant contemporary expressions of cultural practices and productions in fashion, film, music, and drag culture. M·A·C's early advertising further resonated with the emerging social acceptance of androgyny and gender fluidity.

Viva M·A·C: AIDS, Fashion, and the Philanthropic Practices of M·A·C Cosmetics concludes with the transition of M·A·C to Estée Lauder's full oversight. Twenty-five years after the inception of the M·A·C AIDS Fund, Frank Toskan, the late Frank Angelo, and M·A·C epitomize the moment when Toronto fashion decided to "Rise Up" against AIDS. In doing so, M·A·C Cosmetics has indeed become one of Canada's most renowned success stories. *Viva M·A·C* tells that story.

PART I
Spaces of Original Possibilities

CHAPTER 1

The Kitchen Sink

The year 1984 is widely touted as the year of M·A·C's inception, even by M·A·C itself, but the forces that created M·A·C were in play much earlier than this. M·A·C Cosmetics began when its co-founders sensed opportunities and chased creative ideas, informed by their smarts and intuition, and evolved through a series of businesses. M·A·C also emerged during a particular moment – historical, economic, and cultural – and the company was in many ways a logical outcome of these convergences: a small, niche brand, committed to diverse beauty ideals, was able to respond quickly to a local market and to demonstrate a social conscience amid a devastating epidemic. In a practical sense, however, it is likewise evident that M·A·C's day-to-day organizational logic, such as it was, did not follow any rules, let alone the "rules" of the cosmetics industry. A new and different arrangement of practices in working, hiring, acting, and reacting formed the foundation of M·A·C's distinctive corporate ethos, which was eventually encapsulated in the mantra, "all ages, all races, all sexes." By having a keen sense of what was appropriate for themselves and their immediate community and by following their own instincts, Frank Toskan and Frank Angelo effectively challenged all of the existing rules. The origins of M·A·C are often simplified, since few sources exist that document the company's founding and its early days and struggles, and in many ways, this makes sense, because Frank Toskan and Frank Angelo began their business just like so many other hardworking entrepreneurs and immigrants to Toronto in the mid-twentieth century. Both Toskan and Angelo were propelled by tough personal circumstances and working-class backgrounds that emphasized hard work. And like so many others, their stories begin as stories of ordinary people working hard just to get by.

Frank Toskan (PLATE 1) was born in Trieste, Italy, in 1951 and immigrated to Canada with his parents when he was six years old. The family – young Frank, father Guido, and mother Sylvia – arrived by steamer at Halifax, Nova Scotia, in March 1957 and then travelled by train to work on a farm in Edmonton, Alberta. It was a challenging transition for the small family. By 1959, they were ready to return to Italy, discouraged, but when they stopped in Toronto to visit friends and relatives, they decided to stay in Canada. Toskan's three siblings – eight-years-younger Steven, ten-years-younger Walter, and Julie, sixteen years younger – were all born in Toronto. While their parents worked, big brother Frank took care of them, changing diapers and mixing formula, and he became the *de facto* chief babysitter. He resented it at the time but later said he was grateful for the time he had caring for them. He realized that his parents "came here totally unaware of what was waiting for them. It was difficult for me, too. I became interpreter for them by Grade 2. But that's also what gave me the drive to succeed."[1] Indeed, Toskan credits his demanding upbringing and early life experiences for preparing him well for his later entrepreneurial challenges. A childhood spent taking care of his younger siblings and watching his parents working hard, being frugal, and doing without shaped Toskan's disposition, which was grounded in strong family bonds that would later underpin M·A·C's corporate character. Toskan attended elementary school and then the Central High School of Commerce (now the Central Toronto Academy) in downtown Toronto's Little Italy neighbourhood. Toskan briefly studied hairdressing and architectural design after high school, on a constant search for creative opportunities.

Frank Angelo, originally Notarangelo (PLATE 2), was born in Montreal in 1949. Angelo most likely knew as a child that he would inevitably be a business mogul. Angelo's business acumen apparently developed early on: he had his first business, a lemonade stand, at age six. A saxophone player, Angelo's first love was music, and he was playing in bands by the time he was fourteen, first in a group called The Fem-Males, then in another called The Young Canadians. Already an entrepreneur with keen survival instincts honed from growing up in a tough neighbourhood, Angelo hustled to get musical groups together and promote them around his hometown of Montreal. At fifteen, Angelo somehow found a way to play music at army bases in the United States, including in Washington, D.C., and in the Bahamas. When he arrived in Toronto in 1969 with his then life and business partner, Blair James, he immediately began a new business – a chain of hair salons called The Haircutting Place. Their first salon was on Scollard Street in Toronto's Yorkville neighbourhood, the epicentre of Canada's hippie movement. Angelo and James opened their salon in the 1970s at a fortuitous moment, just as the "scene" was winding down and the hippies were starting to cut their hair.[2] The Haircutting Place was Toronto's first chain of unisex salons; not only that, customers could walk in right off the street and sign up for a haircut with any available stylist. Because of the constantly changing clientele, the hairdressers did not develop their own client base, and this allowed Angelo tight control over his business, a habit he would maintain with M·A·C. By the time Angelo was twenty-one, he had thirty-seven hair salons in Toronto at prime locations in department stores like The Bay (the Hudson's Bay Company) on Bloor Street near Yorkville and the Simpsons flagship store at Queen and Yonge streets. By all accounts, Angelo's passion, and his forte, was identifying creative people and inspiring them and shaping them into something bigger, something he thought they deserved to be. Frank Angelo "admired people who were able to do things that he couldn't do. He wasn't really an artist in any way." But he had great common sense and a strong gut instinct. "He was fair, he was kind, and loved people who were talented, and was thrilled with the power of celebrity," remembers Toskan.[3]

When Frank Toskan and Frank Angelo met at the Manatee, a Toronto gay bar, in 1970, there was, according to Toskan, an immediate attraction and friendship, and they soon became romantic partners, known to everyone as "the Franks." By 1976 the Franks were also business partners. Frank Toskan had recently lost his photography job at Eaton's when its famous catalogue folded with the Spring & Summer 1976 edition, so he embarked on something completely different: he bought 30,000 towels and a laundromat on Victoria Park, in Toronto's east end. Hair salons use hundreds of towels a day, and Toskan's idea was that this new business would be the primary towel service for all of The Haircutting Place salons. The Franks named this new business Creative Salon Services. During the day, the laundromat was open to the public; but nights were when it came to life. Toskan's sister Julie and their mother Sylvia helped Toskan do the massive towel laundry after hours. During these all-night shifts, Toskan continued experimenting with his creative work in photography and also make-up artistry. He owned his own photography equipment and began shooting the posters that displayed the new, frequently changing short hairstyles of the day that hung on the walls inside The Haircutting Place salons. Everyone liked these posters, and Toskan began selling these images to other salons. Every week, Toskan would launch approximately twenty new posters with trendy hairstyles featuring quintessential 80s feathered looks, mullets, and asymmetrical cuts sporting names like "Blazing Star" and "Football Hero." Toskan was also photographing strippers and drag queens, friends who stopped by the laundromat on their way home from work late at night or in the early morning. Creative Salon Services soon expanded beyond the towel service, distributing salon tools and other industry equipment like capes and hair colour. Toskan began developing salon products sometime in 1977, starting with a shampoo he called The Hairdresser's Choice. The seeds of what would become M·A·C Cosmetics had been planted.

    Always an imaginative person, Toskan explored numerous creative avenues. On his many trips to Los Angeles, he had noticed Il-Makiage, a cosmetics line available at the Italian fashion house Fiorucci, which had a retail location on Rodeo Drive and was one of his favourite stores. Elio Fiorucci had opened his first store in 1967 in Milan, where he focused on the hippie consumer and the attendant countercultural moment, encouraging creative expression among customers and staff. In 1974, Fiorucci was acquired by the retail chain Standa and expanded into America, where the clothes were closely linked to the Disco era. It was during this time that Toskan became acquainted with the brand and its focus on a "radically new model of design and innovation."[4] Toskan admired the Il-Makiage make-up line's bright, unusual colours and was fascinated by their strong pigmentation, surprised that people would actually wear such vivid colours. Toskan asked himself, how could I apply these colours to my painting? Could I mix them with water? Toskan stayed intrigued and made subsequent visits to Fiorucci. He decided to visit the head office in New York with a proposition: would the owners be interested in having Toskan distribute Il-Makiage in Canada? They said yes, as long as Toskan took the entire product line, which included their Avigal shampoo. Despite the prospect of selling a hair care line that would compete directly with The Hairdresser's Choice, Toskan planned to bring this entire line back to Toronto and sell it at The Haircutting Place. Toskan convinced Angelo that there was nothing like Il-Makiage on the market, and he was positive this unconventional make-up line would sell in Toronto.

But to retail Il-Makiage at The Haircutting Place, Toskan also needed to persuade Simpsons, the department store in which the hair salon was located, to get on board. Simpsons was a Canadian department store institution, and the flagship location in downtown Toronto on Queen Street was famous for its Christmas window displays, upscale ladies' designer wear, the St Regis Room (always known as "The Room"), and its top-floor restaurant, the Arcadian Court.[5] Convincing Simpsons to agree to this plan was a different matter than winning over Angelo, who steadfastly supported and encouraged Toskan. An appointment was set up with Rod Ulmer, then divisional merchandise manager for cosmetics, and Toskan pitched the Il-Makiage concept to him. Ulmer was interested, but Simpsons' management thought the product and concept were too "out there" for their more traditional clientele and did not like the way the line looked – or perhaps, Toskan speculated, they did not like the way that Toskan himself looked. Frank Toskan always had a stylish and youthful appearance, and perhaps management thought he was just a little too creative-looking to be taken seriously. Whatever it was, Simpsons vehemently stated it would *not* launch this wild new make-up line in the main floor cosmetics department, alongside established prestige brands like Clinique, Estée Lauder, Christian Dior, and Chanel. Ulmer recognized, however, that Toskan's outlandish cosmetics line had something special, so he arranged for Toskan to have his own retail space, a stand-alone make-up counter on the second floor (PLATE 3). Toskan rented his new space from Simpsons directly; this separated him from the main floor cosmetics department but also furnished him with unusual freedom. The fledgling company was called "Il-Makiage Canada," and Toskan incorporated his new business as "Make-up Art (Cosmetics) Limited" in February 1981, although, he recollects, he was probably doing business in Simpsons a little earlier than this.[6]

A large neon sign identified Toskan's new retail outlet as the "Make-up Art Centre"; another sign directly underneath featured Il-Makiage. These signs framed the small counter Ulmer had provided. Toskan's counter was, as promised, on the second floor, in front of The Haircutting Place and a Cultures restaurant, adjacent to the "Young Teens" clothing department. Along with Il-Makiage, Toskan's Make-up Art Centre carried professional make-up brands like Ben Nye, as well as other theatrical lines, which Toskan now curated into a one-stop shop together with The Hairdresser's Choice hair care products. The products Toskan chose to sell were an extension of the things his friends were interested in: professional-grade cosmetics with intense pigments that "read" well on photographic film. Products like these were necessary for make-up artists and models as well as the drag queens Toskan continued to photograph, who needed suitable products to cover beards, for instance. The glass showcase contained product displays, and the hair products were stacked neatly behind the counter. On the counter, single round blush and eye shadow testers were attached to pyramid-shaped plexiglass units. Lipsticks were stacked in a row in a separate unit. The counter had several chairs for customers who wanted detailed consultations and lessons, as Toskan always offered information and instruction when selling these professional-grade products. A very early profile on Toskan, accompanied by a flattering headshot, that appeared in the *Globe and Mail* in mid-1981 described Toskan's "casual approach" to make-up application at this "new unisex salon," referring to The Haircutting Place. The article emphasized how the salon, connected to Il-Makiage, was affordable in its offerings and was especially welcoming to young people, male and female. In fact, the counter, along with The Haircutting Place, often hosted special events (PLATE 4). Michael Damian, an actor on *The Young and the Restless*, once made a guest appearance, much to the delight of both Frank Angelo and Julie Toskan. This article marked the first of many times that Toskan's cosmetic advice would be featured in the Toronto newspapers.[7] In its first year at Simpsons, the Make-up Art Centre had sales of about $300,000.[8] Toskan began referring to the Make-up Art Centre by an informal acronym, "M·A·C," and it stuck. A brand was born.

Toskan's much younger sister Julie had long been involved in Toskan's businesses; besides working at Toskan's laundromat, she had been the receptionist since her early teens at The Haircutting Place, where Toskan applied her make-up so she would appear older than the teenager she actually was. Julie had even been a model in a television commercial for the salon. In 1982, she began dating Victor Casale, whom she had known since they were in the same grade nine English class. By 1984, Casale was a first-year chemistry student at the University of Toronto. Now, she brought Victor Casale home and, inadvertently, into the family business. Casale appeared just as Toskan was experimenting with new formulations of The Hairdresser's Choice shampoo for Creative Salon Services. The hairdressers at the salons needed a shampoo with low lather that would rinse out quickly and easily, so Toskan and Casale studied Casale's chemistry textbooks and analysed ingredients. While removing the surfactants, which are the traditional lathering ingredients, they also figured out how to achieve the exact product the hairdressers required. By this time, Frank Angelo was also running his own hairdressing school, and the students as well as the stylists in the salons would test the various formulations, which they enjoyed doing because it made them feel like they were participating in the creative process. Once this new formulation of The Hairdresser's Choice shampoo was rolled out, the hairdressers became an informal but powerful promotional network, personally spreading the word about this new product. Around the same time, Toskan also made a hair product for the singer Gladys Knight, a personal friend, who needed something effective to condition and strengthen her hair.[9] The resulting product, called Formula K, was made and distributed through Creative

Salon Services. To sell it, Toskan loaded the product onto a truck and sold it himself at trade shows across the United States. Formula K was the driving force behind the Creative Salon Services banner, and together Casale and Toskan became its product innovation team.

Soon after the Make-up Art Centre opened, with the Canadian dollar continuing to drop in value, Il-Makiage became too expensive to import from the United States. Toskan's creative but thrifty clientele would not pay for such expensive make-up products. Toskan had been developing the Make-up Art Centre alongside Creative Salon Services and the towel business, and those other concerns were distracting him. To move forward with the Make-up Art Centre after dropping Il-Makiage from its roster, Toskan knew he would need to develop his own cosmetic line to replace it, and if he wanted to stay on top of what was happening creatively in Toronto, he would have to move quickly. Toskan wanted to continue accommodating his make-up artist and fashion communities and their diverse professional needs. Having photographed strippers and drag queens, he also realized that matte finishes and heavier coverage provided the necessary dimensionality in photographs. He was still influenced by wild colours, like those of Il-Makiage, but Toskan's collaboration with Gladys Knight on the Formula K hair care line had made him realize that women of colour had few cosmetic choices. The products that were available were generally greasy, the colours were not precise, and the packaging was not elegant. These insights inspired Toskan to look at that market more closely. He grasped that there was nothing available for them at the make-up counter and there was a real need to service a market so neglected. Creating colour products appropriate for women of colour became paramount. Toskan already knew that the cosmetics industry did not offer colour cosmetics that suited his own creative photographic needs, nor did it offer enough colour variety in general; other cosmetics companies were very prescriptive in what they sold. Toskan's creative ideas converged around all of these realizations. Toskan thus had a tall order for his new make-up line: he wanted to offer professional-grade cosmetics in a wide range of long-wearing, diverse, sometimes outlandish colours with intense pigmentation and high coverage that could also provide the appropriate effects for photography and theatre. He again turned to Victor Casale.

As Toskan's right hand in product innovation with The Hairdresser's Choice shampoo, Casale now helped develop Toskan's various cosmetic concepts, and together they formulated new products. It is no exaggeration to say that Toskan could not have done this work without Casale by his side. At first, Toskan would buy pre-made products and heat them up in his kitchen and experiment with his own mixtures, but soon he and Casale began ordering pigments and raw ingredients, playing with new combinations until they got exactly what Toskan envisioned. Since Casale was still in university, he learned about cosmetic chemistry "organically" and with no preconceived ideas, so "it was my imagination that helped create the products." Driven by Toskan's creative vision, Casale would "see what the industry was doing in formulations, [and] I'd try totally different things, things that chemists today wouldn't even use in a formula. But it worked."[10] Toskan delegated a room for Casale at the laundromat (this was the second location; the first had burnt down) in Thornhill, where Toskan's parents and sister Julie lived – "there were towels everywhere," Casale remembers – and Casale set up his own version of what he thought a cosmetics lab should be. Casale's labs, first in Thornhill and later in Markham, Ontario (both just north of Toronto), were never bigger than about twenty feet by fifteen feet and were always configured in the same way: white walls with a grey floor; dark-grey industrial shelves divided up with drawers and cupboards for storing raw ingredients, with sections or "rooms" to stock the finished products; and a metal bench with a stainless-steel countertop. He and Toskan used a hot plate, a scale, a powder press for compressing eye shadow and powder pans, a mixer to make foundation, a Cuisinart to mix powders, and, later on, a colour computer, and they made all the products themselves by hand. With such a small set-up, Casale and Toskan could only make small batches; for instance, the lipstick mould could hold only ten lipsticks, so they produced either ten or twenty lipsticks per day. They hand-pressed all the eye shadows and complexion products, which was very slow and careful work. Frank Angelo stayed behind the scenes as the business "brains," overseeing all the business processes and driving the company, pushing Toskan, with his inimitable style, to the forefront and inspiring him to achieve even more.

Toskan was never satisfied with their results. Casale remembers how a new product was never really finished because Toskan could never make a final decision on it – he always wanted to play with it some more. Toskan kept saying no to Casale's efforts – "Frank's a creative guy; that drove me crazy but was part of his genius" – so they kept working on a prototype until finally they got it right. Toskan and Casale's first major product innovation came in 1985: the highly pigmented lipstick of Toskan's dreams, with an extreme matte finish in appearance and texture, devoid of any frost or shine. Casale recalls that this matte lipstick was a very challenging product to make because there was no precedent for it anywhere in the cosmetics industry. One of its ingredients was a medical-grade silicone, dimethicone, which was used at the time for breast implants, not cosmetics. It was so unusual to use it in cosmetics that Casale had to have a notary public attest that he and Toskan were not using this ingredient for surgical procedures![11] Toskan named this first matte red lipstick "Russian Red." The packaging looked very different, with a minimalist, gender-neutral black-metal bullet-shaped lipstick container. The eye and cheek colours came with screw-top lids. Toskan sold each M·A·C colour product individually (PLATE 5). This approach appealed to make-up artists, who preferred to create their own colour collections rather than purchasing the pre-assembled, colour-coordinated "looks" offered by other cosmetics companies.

M·A·C's research and development strategy, such as it was, reflected Toskan's entrepreneurial and experimental spirit. Once they had perfected a product and it was ready for the market, it was priced according to how much it cost to produce, not according to how much research, development, or advertising had gone into it, as other cosmetics companies did (there was no advertising at M·A·C, in any case). Around 5 per cent of M·A·C's sales were allocated to R&D, but that amount was not directed to any specific product development; Casale recalls that they never really had a set budget.

The Franks maintained strict control over all aspects of their new make-up business. Since both Franks' families had had hard backgrounds and always struggled, the Franks remained prudent, even tight-fisted; Toskan and Casale both stated later that they would rather have shelved or repurposed products and ideas or make something work in another area than spend money wastefully.[12] Yet this ethic allowed for great freedom and innovation: Toskan and Casale developed anything they wanted, however outrageous, and refined it as often as necessary. Toskan would explain new colour and texture ideas to Casale, often by blending pigments on a piece of white paper. Casale would make samples for Toskan, and they would send them out to professional make-up artists for feedback. One such artist was Frances Hathaway, who recalls that she felt that "this was the very first time that a cosmetic company actually reached out and did something for the make-up artist; before, it was all consumer-driven. No one had ever thought about it before."[13] Toskan was soon being asked by his other make-up artist friends to make custom products especially for them. M·A·C's niche was thus established: a make-up line created *by* a make-up artist, *for* make-up artists, that relied on a communicative network based on shared cosmetics practices that were distinctly different in aesthetic, style, and focus from the mainstream consumer cosmetics brands.

From the start, M·A·C implemented several ethical corporate policies that would remain embedded in its business practices. One defining feature was that the product boxes listed all of the ingredients – something that was not a Canadian cosmetics industry requirement at that time and that was certainly uncommon in the cosmetics industry in general. As Casale put it, M·A·C "had nothing to hide." Consumers were becoming more aware of products that might be "comedogenic" (causing acne), such as those containing oils, especially mineral oil, or added fragrances, and they were increasingly interested in cosmetics with additional skincare benefits. Casale's goal was to make M·A·C's products as good as he possibly could, and he constantly sought to improve them with ingredients such as vitamins A and E. M·A·C's bullet-shaped lipstick tubes were first manufactured by Colt's Plastics Company, once a division of Colt's gun company, Colt's Patent Fire Arms

Manufacturing Co., and were made in Indonesia. The lipstick packaging's guts were made of metal (tin), and the plastic caps were attached afterwards. But the metal would sometimes bend, so Casale chose all plastic guts, which offered a more precise fit than metal. The new tube's lighter weight was also more economical, environmentally sounder to ship, and easier to recycle. Then they created the "Back to M·A·C" program, whereby customers would receive a full-sized lipstick of their choice when they returned six empty M·A·C cosmetic packages to the counter. In these early days, "recycling" was not a consumer buzzword, nor was it a standard practice for businesses, and it was definitely uncommon within the cosmetics industry. M·A·C was ahead of its time in recognizing the need to avoid waste and to take responsibility for implementing production and consumption practices that were less environmentally damaging. This innovative stance proved to be a precursor to the larger environmental movement that was only just gaining momentum. The relative lack of sophistication in recycling processes at the time offers evidence of this. The packaging went back to M·A·C's production facility in Markham, and the staff took everything apart themselves and separated the pieces into different buckets, which were then sent off to various recycling centres. Once local recycling was in place, there was no need to personally sort the pieces – everything could be sent directly to local recycling facilities.[14]

The Franks also eschewed one other standard cosmetics industry convention: advertising. Toskan was sceptical of promotional tactics that involved advertising, a beautiful brand spokesmodel, the ubiquitous gift-with-purchase, and other product giveaways, and he was contemptuous of misleading and disingenuous advertising images. Instead, M·A·C offered a 40 per cent discount to professional make-up artists, hairstylists, models, and actors in order to get the products out in the field and actually used in creative ways. This was an unheard-of strategy for a cosmetic brand and further facilitated and strengthened the word-of-mouth network by then developing among Toronto's fashion insiders. M·A·C became known through this interpersonal form of publicity, and in any case, it did not seem to need the promotional lift provided by traditional advertising. Although the Franks could not have realized it at the time, M·A·C was beginning to change standard cosmetics industry practices with the experiments begun at the Make-up Art Centre.

Cosmetic Mavericks

As their early history suggests, Frank Toskan and Frank Angelo's make-up company was shaping up to become an unusual chapter in the history of cosmetics entrepreneurs whose experiments with formulas and colours and new business models were leading to monumental success in the industry. Toskan himself later realized his place in this history, recalling that he had begun in the kitchen "like Estée Lauder."[15] Toskan was also similar in several ways to Max Factor in that he started out developing cosmetics appropriate for a specific medium. Factor, a theatre make-up artist, had begun his career in the United States, distributing and selling theatre cosmetics. In the early twentieth century, the advent of motion pictures offered him a unique entry point into the cosmetics industry. Film actresses wore heavy, greasy stage make-up that did not photograph well and that made facial features look harsh and distorted. Factor created the first cosmetics for film in 1914 and adapted Russian theatrical application techniques for this new medium. He created new products scientifically, with formulas and techniques designed to optimize facial features on film. The first product was a thin grease paint made in fourteen shades that did not crack or cake. Factor soon gained a reputation as the "make-up artist to the stars." As film actresses began to wear his products off-camera, ordinary women, always fascinated by what the stars did, became interested. By 1916, Factor was creating mass-market products branded with the aura of Hollywood. In 1920, he introduced a new line called "Society Makeup." By 1927, he had developed national distribution channels; a year later he had begun advertising. Factor's Pan-Stik make-up, an opaque foundation for use in all three media – print, film, and now television – was introduced in 1947 and was a mass-market success for decades. Indeed, the Max Factor brand set the standard for all television make-up. Factor was astute enough to realize that television would have a profound influence on cosmetics marketing. Up to the 1940s, brands had been advertised in women's magazines and on radio. With television, the diffusion of Western beauty brands, products, and ideals became possible. By the early 1960s the American beauty industry was spending $152 million per year on TV advertising.[16]

Another notable cosmetics pioneer was Charles Revson. As historian Geoffrey Jones reveals, Revson began his cosmetics firm in 1937 with a line of nail polish. He capitalized on the emerging white, middle-class beauty salon culture, becoming a formidable corporate player in the cosmetics industry with his new company, which he called Revlon. Revlon products closely followed fashion rather than film or television; its lipstick colours especially were inspired by seasonal fashions. The 1950s saw the rise of Revlon's "lipstick wars," particularly with rival Helena Rubinstein, when Revlon began introducing new colour "stories" – themed colour groupings – in accelerated three-month cycles. Fashion's constant search for the latest "look" was matched by Revlon's intensified production of new lip and nail colours. The entrepreneurial spirit was not confined to men. In fact, many female entrepreneurs built successful cosmetics businesses in Europe and North America. Helena Rubinstein, born in Hungary, developed a cream from a secret family recipe that launched her empire. Women's access to beauty culture through hair and beauty salons allowed those with an entrepreneurial spirit to gain a foothold in the industry. Elizabeth Arden (née Florence Nightingale Graham) was born in Canada in 1878. She moved to New York in 1908, changed her name, and created a new elite persona to build up her eponymous business. Rubinstein and Arden sold their aspirational products through beauty salons to build their empires in the early twentieth century. African American businesswomen Madam C.J. Walker and Annie Turnbo Malone both created successful hair care companies for women of colour and became millionaires during the 1920s and 1930s. Estée Lauder (née Josephine Esther Mentzer), the Brooklyn-born daughter of Hungarian immigrants, started a luxury perfume and cosmetics business in the 1930s, distributing products in premium department stores by emphasizing product demonstrations and applications.[17] However, unlike these entrepreneurs, many of whom were creating mass-market products from the outset, Frank Toskan did not start out with the same commercial vision for M·A·C.

In the very small Canadian cosmetics industry, M·A·C clearly stands apart. M·A·C is one of a small number of Canadian-based cosmetics brands that emerged in the twentieth century. One of the oldest brands is Marcelle. In 1949, Dr Phil Blazer from Chicago approached Montreal pharmacist Victor Cape. Blazer manufactured the hypoallergenic Marcelle cosmetics line, which had launched in Montreal in 1933. He asked Cape to be the brand's Canadian distributor. It was a slow and steady success. Borden Inc., a food company, bought Marcelle in the 1950s. In 1974, Michael Cape, son of Victor, bought the brand back from Borden and concentrated solely on the Canadian market, pulling the brand out of the United States. Marcelle Cosmetics is produced in Lachine, Quebec, and is fully owned by the Cape family and distributed across Canada through mass retailers.[18] Another entrepreneur is Morrie Cohen, who created Caroline Cosmetics Inc., named after his daughter, in Montreal in 1968. Cohen focused strongly on the French Canadian market, which he felt was being ignored by the unilingual cosmetics multinationals. He saw his direct competition as mass-market brands such as Maybelline and CoverGirl. He then developed a secondary line geared to consumers aged eighteen to thirty-five called Annabelle (named after his mother-in-law). Some of the products were made locally; others were sourced in the United States. Annabelle entered the US market in the late 1990s. In 1999, Marcelle's parent company, Professional Pharmaceutical Corp., purchased the Annabelle and Caroline brands for $11 million.[19]

Several entrepreneurial women have experienced success in the Canadian cosmetics industry. Caryl Baker, a one-time model, began importing cosmetics from US manufacturers in 1969. Her company was called Caryl Baker Visage, a name that translated easily into French. She sold her products through representatives who held in-home parties, similar to the American-based brand Mary Kay, and within five years had three hundred representatives. When The Bay opened its downtown Toronto location on Bloor Street in 1974, it asked Baker to open a store there. Baker's operation grew, and she decided to manufacture the products in Canada, since, as was Toskan's experience with Il-Makiage, importing some three hundred different products from the United States was becoming too expensive. A point of distinction for Baker was that she also offered make-up lessons, developing her business into a full-fledged school of make-up artistry. Lise Watier is another Canadian success story. She opened the Institut Lise Watier in Montreal in 1968 to teach women about make-up and skincare. Her mandate was to empower modern women through cosmetics, in line with their newly achieved professional status during the second-wave feminist movement. Watier's cosmetic line launched in 1972. Having become a household name in Quebec, Lise Watier began making its products available in Ontario in 1980 and in western Canada in 1984. While these examples may suggest there is a thriving Canadian cosmetics industry, this is a relatively small number of brands compared to the dozens that emerged in the United States and Europe during the twentieth century.

Toskan's products and creative practices diverged in many ways from those of his Canadian contemporaries in the cosmetics industry; so did his attitude. He rejected what he felt was a "paint by numbers" approach to make-up and fashion choices. At this time in the 1980s, it was fashionable for people to have their "colours" done and their "season" determined. Depending on their skin's undertones (cool or warm) and intensity (lighter or darker), a customer was a "Spring," for instance, and a suitable palette of colours was then suggested for clothing and cosmetics. Caryl Baker endorsed this method for choosing make-up colours, and for her it was successful, but Toskan felt that this approach was too formulaic and deprived people of choice and of the chance to express their individuality. For a time, some customers did come to the Make-up Art Centre counter with their fabric swatches to match their make-up colours to their wardrobe, but Toskan quickly discouraged this habit. Pre-planned colour assemblages offended Toskan; people should just wear what they like, he thought, not what they are told to wear by magazines, ads, or cosmetics companies.[20]

Jean Macdonald, a former model, started a cosmetics business in Toronto in the 1970s called Jean Macdonald Beautyworks. Primarily catering to fashion models, she taught more advanced cosmetics techniques such as contouring, but she really designed her line and education for models' faces. Toskan thought her application and teaching methods were excellent, if also somewhat formulaic, since they tended to make customers all look model-like, and this did not always translate well to real people with irregular, decidedly non-model features. Toskan considers

Macdonald influential in that she helped customers change their attitude towards make-up by getting them directly involved in the process. Still, Toskan felt that Baker and Macdonald and others in the industry were dictating *to* customers instead of having a dialogue *with* them about achieving their own unique look. Advancing an individualistic beauty aesthetic reflected Toskan's personal approach to working with customers that embraced everyone's character. It also revealed an implicit political commitment that resonated with a new and emerging beauty culture.

Business historian Geoffrey Jones describes in *Beauty Imagined: A History of the Global Beauty Industry* how the cosmetics industry's rise as a global economic force influenced the diffusion of various beauty ideals throughout the twentieth century. Before Western companies began exporting their products in the early part of the century, beauty was local in its products and traditions. In the early to mid-twentieth century, major Western brands imbued their products with the glamour of locale. Luxury brands were less likely to adapt to local variations; for example, the prestige French company Lancôme's brand identity rested on a more universal understanding of its meaning for consumers, that of Parisian style and glamour, and a standard version of beauty accompanied the brand's images. Jones notes that sales, acquisitions, and mergers beginning in the 1960s created cosmetics conglomerates out of Procter & Gamble, L'Oréal, and Unilever. Trustworthy figureheads like Elizabeth Arden and Helena Rubinstein had died and family businesses had disintegrated, a trend occurring at the same time that corporate control expanded. The intensification of globalization saw huge cosmetics conglomerates continue to form. With these mergers came a more homogenized version of beauty.[21]

The diffusion of a Western beauty ideal – that is, fair skin, blonde hair, blue eyes – had been propagated for decades by mass media and cosmetics companies, but it was during the 1960s that political movements in the United States around civil rights brought discussions about beauty culture to the forefront. The African American beauty salon was a women-only safe space where information about the civil rights movement was shared, resistance originated, and political organization came together. Yet while the civil rights movement dominated the political landscape, it was barely represented in beauty advertising. Beauty itself now became a legitimate political concern within this dialogue. Historian Kathy Peiss notes in *Hope in a Jar: The Making of America's Beauty Culture* that "[m]ass-market cosmetics firms responded more slowly and often reluctantly to criticisms from women of color about racist beauty images and exclusionary marketing." Brand extensions that incorporated ethnic and especially African American consumers' needs for more diverse skin-tone colour products – for a new fashion "aesthetic" – started to emerge. However, the offerings were limited.[22]

Using – or even rejecting – cosmetics became a political action, and not just in African American communities, during the burgeoning counterculture of the 1960s. Some women viewed cosmetics as tools for women's acceptance of their role in their own oppression, a complicit adherence to both the dominant beauty ideal and the patriarchy. Thus refusing to wear make-up became a form of political action. For others, cosmetics were empowering and wearing them symbolized hard-won gains, just as Canadian cosmetics entrepreneur Lise Watier envisioned. The 1970s also marked the beginning of second-wave feminism and the women's liberation movement. Having joined the workforce in ever-increasing numbers, women had more disposable income to spend on cosmetics. But it was still debatable whether the cosmetics industry empowered or oppressed women. As business and communications scholar Linda M. Scott recounts in *Fresh Lipstick: Redressing Fashion and Feminism*, the "natural," un-made-up look was soon co-opted by mass-market cosmetics companies in the 1970s and became a new signifier of the "liberated" woman and a new advertising trope – as reflected, for example, in CoverGirl's ubiquitous ads featuring all-American model Cheryl Tiegs.[23]

As globalization continued throughout the 1980s, however, the homogenizing trend in beauty ideals started to reverse, and diverse, non-Western beauty standards and norms began to spread. For brands to expand across a global landscape, a consistent and unified brand identity across different markets was required, but now brands also needed to be more flexible in the beauty standards they espoused, and the products they offered had to accommodate local differences.[24] Brands now needed to be more sensitive to cultural norms, traditions, and habits. Thus by the mid-1980s, cosmetics companies were generally responding more to local needs and local markets. Meanwhile, consumer groups were increasingly targeting the beauty industry, particularly advertising, accusing it of manipulating consumers through misleading promises. There was a perception of brand inauthenticity. Product integrity came to the forefront, and ingredients were questioned not just for their efficacy but also for their safety (concerns that continue to the present day).[25] The green movement pushed for more "natural" ingredients, which, despite various and vague definitions, were perceived as safer and more effective. Concern for the environment led to a push for recyclable packaging and, increasingly, attention to social causes.

A space developed for specialized, local cosmetics firms like The Body Shop (1976) and Aveda (1978). Both these brands were proponents of natural ingredients, ethical production practices, and transparent promotion, all of which gained purchase by the 1980s. Anita Roddick, The Body Shop's British founder, started her company by making products in her kitchen. She packaged them in plain bottles, did not advertise, and refused to make dubious product claims, especially about anti-aging properties. The Body Shop was one of the very first companies to claim it did not test its products on animals. Aveda founder Horst Rechelbacher was intrigued by aromatherapy, and he used herbs and plants in his hair, skin, and body products, which he also initially developed in his kitchen. His US company sold its products through salons called "lifestyle" stores. Cosmetics brands like these, which were still far from mainstream in the 1980s, helped open up a space for very niche products and brands that were unique and original almost by definition in that they responded to local needs and deployed innovative, rule-breaking ways of doing business.[26]

As Frank Toskan realized after working with Gladys Knight, quality cosmetics for women of colour were still hard to find, even by the 1980s. Toskan's small company thus found a favourable response in its local creative market when the large cosmetics brands failed to effectively service those markets, especially the multicultural consumers in Toronto, and M·A·C effectively filled this niche with diverse colour products. Suzanne Boyd, former editor-in-chief of *Flare* magazine, was herself an early M·A·C customer for this very reason, and she remembers how M·A·C quickly became known in Toronto for its colour range, especially for darker skins: "you could go and get a foundation that matched your skin tone."[27] For women like Boyd, finding a foundation that matched dark skin and was not too pale and did not read as "ashy" was one of the biggest cosmetics challenges, because of the dearth of options available. The beauty industry was, and still is, subject to critique for promoting narrow representations of beauty ideals – ideals that Toskan set out to challenge with his new company.[28] Toskan, too, was working in a climate of being able to respond quickly to immediate demand within his own professional circle of creative colleagues who became customers and friends.

M·A·C Girls and Boys

From its inception, M·A·C was far more underground and subcultural than its cosmetics competitors. This fact was immediately clear from the people who worked at M·A·C's retail counter and the creative practices they exhibited. Cosmetics companies usually hire salespeople into the department store setting who represent their brand and company image, making sure they fit a certain visual template. For instance, Clinique's image has always been clean and antiseptic, and its scientific image is reflected in the white, lab-coat-style uniforms worn by its sales associates. By enforcing a standard, homogeneous visual presentation that suggested conformity, many cosmetics companies stripped their salespeople of their individuality. In stark contrast, Toskan liked his staff "fresh" and a little "raw" and wanted them to be themselves: "You can't really take a creative person – it was necessary to hire creative people – and tell them what to say or do," he said. M·A·C's salespeople came straight from Toronto's Queen Street West fashion, music, and art scenes. M·A·C's retail staff were all trained artists, some in make-up, but frequently in other visual arts (a quality that still defines M·A·C's retail staff), and often had never worked for a cosmetics company before. If they had, Toskan often needed to "reteach" them according to his own style and values. Many of these people did not work at M·A·C for long.

Suzanne Boyd remembers how M·A·C's visual presentation played out in the department store setting. For the traditional prestige cosmetics companies, the "right" look was definitely female, but it was

> not just [about] their skin tone or their weight or any of that; it was a particular point of view – almost very corporate looking, middle of the road, "corporate pretty"; everyone looked exactly the same. [But] when you went to the M·A·C counter, you saw individuality and very bold expressionism. There'd be bigger, smaller, Asian, Black, white, boys in make-up. That was unheard of at the time. It was shocking, and for someone like me who'd see that in the nightclub – you're seeing this in the broad light of day, in the department store – that's great ... It was almost like you'd get the "club nod."[29]

Tattoos, piercings, and coloured hair were accepted, even encouraged among the artists, alongside "the freedom to make their own choices," said Toskan.[30] Boyd's observation helps bring into focus why Simpsons insisted that the Make-up Art Centre be located far from the main cosmetics department on the main floor. Toskan understood and respected Simpsons' rules, and he did not want to offend anyone there, but he also did not want to be part of this kind of corporate structure, and he did not want to be managed or told what to do with his business and the people who worked for M·A·C.

Toskan hired primarily on the basis of what he calls "niceness." M·A·C was inclusive of everyone, as long as they were "nice people" and capable of sharing the M·A·C philosophy of individuality, not just selling the products. Toskan gave people who looked different, who did not seem to fit in anywhere or did not have more conventional employment opportunities elsewhere, a chance at M·A·C. Senior M·A·C artist Jane McKay recalls that in the early days, M·A·C staff comprised "people who didn't necessarily fit into the big corporate world and they saw themselves in this place of artistry, social compassion, [with a] sense of community."[31] Toskan encouraged M·A·C's artists to express themselves, and this gave them pride in themselves and their employment, which in turn created employee loyalty. Toskan knew that, like himself, "creative people like to be free. If you take that away from them then you've kind of lost the soul of who that person is. We understood that very early on. To have that kind of person working with us and supporting what we were all about – we needed to give them freedom."[32]

Toskan ensured that training and practices were consistent among the artists and with the M·A·C brand, but he always allowed space for the artists' personal expression. Everyone on the M·A·C staff was young and wanted to be different, and they respected similarly minded people who unabashedly expressed their individuality and creativity. "We were all 'like' people," said Toskan, "and we were all 'underdogs.'" In fact, M·A·C's early community was essentially composed of these "underdogs." Being gay, especially, was for many people very much about being an underdog or an "outcast," Toskan recollects. Frances Hathaway clearly remembers the sense of inclusion that M·A·C offered its staff – an inclusion that embraced the LGBTQ community, including herself, from the beginning.[33] This camaraderie and practice of working together gave them the strength to support one another as well as others who perceived themselves as being different, as also being an "underdog," and to help those who were most in need or having a difficult time. When Toskan interviewed new staff, he looked for that type of person. This hiring practice was both personally and professionally rewarding.

Another glaring difference at the M·A·C counter was the presence of men, androgynous-looking staff, and sometimes drag queens. Toskan remembers that some female customers were clearly uncomfortable with, even offended by, men working behind the cosmetics counter. Some would even ask Toskan outright, why are *you* here? They did not want a man to apply their make-up. In the 1980s, the only men who were associated with make-up were the superstars who came to a store from Paris or New York for a special appearance. In New York, men did apply and sell make-up at the beauty counter, but this practice was not yet widespread in Toronto, Toskan recollects. Department stores by nature were highly risk-averse, and management listened intently to any kind of negative customer feedback and took it very seriously.[34] Toskan would tell female customers that a man's eye was skilled at determining a woman's most flattering beauty look, and his honesty and sense of taste soon cultivated a loyal clientele.

Taste is manifested in knowledge or cultural capital that marks one as "distinctive," and it certainly characterized Toskan and his staff.[35] Such assessments can also be considered part of the bodily dispositions reproduced by the *habitus*. Toskan and his team worked hard to overcome management pushback and customer bias about M·A·C's staff. But there was, Toskan remembers, always "a struggle to learn things from the bottom up."[36]

In further defiance of standard retail management practice in the cosmetics industry, Toskan did not pay his staff by sales commissions; rather, he paid his artists a high base salary. Sales commissions foster competition among staff, especially in cosmetics. Toskan would have no part in an environment where competition, rather than community, defined work practices. Instead, the M·A·C artists worked as a team to service M·A·C customers by focusing solely on the creative aspects of make-up and on what the customer wanted. In fact, M·A·C also encouraged its customers to work with different artists and obtain different perspectives so as to experience various styles and tastes, something that cannot easily be done when staff are paid by commission. Toskan again found his champion in Rod Ulmer, whose smooth negotiating style facilitated M·A·C's independence and allowed the Franks to hire their own staff and work out this unusual pay structure. Ulmer knew that Simpsons' financial department would not "get" what the Franks were doing; in a later interview he recalled that "I kept the financial people away, I kept the store managers away. Nobody's allowed to talk to these people [the Franks] except me. I set up the financial arrangements with their staff, so they own their own staff. Nobody can touch their staff."[37] Since retailers generally hire the cosmetics staff, with remuneration split between the retailer and the cosmetics company, in this regard the Franks also played by their own rules.

The staff's all-black clothing lent a dramatic look to the retail counter that reinforced the brand's "cool" factor and difference. Toskan could not afford – and did not want – a company uniform of any kind, but he noticed that his staff wore black most of the time anyway. They all had a similar aesthetic; this was the time in fashion in Toronto when all-black was what "alternative" people wore; "it was a rebellious colour" in the 1980s, Toskan recalls.

This attitude and colour had, in different ways, also defined the 1960s beatniks, the punk scene of the 1970s, and now, in the 1980s, Goth music. So for M·A·C's staff, wearing black as a visual brand identity came naturally. This all-black look for M·A·C just seemed right to Toskan, who surmised that this was also due to his Italian background, where the women always wore black. Wearing black was subversive in the cosmetics industry because heretofore it had been strictly forbidden; as an unspoken rule, black was never worn in the hair industry either.[38] Frances Hathaway remembers that her mother, Evelyn, a close friend of Frank Angelo's, advised him that black would look chic and stand out yet still work for the more practical aspects of the job. And black has historically been a fashion colour, as fashion scholar Jennifer Craik observes. She notes that black has connotations of sophistication, mystery, and death, thanks to its association with mourning. But, following French designer Coco Chanel, black also denotes being chic and stylish – recall, for instance, Audrey Hepburn's "little black dress" and pearls in the 1961 Blake Edwards film *Breakfast at Tiffany's*. The colour black also acts as a default "blank slate" upon which any identity can be projected, whether consumer or designer.[39] Thus, black as a brand colour was perfect for a company like M·A·C that did not wish to impose a particular identity, either on its staff or on its customers. Furthermore, this all-black look was antithetical to the white uniforms sported by other cosmetics brands. Often, when Toskan travelled with his staff to an event, people would ask if they were in a rock band!

Just after launching the Make-up Art Centre in Simpsons, in 1982, the Franks opened their own professional retail store at 233 Carlton Street in Toronto's Cabbagetown, an Irish working-class neighbourhood that was just on the edge of becoming upscale when the Franks moved in. It was here, in their own place, that they had the ultimate creative and business control, away from the dictates of the department store. In the all-white space, the M·A·C make-up line and the hair salon were ensconced on the first floor, the offices took up the second floor, and the Franks lived on the third floor. This space quickly became a community hub where industry professionals would network, demonstrate new cosmetic techniques and practices to one another, and drop off their portfolios.

Customers began socializing at the counter, too: Toskan often had to put out extra chairs to accommodate everyone because so many people would stay for hours. Frances Hathaway remembers always being there: "It was like the clubhouse for me. It's where we hung out. It's what we did."[40] In its first year, Toskan sold $20,000 worth of products at the Carlton Street store. Toskan experienced every aspect of his new business every single day, from morning until night: creating, producing, and packaging the products with his family beside him; standing behind the counter and selling his products alongside his staff; doing make-up applications – not "makeovers," he stressed – on his clients, cleaning the counter and the testers; and, sometimes, dealing with difficult customers. He began his day at the Markham factory, just north of Toronto, worked at the Simpsons counter in downtown Toronto, then went on to the Carlton store, finishing at night photographing strippers and drag queens and the models for The Haircutting Place's promotional pictures. From all this, day after day, Toskan knew exactly what it took to build his business from the ground up.

According to sociologist Andreas Reckwitz, practice theory locates the social not just in mental qualities, discourse, and interaction, but also in routinized behaviours consisting of various interconnected elements: bodily activities; mental activities; "things" and their use; background knowledge and understanding; know-how; states of emotion; and motivational knowledge.[41] A practice cannot be reduced to any one of these elements, for they are all interrelated: "A practice is thus a routinized way in which bodies are moved, objects are handled, subjects are treated, things are described and the world is understood."[42] As such, social fields and institutionalized complexes "from economic organizations to the sphere of intimacy – are 'structured' by the routines of social practices."[43] The temporality of social practices includes repetition and sequence, since practices occur in the "everyday crises of routines" as people constantly face familiar and challenging situations that constitute a form of social reproduction. The social itself is composed of these different practices. Negotiating an interaction at the retail counter often requires very intimate physical contact and, frequently, emotional connections, and this requires practices and skills that must be deeply embodied by the make-up artist.

Frances Hathaway describes this relationship: "Make-up is more intimate than hair; a hair artist stands behind, generally, and they look into the mirror to have a conversation. A make-up artist is in front and looks directly into the eyes of the person, at a very close distance. You have to make whoever's in your chair feel comfortable, confident, relaxed, immediately ... [T]rust and respect are the two things" a make-up artist must establish with the person sitting in her or his chair.[44] Wearing make-up itself is an embodied act, a bodily technique enacted as a set of practices of creative personal expression.

At the cosmetics counter, such practices are complex and essential: the make-up artist's self-presentation and conduct at the counter; how the customer is approached; the delicate ways in which the interpersonal and physical space between the artist and the customer is navigated; and, if there is a cosmetics demonstration, the manner in which this encounter is negotiated and concluded. This work entails other routinized movements and performances, which manifest themselves in how objects such as cosmetics, make-up brushes, and other tools are handled, but also in knowledge and speaking. The make-up artist also imparts highly specialized knowledge to clients. As M·A·C senior make-up artist Jane McKay explains, artists know "colour theory, theory behind shape, theory that goes into make-up," and they offer their expertise like an "insider's report."[45] Frank Toskan transposed his own practices, routines, and behaviours as a make-up artist and entrepreneur directly onto his creative product development, decision-making, and interpersonal dealings with employees and clients in the retail setting. He acquired deep knowledge of his business from years of routine, working closely with his products, his customers, and his staff from morning to night. These practices – speaking with clients, selling them cosmetics, often touching them – became embodied ways of behaving, even though they might appear to be banal, and they were, for Toskan and his staff, a part of their *habitus*. Since Toskan insisted on working the retail counter alongside M·A·C's make-up artists to ensure they followed his own methods and creative practices, these practices became routine at M·A·C, inculcated in the staff, and this ensured their reproduction within M·A·C's internal organization and culture.

The Kitchen Sink

These qualities, features, and practices thus became the foundation for M·A·C's distinctive community and sociality – M·A·C's own culture.

Toskan encouraged M·A·C's customers to have fun with make-up and not to be dictated to by others – people or cosmetics companies – and he taught them techniques that empowered them to create the individual look they wanted. Indeed, demonstration and education were very important to Toskan and became the foundation of his customer service ethic and practices. He encouraged his artists to spend as much time as they needed and wanted with each customer and to really *instruct* customers on how to use the products. Face charts showing make-up application placement were often used (PLATE 6). Such education was partly due to his new make-up line being, to his surprise, very appealing to many non-professional customers, including the everyday, albeit adventurous, professional woman. Customers got directly involved in this creative process, during which they were shown how colours worked together so that they would know what to do with the products themselves. Toskan insisted that M·A·C staff provide their best make-up service, and be friendly and never exclusionary, and he insisted that no one sell anything the customer did not want. The artists would demonstrate new items and techniques or more outlandish fashion colours, and if the customer liked the look, Toskan knew they would return to purchase. M·A·C was about the service, not the hard sell. To help with customer education there were always brochures about the products, guides to application, colourful postcards with make-up tips, and pictures of the new professional make-up brushes and how to use them, all of these stocked at the retail counter. Toskan even made VHS videos of make-up lessons to give away to customers, such as *Frank Toskans'* [sic] *Do It Right Basic Make-up Techniques*, decades before the era of YouTube make-up tutorials (PLATE 7). Toskan often signed his name to these various M·A·C communications, and his signature ensured that his message was very personal and authentic. He believed that those messages had to come from a real person to have any legitimacy or power. In fact, he insisted that everything coming from M·A·C be his own message. It was very important to Toskan that M·A·C have a "human element" that was never corporate.[46] This formula was a success; customers swarmed the counter.

"The Hippest Thing to Come Out of Canada"

M·A·C's world expanded in 1989 in several new and unexpected ways. Toskan's friend, the make-up artist (and later actress) Debi Mazar, was preparing for Madonna's 1990 Blonde Ambition tour and asked Toskan to create some new cosmetic colours for Madonna, which he did. M·A·C's star product was still Russian Red lipstick, the intense, cool, matte red that had been a strong seller since it was created in 1985. When Madonna revealed in an interview that she, too, wore M·A·C Russian Red, Toskan was immediately inundated with phone calls from potential retail partners interested in selling M·A·C. The first call was from the exclusive store Henri Bendel in New York City. Bendel had quite a different style and clientele than Simpsons, and Toskan liked Bendel because it was eclectic and took artistic and creative risks, so he agreed to open the first international M·A·C counter there. Toskan hired several New York make-up artists to represent M·A·C, and in its first week M·A·C had the top sales in the department. Toskan travelled to New York every weekend after that, and the sales figures grew.

Toskan disliked Simpsons' sales goals and individual sales quotas, which were also in place at Bendel, even though M·A·C always made its daily sales figures, outselling Chanel, Prescriptives, and Estée Lauder three times over. With this success, though, came growing sales pressure. Toskan soon realized it was not advantageous to always meet, let alone exceed, management's sales goals, as it brought unwanted added pressure to sell more the following day, week, and month. He did not explicitly say this to the artists, however; Toskan's strategy instead was to just inspire his staff to be creative and service the customer, and, as at Simpsons, to keep management away as much as possible. M·A·C's Bendel artists were very happy, he realized. There was no force selling, and the artists loved what they were doing, especially the fact that they could spend as much time with customers as they wanted, just as the Toronto artists did, not the standard five minutes before moving on to the next customer. The M·A·C counter at Bendel also attracted many women of colour. Until M·A·C entered the store, Bendel's cosmetics brands had not catered to the unique needs of women of colour, so early M·A·C customers included supermodel Naomi Campbell and her friends and the drag queens. Toskan recalls how it was almost "like a party" because Bendel's staff knew all the customers, and everything at the counter became a "happening." Bendel's management was pleased with the sales numbers but was definitely not used to the way they were "happening" at its M·A·C counter. Toskan delivered morning talks to Bendel's entire cosmetics department, often giving them more attention than they received from their own brand representatives. Before long, everyone wanted to work for M·A·C, and there were many job applications, creating a new set of issues within the store's dynamics.[47] M·A·C then opened a counter at the American department store Nordstrom, and M·A·C's expansion across the United States began, albeit very slowly. By 1988, M·A·C was being carried in these two American locations and fourteen Canadian department stores – twelve national branches of The Bay, Simpsons in Toronto, and the specialty department store Ogilvy in Montreal – as well as at the M·A·C store in Toronto, where the head office was located. Total M·A·C sales were around $10 million in 1989.[48] This was good news, since the Franks had invested more than $1.25 million of their own (and their families') money in the business up to that point.[49]

With M·A·C now expanding across the United States with Nordstrom, Toskan unexpectedly found himself having to periodically do damage control at the counters. This was not because of poor service on the part of M·A·C staff; rather, Nordstrom expressed concern about how some of the staff's visual presentation at the counter was perceived by customers. Toskan recalls that one male M·A·C staff member was fired for wearing make-up, an odd charge considering that cosmetics was the product he was selling. A number of people soon found out, including singer Linda Ronstadt, since this particular staff member was her favourite make-up artist and a friend. Ronstadt organized a demonstration – more like a picket, Toskan remembers – outside Nordstrom. The staffer was hired back. Nordstrom subsequently rewrote its hiring policy to be more inclusive and accommodating around gender presentation. Toskan remembers a similar situation at another store, when a man was fired for dressing androgynously. There, Nordstrom's claim was that this staffer was offensive and did not fit in with the store's lifestyle, image, and definition of a family. But Toskan insisted that he, his artists, and M·A·C would not compromise to suit corporate dictates, and he threatened to pull the counter out of Nordstrom if it did not hire the staffer back. The store thought Toskan was "crazy" to pull what was by now a $2.5 million counter out of the store over one staff member. But Toskan stated that it was not just about this single incident; this attitude resonated through all of M·A·C, and capitulating to Nordstrom would damage his personal and professional integrity and compromise M·A·C's ethos. If Nordstrom did not rehire this employee, they *must* pull out. In the end, Nordstrom did hire the staffer back and rewrote its hiring policy specifically to respect the gender identity of the person as it was presented at the time of being hired. Toskan recollects that it was "pretty major" for such an about-face to happen, especially in the southern United States, and especially in the late 1980s, and it brought M·A·C a great deal of favourable attention in LGBTQ communities. Those communities celebrated M·A·C because they felt that M·A·C stood up for them; they also thought of M·A·C as successful and even "mainstream" due to its location in a department store – something that offered a rare type of legitimacy to those marginalized communities.[50]

Frank Toskan and Frank Angelo chose not to play by the rules of the cosmetics industry; they followed their own instincts and interests, responding to the social and cultural worlds around them and encouraging their staff to do the same. M·A·C's products, packaging, style, aesthetic, staff, and service ethic, not to mention its focus on acceptance, inclusivity, and respect for individuality and difference, all ensured that M·A·C did not and, moreover *would* not fit into any traditional beauty business model. In any case, M·A·C and its staff had always been more intimately connected to their local environment: the Toronto fashion scene that was flourishing all around them.

CHAPTER 2

Fashion Capital

M·A·C's creative and innovative products and Toskan's practical knowledge, along with the practices he fostered among his similarly minded artists and his tight artistic community in Toronto, were distinctly at odds with how things were traditionally done in the cosmetics industry, but they made a great deal of sense when considered within the realm of fashion, especially within the Toronto milieu of the time. As Suzanne Boyd asserts, M·A·C was "a beauty company, but I consider it all fashion" – an opinion that was shared by many in Toronto back then.[1] Being successful in fashion requires the correct knowledge, abilities, and "feel" for fashion at any given moment – it is not merely about style or the latest trends. Toskan worked not only with customers at the M·A·C counter but also with designers, retailers, models, stylists, journalists, and media personalities in Toronto's fashion industry. All of these people were linked together by the activities, practices, positions, and struggles that defined the Toronto fashion field's cultural production in the 1980s. It is within this cultural milieu that Toskan's artistic inclinations and his own increasing cultural and symbolic capital – and M·A·C's – developed. In the 1980s, a global fashion industry was about to be born, modern forms of branding were emerging, and the fashion market was about to align itself with financial globalization. At that time, specific fashion centres defined the production and reproduction of fashion: Milan, New York, and London, with Paris still the fashion capital, identified by its haute couture heritage and elite origins. And Toronto, for the first time, seemed poised to join this group.

Riding this 1980s momentum, fashion and music subcultures converged and thrived in Toronto's underground dance clubs, just as they were doing in New York and London. Suzanne Boyd was a struggling student at York University in Toronto during the early 1980s who loved fashion and the arts, and she soon became part of this scene. After being photographed by Mario Testino for Vidal Sassoon, she was signed by Judy Welch, a premier Toronto modelling agency that represented some of Canada's top fashion talent. Boyd was one of many fashion insiders who frequented The Twilight Zone dance club at Richmond Street and University Avenue in downtown Toronto, where much of what was happening in Toronto fashion converged on the dance floor. The Twilight Zone was the first legal after-hours nightclub in Toronto. The Assoon brothers – David, Albert, Tony, and Michael – from Brooklyn, New York, came up to Toronto and modelled "The Zone" after the Paradise Garage, which itself was apparently a "cooler" version of the famed disco hotspot Studio 54. The DJs and music flowing out of New York and London (and Washington, D.C., and Atlanta) inspired and influenced the fashion and arts scenes in Toronto.[2] According to Boyd, each week the Assoon brothers would bring new records to Toronto for the upcoming weekend; sometimes Boyd would drive down to New York City with them. She recalls, "We felt we were on the circuit of what was happening in culture." Toronto's close proximity to New York meant that many people and bands regularly visited Toronto. The Zone represented "a bubbling up of culture," Boyd said, a place where people represented themselves in fashion to become "the biggest expression of themselves" in a place where "it was all about identity."[3] Rick Mugford, manager of WOW, a trendy fashion boutique on Queen Street West, agrees: "In the late 70s and 80s, art, fashion, and music all melded together. It was a pretty unique time and all these things cross-pollinated with one another. If you went to a fashion show you'd see people you saw at art things; if you went to an art show, you'd see people you saw at fashion things. The crossover was really palpable. It was all interlaced."[4]

This was a very subcultural and non-commercial scene, and people made their own clothes and spent all week creating looks to debut at the club that weekend. People wanted the Toronto clubs to be like Andy Warhol's Factory, where art performances and small fashion shows took place, Boyd remembers. The fashion brand Parachute held numerous shows and hired the clubgoers to model in them. Twin designers Dean and Dan Caten were there and they designed their first dress for their eponymous label on Boyd. Joe Mimran of the Mimran Group, soon-to-be purveyor of the Alfred Sung and Club Monaco brands, was there, too, as was the shoe designer Patrick Cox. At The Zone, Boyd met make-up artists and the people "who made the shows tick." Boyd remembers them as "outsiders and not part of the establishment," who formed a community. "We thought we were making some sort of social statement with fashion." Everyone's thinking was, "we're part of the cool Queen Street scene, and there's the Hoax boys and the Babel boys and Karim Rashid and very cool artistic people doing seemingly new things, so it was very exciting." Here, Boyd was referencing the Queen Street label Hoax Couture designers Chris Tyrell and Jim Searle, and Babel designers Scott Cressman, Pauline Landriault, and Karim Rashid; the latter would go on to become a global industrial designer. This was a time when fashion was "seeming to find itself," and street fashion, originating in the clubs, was more important and more relevant than the haute couture seen at the Paris designer shows.[5]

Frank Toskan was an avid clubgoer and was very much inspired by these scenes. Several people in the fashion industry with whom Toskan collaborated in the 1980s shared M·A·C's ethos and became integral to developing the M·A·C brand. Freelance make-up artist Frances Hathaway was always an influential ambassador for the M·A·C brand. She had known Frank Angelo since she was a teenager. Her mother, Evelyn, who owned several hair salons in Toronto, had been close to Angelo for years and had even helped him establish his hair business in Simpsons by arranging for an introduction with its president. When Hathaway began her make-up career in Toronto in 1981, she turned to the Franks for products. She sold M·A·C products privately at Toronto's upscale Robert Gage salon and had several artists working with her there. By the mid-1980s, Hathaway was travelling to Europe and using M·A·C products on singer Linda McCartney and model Jerry Hall, who were among M·A·C's first celebrity clients. Hathaway famously used M·A·C products on Princess Diana for the portrait by David Bailey that hangs in the National Portrait Gallery in London; Diana later asked to keep the products Hathaway had used. An early promotional piece from the mid-1980s featuring Hathaway and photographed by budding Canadian fashion photographer Walter Chin encapsulated M·A·C's working directive of inclusivity and creative expression, directed to fellow make-up artists (PLATE 8). Its copy reads: "Only Make-up Art Cosmetics gives this acclaimed make-up artist the freedom to create, to imagine, to reach for perfection. To perceive what will be. Frances Hathaway works with Make-up Art Cosmetics. So should you."[6] This attitude reflected the broader sense of inclusion within the fashion industry in Toronto. As Toronto-based fashion stylist Susie Sheffman recollects: "I think that ethos or that sentimentality, that mentality, was very much a part of the Toronto downtown artsy fashion scene, Queen Street scene. We were very much about embracing diversity, whatever that meant back then. I think that we were this little utopian society. We were open; we were open and embraced all. I think that M·A·C was definitely, probably, one of the first of the corporations that took that line."[7]

Beginning around 1985, the Franks developed a vital and long-lasting professional relationship with the visual artist Donald Robertson, now creative director at Estée Lauder. An illustrator by training, Robertson briefly attended the Ontario College of Art (now the Ontario College of Art and Design) before trying his luck in Europe, at one point sleeping on Frances Hathaway's sofa after she moved to Paris.[8] Hathaway remembers telling Frank Angelo about Robertson shortly after he landed on her couch. She told Angelo that Robertson's ideas and aesthetic were perfect for M·A·C: "If you want to set yourself apart, get an illustrator. You do *not* want a real face, because how can you say everything you want to say about M·A·C on a face? [You want] something that can bring another element, another dimension, to the feeling of your company."[9] When Robertson first came to M·A·C, he did not have much work in his portfolio, but as Hathaway had promised, Toskan loved what he had done, especially his tactile pieces such as cut-outs and collages, which Toskan thought were more interesting and artistic than photography. Robertson's work was "brilliant – but also cheap," and it was not commercial in any way, and he believed in M·A·C's ethos. Robertson was never a M·A·C employee; he freelanced for many Toronto clients, and his signature style could be seen in numerous 1980s advertisements and visual communications in fashion publications such as *Toronto Life Fashion* as well as in M·A·C's communications (PLATE 9). Creativity was the driving force behind M·A·C, and Robertson contributed considerably to the company's developing visual aesthetic: "Everything I did for M·A·C at the time was just painted faces," Robertson recalls. "We just decided that art was our way to go, as opposed to advertising and traditional model booking."[10]

An early project Robertson worked on with Toskan was M·A·C's new logo. One immediate business problem Toskan had faced when setting up his business was the confusion between M·A·C and Toronto's School of Makeup Art, which was often – and mistakenly – linked with Toskan's Make-up Art Cosmetics business. Toskan needed to cut the mental association that customers had developed between his company and this unrelated make-up school. He already had a working logo for M·A·C, of sorts: "Make-up Art" was spelled out in a hot-pink, sharp-edged script, with "Cosmetics" underneath in block letters. The script channelled the 1980s post-disco new wave aesthetic, and the block letters suggested the brand's artfulness and cutting-edge stance (PLATE 10). Up to this point, Toskan had created M·A·C's visual identity and communications himself, primarily because he could not afford to hire anyone else to do them. Toskan created the earliest version of the now-familiar M·A·C logo: white, block-letter script that simply spelled out "M·A·C." Robertson, along with graphic artist Tom Burton, turned this into something more distinctive. The new logo was in a much leaner white script set against a black background. It was clean, it stood out, and it was "in your face," Toskan said, and he felt it represented M·A·C's persona.[11] They made it on one of the first Macintosh computers; Robertson then used more new technology to toy with it further: "At the time, companies were starting to get their own Xerox machines, which was unbelievable; it was the most exciting thing. It was like getting an iPhone today. And I figured out that I could fuck with the *xy* factors on the settings, and I literally stretched the logo on a Xerox machine as wide as I could make it so that the circles became ovals."[12] The instantly recognizable, iconic M·A·C logo was born.

With so much creativity around him, Toskan produced outlandish fashion colours for his new make-up line, such as blue, silver, red, and yellow, adding a metallic edge that made them a hit with what Boyd called "the club people." "It felt like a grassroots, organic, very inspiring sort of time," Boyd reminisces, "where you just could be very expressive with clothes, and your hair, and makeup; it was that kind of thing."[13] One of Toskan's first "collections" comprised electric neon colours meant to be worn specifically in the dance clubs: glow-in-the-dark pink, yellow, green, and orange pigments to be applied free-form. To promote this collection, Toskan produced small events at The Twilight Zone, painting people himself and handing out his ubiquitous self-made brochures about the products. For Toskan, it was a "no-brainer" to craft ideas and products that the club and fashion people wanted. In fact,

> it was always about staying ahead. We didn't even have to try to stay ahead, because we would be ahead because we'd be experimenting with stuff, and then I'd go back and I'd make the stuff and then a year later when editorial would come out, we'd already have it; it would be there ... Most companies make a product, figure out how to sell it, and then they put it out in the market, and create a demand. Our demand was already there. We were very fortunate in that way, that our demand always existed before we'd make it.

Because Toskan was always in touch with what was going on in these creative subcultures and was inspired to discover what was hot, he knew what kinds of fashion were happening. Also integral to M·A·C's production process was its collaborative ethos. Besides working in the field with Hathaway and Robertson, Toskan sent the M·A·C make-up artists out on photo shoots and other creative and fashion jobs. The artists

> were able to tap into what was going on in the industry and bring me back the ideas. I would go back and make the ideas, and then take them back to Donald, collaborate with him, and see how we could put them

out. But we had an inside track for years. We developed the industry. So, we developed the colours and the product that would, a year later, be in demand.

Toskan never had to create a demand for his products through marketing or advertising; that demand already existed, and he recognized it because he was part of it.[14]

Toskan was soon demonstrating his fashion acumen outside the club, routinely dispensing cosmetics advice and communicating his vast knowledge of professional techniques and trends in the media. Fashion columns in the *Toronto Star* and the *Globe and Mail* increasingly featured Toskan and M·A·C products, in articles on the latest fashion and cosmetics trends, or in profiles of local personalities' beauty regimes. In Montreal, the *Gazette*'s holiday feature in December 1986 displayed a "Fantasy Face" consisting of M·A·C's "T.V. 2 Special Effects Foundation," along with red, green, and metallic holiday colours available in a creamy powder product called "Special Effects": the model's features were highlighted with "Silver Special Effects."[15] For the 1987 holiday season the following year, Nancy Hastings wrote in the *Toronto Star* that "this season, make-up artists still share special-effects secrets."[16] In September 1988, the high point of the fashion year, the *Toronto Star*'s Bernadette Morra covered M·A·C's "Soft Focus Fall Beauty" offerings, which were coordinated with the season's fashion and hair trends but still neutral and suitable for individual skin tones. Toskan advised:

> There's a resurgence of color in clothing, but not in makeup ... We're seeing clothes in fuchsias, pinks and greens, but the face is still neutral. It's a warm palette with soft browns, peaches, warm reds with a lack of emphasis on blue, green and purple. But that's what's giving it a new look. Three years ago if you had an electric blue dress, you would try to match the makeup to that. Now the makeup stands as a neutral background to clothes and complements the skin ... The mouth is more natural. We're eliminating lip liner for day but for darker shades you still need it to define. Softness on the cheeks is definitely back. They should look like the color is coming from within the skin and not look like it's been painted on top. The color should be a few shades warmer but close to your own skin tone and softened with a translucent powder base and finish.[17]

Clearly, Toskan had a practical knowledge of cosmetics that enabled him to become an opinion leader on the local fashion scene. Indeed, Toskan very much saw himself as a leader, not a follower, of fashion trends: "I am as much a designer as someone who's designing clothing." He looked for inspiration in diverse sources, from European textiles to the latest street trend of short hair.[18] This sort of cosmetic knowledge clearly overlapped with fashion knowledge, especially since cosmetic and beauty looks often result from designer collaborations with artists at fashion shows, and cosmetics collections are often inspired by seasonal fashion trends. Fields can and do overlap, and Toskan moved seamlessly between the cosmetics field and the fashion field.

In 1988, in one of the earliest newspaper articles about M·A·C, Toskan expressed his irritation with the big cosmetics houses. For one thing, they all featured the same type of products: "I hate it when you can get every shade of frosted shadow possible when all you want is a matte. I hate it when somebody has 30 lipsticks in their line, but they all look alike – either all corals, or all reds, or all pinks." This, he felt, did not respect the customer's vision, desire, and sense of individuality. As evidence of this frustration, by 1988 M·A·C had approximately three hundred products. Toskan was adamant that his cosmetics line not mislead consumers with false claims and especially with advertising that induced anxiety about age. M·A·C products performed well, and furthermore, they were not overpriced; they hit price points above mass-market drugstore brands like CoverGirl and Revlon, but well below prestige cosmetic lines like Estée Lauder, Elizabeth Arden, Lancôme, Chanel, and Clinique. In 1988, M·A·C lipstick was priced at $8.50.[19] That price was competitive with mass-market brands such as The Body Shop at $7.95 but well below Canadian department store brand Lise Watier at $11.50 and prestige brand Estée Lauder at $14.[20]

Toskan continued to stay attuned to the ever-changing fashion cycle while advising customers on individual make-up regimes that respected their needs and styles, all while maintaining M·A·C's professional-level standards for its make-up artist clientele. M·A·C's innovative and fashionable products were becoming highly desirable. Lisa Tant noted in the *Vancouver Sun* in June 1989 that the "new understated colors from M·A·C Cosmetics sound good enough to eat; mango, yogurt (pale lilac), vanilla and mocha.

M·A·C's line of satin lipsticks ranges from pale peach to warm saffron and Salsa, a brilliant orange/red shade."[21] That summer, Tant wrote about M·A·C's arrival at The Bay, where the full variety of M·A·C's offerings was on display:

> The M·A·C line features seven different lipsticks for every occasion: frosts; creams – for shine without a frosty glitter; mattes; rich satins; glazes – translucent yet shiny; natural lip tones; and tinted Vitamin E sticks to protect lips from chapping. Three different eye shadows, in a full range of bright to neutral tones, are also available. Colorful stage and photography makeup used to have a bad reputation for being thick, cakey and hard on skin. M·A·C's professional line contains natural vitamin preservatives, sunscreens in their foundations, and no mineral oils or lanolin which tend to be comedogenic (acne-causing). Every product is custom blended and tested without risk to animals. For those sensitive to certain oils or powders, all ingredients are listed on the box.[22]

For all this media attention, Toskan was very uncomfortable being in the public eye. For a time, Donald Robertson and Toskan had considered using Toskan's name as the brand name. Robertson even suggested at one point that Toskan change his name to "Frank M·A·C." But Toskan felt that he was *not* M·A·C and that calling it "Frank M·A·C" or "Frank Cosmetics" would detract from the company's collaborative ethos. Toskan wanted everyone who worked at or with M·A·C to participate in the company as part of a community, and he never wanted to steal anyone's spotlight because he felt there was so much talent in the company. He wanted to have a presence, and he did not mind his name being known as long as it was not his own image that dominated the brand's identity. He definitely did not want a "face" for the brand, and he especially did not want to be the face of M·A·C himself. Robertson and Frank Angelo were constantly pushing Toskan, and he sometimes resented it: "I liked making my products, I liked talking to people. I liked sharing part of who I was and making that into the business," he recalls, but he did not feel it was really his nature to put himself "out there." The business-minded Angelo recognized that he was not the image of M·A·C and that Toskan epitomized the brand. But despite his protests, Toskan by default became the unofficial "face" of a brand that was breaking new ground in the cosmetics industry and becoming an influential player in the Toronto fashion industry.

Now that M·A·C had expanded to Henri Bendel and then to Nordstrom, Toskan needed someone to manage the M·A·C vision in the United States and to train M·A·C's staff to ensure that education and, eventually, in-house certification were standardized. The Franks hired freelance make-up artist Jane McKay in 1989 as Director of Technical Training. McKay arrived in Toronto from Calgary, Alberta, via Milan, having achieved a great deal of success in Europe and then in Toronto; her prestigious first booking in Toronto was for Alfred Sung Couture. McKay's friend Debra Berman, who was dating Donald Robertson at the time, introduced McKay to the Franks. She and Toskan clicked immediately, and he really liked her work. Her initial meeting with Angelo was less cordial, but over time, he became her "greatest fan" as she worked with him on M·A·C's organizational activities. Six months in, McKay established a training program for new artists and hired more people to help her, eventually creating the "Pro" Artist program, expanding the professional product offerings, and developing a roster of Senior Artists. (McKay herself remains a senior artist at M·A·C.) Always, the overarching directive for new staff was to focus on the service, not the sales; if the service was good, sales would naturally follow. McKay recognized the value that M·A·C offered to the professional make-up artist, and vice versa:

> If you take make-up and you put it in the make-up artist's hands, that's your professional voice; and the trickle down from that is what happened for us, and it was word-of-mouth success. It's funny that none of those other big companies figured it out. I mean, Max Factor kind of did it, back in the 20s, and they lost it, they lost their professional niche. No one has done this and it was groundbreaking at the time.[23]

Toronto Life Fashion

Toronto was trying to establish itself as a new fashion centre, and this inevitably brought about a confrontation with a notable contingent of fashion leaders. The symbolic value of fashion goods as they relate to a place of local production is crucial to the fashion industry; so is the competitive value that such goods yield. Place of origin has become a signifier on the postmodern capitalist landscape, and goods with high symbolic and cultural value have a competitive advantage in the marketplace. Fashion scholar David Gilbert observes: "Fashion's great centres have long contained overlapping fashion cultures and spaces, in which conventional models of the fashion process – trickle down emulation or bubble-up street innovation – prove hopelessly inadequate as descriptions of the interlocking circuits of production and consumption, imitation and intimidation."[24] Gilbert describes London as an early fashion centre and one of long standing, arguing that it successfully blends the cultural with the economic. Such fashion centres exhibit the inherent tensions of Bourdieu's field of fashion, with its autonomous and heteronomous poles. Moreover, London has developed a culture of superiority, albeit one bested, at least in the nineteenth century, by Paris. Paris as *the* source of high fashion, asserts Gilbert, predates even its famed haute couture, going back to courtly fashion systems. London and Paris have been competing for centuries. Gilbert states that by the end of the nineteenth century, New York was well on its way to joining Paris and London, since it had become America's economic centre and the country's primary manufacturing sector, as well as the location of a new class of social elites that had considerable economic capital.

Urban geographer Norma M. Rantisi notes in her work on the New York fashion industry that "[t]he prominence of New York ready-to-wear within the international fashion circuit stems from its ability to temper design and art with commercial interests."[25] Rantisi applies the concept of "path dependency," whereby a projected development is disrupted by seemingly small historical events that privilege certain paths and foreclose others, which she claims can be used to explain economic development. This theory describes a trajectory of commercialism associated with high-volume production (and technology), but one that is disrupted by historical events and crises. Rantisi suggests that as a result of such occurrences (which for New York include war, changing markets, new supplies of labour, and new agents such as designers, as well as trade groups, unions, media publications, stores, and design schools that nurture local talent), new conventions and norms develop over time that come to define how things are done, bringing with them a new culture, new forms of communication and information flow, and new relations between agents. All of this leads to renewal and transformation in the industry and in the city. In this way, localized capabilities form that come to define a region's economy, its products, and ultimately, symbolic images and meanings that connote authenticity and enhance reputation. The theory of path dependency is based on a structural analysis, and Rantisi also acknowledges the interlinking of structure with agency (alongside economy and art) and the tensions inherent in their interface. Rantisi refers here to Anthony Giddens's idea of "structuration," a form of practice theory that bears some resemblances to Bourdieu's ideas about social change. Without digressing into Giddens's work, Rantisi argues that taking account of how various actors exert their agency within a seemingly rigid, even predetermined, structure necessarily offers insight into the transformation of a local economy, and specifically, of New York's fashion industry – in other words, the city's field of cultural production.

Rantisi describes how the early years of New York's garment industry, around the mid-1880s, were strongly affected by the influx of immigrants into Manhattan's Lower East Side. Jewish immigrants had brought their tailoring skills with them, and this made for a consistent supply of cheap, dependable labour to support America's increasing industrialization. This coincided with the advent of department stores, fashion magazines, and mail-order catalogues. The inspiration for the ready-to-wear garments that consumers wanted, and that mechanized production could now provide, came from Paris and its haute couture. By the 1920s, the city's centre of production had moved to the western side of midtown Manhattan. Other support and service institutions took hold there, in tandem with a new focus on merchandising to increase sales, and the proximity to Penn Station offered optimal access to travellers. The retail market along Fifth Avenue became crucial; Henri Bendel was one of the first to set up shop there, in 1910, and was soon joined by other retailers. By the 1920s, advertising had become instrumental to the promotion of fashion goods in the new fashion magazines, and this helped maintain the balance of production and consumption by managing consumer tastes.[26] But those tastes were still heavily influenced by Paris, a fact made evident not just in the competition with French designers, such as Gabrielle "Coco" Chanel, for media space in American magazines, but by the strong Parisian influence in design and teaching at the fashion schools.

Local American talent began to push through in the 1930s. The Fashion Group was formed in 1931, bringing together design talent such as cosmetics moguls Helena Rubinstein and Elizabeth Arden, as well as Eleanor Roosevelt, who was then a labour activist and the First Lady of New York State, and Dorothy Shaver, vice-president of Lord & Taylor department store. The group's mandate was to represent and advocate for all aspects of the New York fashion industry, and it was strongly women-focused in its efforts. The Costume Institute was founded in 1937, and its annual gala would become the New York fashion industry's biggest social event and fundraiser, making visible the link between fashion and the performing arts in the city. Seventh Avenue in midtown became the official Garment District. Paris's sway as a fashion leader was compromised during the Second World War, depressing that city's influence, and American design talent and ready-to-wear began to fill that gap – a development that was covered extensively by American fashion media. New York was filling the spot in the fashion hierarchy that Paris had vacated.

With the end of the Second World War and the rise of Christian Dior's "New Look," Parisian dominance seemingly returned, but this dominance was more symbolic than actual, for by now the New York fashion industry had developed its own design expertise, magazines, organizations, and influence. Meanwhile, design education was flourishing, with the founding of the Fashion Institute of Technology (FIT) in 1944, alongside the Pratt Institute and the Parsons School of Design (established in 1897). These schools reinforced New York as a fashion centre. A defining feature of New York was its elevation of the New York fashion designer – not just the designs – beginning in the 1960s. This was evident first in the founding of the Council of Fashion Designers of America (CFDA) in 1962; soon after, John Fairchild, editor of *Women's Wear Daily* (*WWD*), began featuring designers, industry news, and gossip rather than manufacturers on his pages.

The 1960s also saw the rise of identity politics and feminism in all fashion centres, in tandem with the rejection of mass culture and the rise of youth subcultures. In the 1970s, designers like Gloria Vanderbilt and Calvin Klein moved their labels from the inside to the outside of their jeans, launching the trend towards designer logos and distinct fashion brands, not just design houses. Meanwhile, Parisian haute couture was declining and French designers were beginning to incorporate American production, manufacturing, and branding strategies.

Coming between Paris and New York, however, was Milan. As economic historians Elisabetta Merlo and Francesca Polese explain, Milan emerged as a fashion capital in the 1970s.[27] Two forces contributed to this: the dislodging of Paris as the fashion leader due to shortages of materials, a drop in personal incomes, rationing, and the wartime occupation (the Germans had attempted to move the haute couture industry to Berlin); and the disruption of trade caused by the war, which introduced America (i.e., New York) to the Italian fashion world. Milan became Italy's fashion capital because of "the emergence of both an international market and a concentrated urban cluster of entrepreneurs and institutions that developed specific skills in production, marketing, and distributing clothing that would satisfy the demands of the new market."[28] After the war, Milan benefited from Paris's retreat as a fashion monopoly. As consumers were increasingly influenced by the American lifestyle and moved away from Parisian haute couture, Milan stepped up, capitalizing on its reputation for producing high-quality fabrics. Not only this, but after the war, America transferred technology, capital, and knowledge overseas. Merlo and Polese note that "[t]he United States helped the Italian textile and clothing industry to become integrated into the new world geography of fashion and supported Milan in its challenge to Parisian dominance."[29] The United States thus helped create a demand for Italian products. In the 1950s, the Italian clothing and fashion industry began to expand; by 1956, Italy had become the main European exporter of textiles and clothing to the United States and Canada, overtaking France and Great Britain, which had been the undisputed export leaders until then. Interestingly, Milan was not the same kind of political, economic, artistic, or cultural capital as Paris or New York; instead it competed with other Italian cities like Florence and Rome. These cities also responded to the expanding fashion industry, with Florence's artisanal production and fashion shows dominating from about 1951 to 1971, and with Rome's links to Hollywood. However, it was Milan that ultimately emerged as the leader. Milan, which had always been an industrial city, distinguished itself by its more severe and even sombre aesthetic, in contrast to the extravagant and glamorous style that defined Rome.

Merlo and Polese acknowledge the power of fashion shows and fashion media to establish a city's identity as a fashion capital. Milan was home to the most powerful and influential Italian fashion magazines. Seventy-five of the 149 fashion magazines published in Italy between 1861 and the 1920s were published in Milan, and much of the fashion press had connections to the corporate world.[30] However, Milan also distinguished itself in the way its economic institutions realized, and exploited, the city's fashion capabilities. Milan hosted its first exhibition devoted to fashion in 1951, the Fiera Campionaria (Milan Sample Fair). All products of the fashion business were represented there: furs, accessories, and jewellery. In 1952, a new fashion committee, the Italian Fashion Service, was founded to promote Italian fashion abroad, with the goal of explicitly linking fashion to industry. Three other actors in Milan contributed to the exploitation of the American market and to the subsequent emergence of Italian (Milanese) fashion: the Associazione industriali dell'abbigliamento (Association of Clothing Industrialists), founded in 1945, which published a bimonthly trade review, *Quaderni*, to educate Italian entrepreneurs in American ways of doing business; the American Chamber of Commerce for Italy (AmCham), whose monthly review, *Italian-American Business*, helped Italian fashion exploit the American market – for example, by organizing exhibitions of Italian products in the United States to demonstrate Italian workmanship and quality; and La Rinascente, the Italian department store, which represented the new, modern way of retailing and diversified its ready-made clothes to cater to upper middle-class consumers.

Many of the historical events – and crises – that those in the burgeoning Toronto fashion industry experienced were similarly mutually constituting, an outcome of the interaction of structure and agency and the playing out of historical developments within the broader fashion field, just like in Paris and especially New York. Toronto likewise saw an influx of design talent, a rise of fashion media, an emphasis on local production, retail, and business organization, and perhaps something more intangible: a certain Canadian flavour that had never been so enthusiastically expressed before. To be sure, M·A·C's timing was critical – it emerged within the cosmetics industry as the right brand at the right time – but its unique strength was its truly fashionable identity. M·A·C was the right brand in the right place *at a moment* when Toronto seemed ready to join New York, Milan, and even Paris as a fashion capital. To be "in fashion" in Toronto during the 1980s was without doubt the result of unique historical and political circumstances; Phillip Ing, a fixture in the Toronto fashion industry since the mid-1980s, agrees that "a perfect storm" of events led to a completely new and "pretty unique time" for fashion in Toronto.[31]

Yet there is no single or unified story of Canadian fashion. According to Canadian fashion scholar Alexandra Palmer, editor of *Fashion: A Canadian Perspective*, no definitive or "official" historical account of Canadian fashion exists; rather, there are disjointed narratives of various times and events. As Palmer notes, Canada's fashion success stories – and she specifically cites M·A·C as one of these – seem to deny, obscure, or neglect a nationalistic basis or a Canadian identity. Toronto's fashion story has yet to be meticulously chronicled.[32] M·A·C's success had much to do with its position within a fashion community that was excitedly defining itself and realizing a newly found potential. As Steven Levy, creator of Canada's first large-scale industry event, the Festival of Canadian Fashion, recalls, "Toronto was in the embryotic stage of what it is today; people were looking at Toronto as a possibility of becoming a big city and that meant culture and events and so on."[33] Jeanne Beker remembers how

> we were so excited by the fact that Toronto finally had that kind of scene, that Toronto felt like it was coming of age. Suddenly, there was this high level of glamour in Toronto. Suddenly fashion mattered in Toronto

in a way that it hadn't been before. The creative spirit in Toronto was starting to really come up, and, really, we're on a level of European and American counterparts. They had started to make a mark. Suddenly you could see Wayne Clark being advertised in the pages of American fashion magazines ... These things were coming in dribs and drabs. We realized creatively we were becoming a force to be reckoned with; and the compassion, wanting to support each other. Maybe it was more of a competitive thing in New York, more of a judgmental thing. New York's that kind of melting pot where people come from all over the place and they finally find themselves in this thing together; whereas Toronto – we were feeling like we were growing up together. I think there was such a great feeling of family in that city.[34]

Some fashion insiders have suggested that the issue of Quebec sovereignty in the 1970s had a discernible impact on Toronto's fashion industry in that it drove some of Montreal's fashion talent to Toronto. Fashion journalist David Livingstone noted that in the 1970s, "politics rendered the Canadian fashion scene even less coherent" after members of the Fashion Designers Association of Canada sent out models carrying Quebec flags at a fashion show, suggesting a defiant, sovereigntist stance.[35] In a chronicle of the Toronto fashion industry's rise published in *Flare* magazine in September 1999, designer Hilary Radley recalled that people "at the head offices of many sectors left and the [retail] sales and buying offices for Eaton's and the Bay left and became part of the corporate head offices in Toronto. The contractors set up in Toronto [and] the colleges were doing well there, too."[36] Steven Levy disagrees with this, saying that the manufacturers who were in Toronto during the 1980s had in fact always been there and that fashion design talent was already well established in Toronto and did not move manufacturing from Montreal: "Toronto was slowly, slowly surpassing Montreal only because of the – I believe – creative energy that was here, because of their forward thinking, that idea of branding born in New York."[37] Bernadette Morra, former *Toronto Star* journalist and editor-in-chief of *Fashion* magazine, points out that many of the freshest Toronto designers, such as Joyce Gunhouse and Judy Cornish of Comrags, were recent graduates of the highly regarded fashion program at Ryerson Polytechnical Institute (later Ryerson

University) and had stayed in Toronto and set up shop there after graduation.[38] Phillip Ing and Susie Sheffman both observed that these designers were the children of the baby boomers who came of age in the 1980s and were the first generation to really explore culture and art and fashion. While there seems to be no consensus, it is apparent that a number of converging historical and material circumstances made Toronto *the* fashionable place to be in Canada during the 1980s.

Toronto's fashion industry received some support from the municipal government and was strong in marketing and retailing. However, the design side was weaker than the manufacturing side, and the latter was the real backbone of the fashion industry in both Montreal and Toronto. According to a report in the *Metropolitan Toronto Business Journal* in April 1987, around 20,000 people were employed in the garment and support industries in Toronto in the mid-1980s, and textile and apparel manufacturers were Toronto's second-largest employer after food and beverage. The specific problem, according to Joe Mimran, who was interviewed for the piece, was that Toronto lacked the infrastructure to support its own design industry. Toronto's textile industry could not sustain the entire design trade, and imports were expensive. European designers did not face this problem. Furthermore, Canadian fashion did not usually invite or receive international attention. Mimran, who was then Managing Director of the Monaco Group Inc., which produced clothing for Alfred Sung, Sung Sport, and Club Monaco, said that "Europe always seems shocked to hear that we do our own designing. New York doesn't perceive of Canada as anything, I can tell you right now. World coverage never emanates from Toronto, only from London, Milan, Paris, Tokyo, and New York. *Women's Wear Daily* has written about Alfred Sung but so much more needs to be done before we can impregnate that consciousness."[39] Nonetheless, many Toronto-based Canadian designers received international attention for the first time during the 1980s, especially Alfred Sung, Wayne Clark, and Dean and Dan Caten, creating a new narrative about Toronto fashion.

Alfred Sung was the leading Canadian fashion designer (though he was born in Shanghai and studied fashion in New York). Sung's partnership with brothers Joe and Saul Mimran began in 1981.

Together they produced casual, classic clothes for men and women that, paradoxically, reflected "a very American look," according to Sung.[40] Club Monaco's first retail location opened on Toronto's Queen Street West, just east of Spadina Avenue, in 1985. The store's opening brought out the "club people," who mistakenly thought the store was a new dance club and dressed accordingly. Another success story was the Toronto-born design twins Dean and Dan Caten, who had studied for one term at the Parsons School of Design in New York and debuted their first collection in March 1985 at the Diamond Club in downtown Toronto. Right after that, they began designing for the Toronto-based high-end label Ports International. Roots is another important Canadian brand, considered one of Canada's most internationally recognized companies, fashion or otherwise, although it offers an alternative design aesthetic. Roots was founded by two Americans who reappropriated signifiers of Canadiana, particularly the beaver, and famously placed them on sweatshirts. Canadian historian Catherine Carstairs suggests that Roots succeeded in fashion not by capitalizing on a secure Canadian identity or the support of the increasingly vibrant Canadian, Toronto-based fashion industry, but by unwittingly exploiting the uneasy cultural and economic relationships between Canada and the United States, and the nationalistic differences between Quebec and the rest of Canada, at a particular historical moment. Even so, Roots clothing and leather accessories were wildly popular with consumers in and outside of Canada.[41]

This new emphasis on Toronto as Canada's fashion capital fostered a new network of fashion designers, stylists, make-up artists, and journalists. Fashion stylist Susie Sheffman remembers how "there was something magical going on" in Toronto fashion at that time.[42] Bernadette Morra recalls that "it was a time when if you were interested in fashion, all of a sudden there were people to follow, a place to go, stores on Queen Street that were supporting them, a place you could go to buy them, you could read about them in the *Toronto Star* and fashion magazines; they were covered. So there was a really strong, thriving scene."[43] Jeanne Beker agrees: "It was that fabulous period when we just really realized fashion's possibilities. Suddenly we weren't the shy, dull Canadians, so conservative, boring. We felt that we really might have the power to be noticed."[44] It was within this milieu that the Franks were building M·A·C and found an audience and a market, and Toskan positioned M·A·C as a fashion brand squarely within that field. The soundtrack to this time, according to Suzanne Boyd, was The Parachute Club's song "Rise Up" – "We were all just rising up to be ourselves. M·A·C was kind of the emblem. If you could put a brand to that, it would have been M·A·C."[45]

One of the most powerful sites in the Toronto fashion industry was the Festival of Canadian Fashion. Organizer Steven Levy was a fashion "outsider," but the Toronto designers Linda Lundström, Wayne Clark, and Marilyn Brooks were his friends. At the time, Levy was working in market research. He was experienced in organizing large-scale events and had founded Toronto's popular twice-yearly One of a Kind Show in the 1970s, a large venue where artists and designers could sell their crafts and unique work. Levy was very interested in how his friends conducted their businesses, and it perplexed him that the fashion industry did not have a large, professional event to promote its designers: "I wondered why we couldn't pull everyone together and yell 'Canada!' and make noise globally." But Canadian designers were not used to promoting themselves, and in typical Canadian style, they did not embrace being outgoing. Levy recognized that there could be no fashion industry without the consumer. The clothes needed to be shown and promoted in ways that would allow their designers to develop a fan base and begin building their brands by creating an emotional connection with the audience. That meant organizing fashion shows. Although there was less emphasis then on the "brand," or a "brand identity," Levy knew that the key to creating mass name recognition and achieving awareness for these designers was by presenting them and their work in new ways.[46]

Appointing himself the unofficial "Minister of Fashion," Levy launched the Festival of Canadian Fashion in Toronto in 1985. Brooks, Lundström, and the twenty-two-member organization Toronto Ontario Designers (TOD) assisted Levy.[47] The Festival's inaugural year brought together the upscale Canadian retailer Holt Renfrew and the Toronto Eaton Centre with the *Toronto Star* and *Toronto Life* magazine as media sponsors of the event, which was held from 24 to 28 April at the newly opened Metro Toronto Convention Centre on Front Street in downtown Toronto. Twenty-four fashion shows were held, and 50,000 people attended. The event was not restricted to Toronto's fashion industry; in an unusual move, it was open to the public, who could buy tickets for each of the five days. The Festival – part fashion trade, part creativity, and part entertainment – generated interest among both producers and consumers of Canadian fashion as well as much-needed publicity for the Toronto fashion scene. Pre-social media, this was the first opportunity consumers had ever had to meet the designers in person, see the clothes up close, and become a part of the fashion "scene," if only fleetingly.

Designers Wayne Clark and especially Alfred Sung were the undisputed "stars" of the Festival. Sung had the largest and most prestigious fashion show, since the Mimrans envisioned turning him into an international brand. Sung's show was on Saturday night, the most coveted spot, and was co-sponsored by *Flare* magazine. Levy recalls how more people than were legally permitted attended the show. Susie Sheffman states that "up until that point, fashion shows were for the very elite. What the Festival of Canadian Fashion did was they threw the doors open and they said, this can be for anyone, anybody who has an interest in fashion can come out and be part of this fabulous few days that was sort of part trade show, part fashion show extravaganza."[48] The Festival democratized Toronto fashion by incorporating consumers into the fashion scene in new, exciting, and inclusive ways.

From the beginning, Frank Toskan coordinated all of the models' make-up looks, using M·A·C products, for the Festival's many runway shows. Other cosmetic brands better known and more prestigious than M·A·C had been vying for that platform, but Levy gave it to M·A·C. Toskan was influenced by the New York creative scene, and he wanted to bring some of that spirit and energy to Toronto, which, despite its exuberance, still felt to him very small-town and narrow-minded in many ways. Susie Sheffman felt differently, attributing an almost avant-garde mentality to the scene, something that she sensed was welcomed by consumers: "There was no conservatism. It was almost bizarre when I think back to that. We think of the 60s, the late 60s, as a time of revolution, and early 70s. But I think that the early 80s was really a huge time of revolution for fashion and art and the confluence of those, and music, and the energy that each of those things brought to the other."[49] The Festival offered what Toskan thought had been missing in Toronto: a unique opportunity to showcase New York energy to a Toronto audience. And importantly, that energy was being translated through M·A·C Cosmetics. Twelve M·A·C artists applied make-up on the hundreds of models all day long. The models then became unofficial M·A·C brand ambassadors. This network of make-up artists and models further strengthened the word-of-mouth Toskan had already been cultivating among his colleagues and retail customers.

For the 1987 Festival, Toskan asked Steven Levy if M·A·C could have its own fashion show (PLATE 11). Levy agreed, and the Franks paid for it themselves, with Donald Robertson contributing his artwork to the program (PLATE 12). Phillip Ing, a recent film graduate from York University and a relative newcomer to fashion, had come on board the Festival's organizing team in 1986 at Levy's request. While model Sam Turkis choreographed the more highbrow designer shows, Ing oversaw the young and often more club-inspired shows, and he was the obvious choice to work with the Franks on this first M·A·C show. The Franks became good friends with Ing right away. The M·A·C show, co-sponsored by *Flare*, was assigned a highly desirable spot – Saturday, ten p.m. Two days before, on 9 April, Nancy Hastings in the *Toronto Star* had billed it as an "ambitious show-spectacle of makeup, hair and fashion design, featuring the Desrosiers Dance Theatre, clothing from Comrags, cocktail couture from Winston, and the much-anticipated return of Zapata."[50] A very different type of audience came to the M·A·C show, Levy notes: the more fashion-forward people and other cultural groups in the city. People were screaming, and the energy was "unreal." Journalist Marina Sturdza declared M·A·C's collaboration "Best of Show" in the *Globe and Mail*'s Festival recap on 5 May, noting that they "produced a stunning spectacle that kept the audience on the edge of its seat."[51] Levy realized that M·A·C had "a great team behind it, with both a strong creative side and a strong business side. They have come up with a very fashion-forward look that they are able to mass-market – they're avant-garde yet they're accepted by everybody." He recognized that the one-of-a-kind pairing of Toskan and Angelo was producing something utterly new on the Toronto fashion scene.[52]

Indeed, after Levy had struggled to get his show off the ground the first two years, the Festival really found its stride in 1987. Designers were less sceptical and more enthusiastic about joining in, if only because their competition was there. Barbara Aarsteinsen reported in the *Globe and Mail* on 28 April 1987 that the $1.4 million Festival had attracted crowds of up to 10,000 people at one time. The 19,000-square-metre space in the Metro Convention Centre was vast, holding a 22-metre runway and 350 booths. The production team of 13 people had put together 27 shows with 3,000 ensembles, wrangled 320 models, managed 20 dressers, and directed 10 hairstylists and 15 make-up artists, besides providing music coordinators, a host of security, and an administrative staff of 15. Over the five days, the Festival drew 70,000 visitors, including 400 from the international media, as well as 1,500 buyers, 100 of them from the United States. American buyers were "pleasantly surprised" by the quality and sophistication of Canadian fashion, having previously not been "convinced that there was much fashion up here," one American buyer said. Buyers were keen to introduce Canadian wares to a hungry American market, ironically seeing "potential in a label that says 'made in America by Canadians.'" The mix of trade, retail, and consumers did dissuade some buyers from attending, but for Levy, the goal was a new type of marketing and advertising of Canadian fashion, a mix that would hopefully put Canada on the map as a fashion capital.[53]

The importance of the fashion show in defining the field of fashion and its centres cannot be understated, as seen in the case of Milan's fashion ascendance. Fashion scholars Joanne Entwistle and Agnès Rocamora observe in their ethnographic study of London Fashion Week that the fashion show has a specific meaning for fashion insiders; unlike a trade event, where commerce is the priority, the fashion show is part of fashion tradition. The fashion show does not simply display goods for sale; it is both a physical space and a "cultural event" where designers showcase their creative vision and where the field of fashion is produced and reproduced. One of the fashion show's main functions is for people to see and be seen so that one's position within the fashion field relative to others can be asserted. And designers are not the only people who occupy powerful positions within the field; other agents – journalists, editors, buyers, stylists, and models – use fashion shows to establish and reinforce their belonging in the field.[54] In a profile on M·A·C in the *Globe and Mail* in 1989, Marina Sturdza observed that Toskan's tactics at the Festival had actually been very strategic in this regard:

> Since cosmetics sales are closely linked to clothing directions, Toskan's route was to align MAC directly with fashion ... Toskan allocated very substantial time and all available dollars to establishing the company's presence at high-visibility industry events, such as the Festival of Canadian Fashion, with huge, extensively staffed booths, where MAC dispensed expert advice and retailed their product. That image was reinforced on the Festival's runways, which provided the perfect vehicle to demonstrate MAC's range and technique.[55]

M·A·C's position and status at the Festival as the official make-up brand for *all* the fashion shows, cemented by having *its own* fashion show, demarcated a special position for M·A·C in the Toronto fashion field that authorized its legitimacy and status within it.

Toskan now acknowledges that, despite his previous scepticism, "Toronto was ready for so many things."[56] The Festival was a watershed moment in Canadian fashion history and was central to M·A·C's early success and identity as a fashion company. Susie Sheffman suggests that, while the Festival of Canadian Fashion was indeed initially a success, this was perhaps not exactly for the reasons first envisioned by Levy:

> The biggest thing that it [the Festival] accomplished was probably not attracting the rest of the world to Canada, but it was probably about bringing people within Canada together, within the scene. I don't think we've ever been successful at bringing the international world of fashion here, home to us. What it did was it was very significant in terms of illustrating that there was an enormous scene here. That may be what it

intended to do, to bring the rest of the world to us, but I think what it more strongly did was unite the fashion world here.

This unifying function did much to solidify the small and tightly knit community, bound by its shared goal of highlighting Toronto fashion for the first time. Interestingly, one quality that especially seemed to characterize the fashion field in Toronto as a whole was the curious fact that despite the Festival's commercial import, the designers did not seem overly concerned about getting rich. According to Sheffman, "the stakes were not as high as they are now. If you made a mistake or screwed something up, okay, so you did something else the next day. The stakes in business were not so high."[57] Donald Robertson recalls how no one in Toronto really set out to make a lot of money: "None of us were influenced by the United States at all. Because, had we been influenced by the United States, we would have been like everybody else."[58] For fashion insiders, the excitement was more about the self-expression and creativity that defined the fashion people and the scene at that time. And this scene was supported by a powerful new media industry in Toronto devoted to this new world of fashion.

Discourses of Toronto Fashion

While M·A·C's success was impacted by how Toskan played the fashion "game," M·A·C, like the Toronto fashion industry generally, benefited from the new media outlets and publications that promoted Canada's fashion industry, including of course Toronto's. As journalist Deborah Fulsang recounted, Toronto media celebrated the fashion industry, articulated in media accounts of the industry's activities in new fashion magazines, television shows, newspaper columns, and even independent publications that came into being in the late 1970s and 1980s; together these generated a new discourse about Canadian fashion. *Toronto Life* had published a monthly magazine on local happenings since 1966, and the women's fashion magazine *Toronto Life Fashion* grew out of that publication in 1977. Its founding editor was John MacKay, a former fashion publicist, and he recalled how the late

1970s and early 1980s were an unusual time for fashion in Toronto. He noted that consumers had more disposable income and that fashion rose to the forefront. As the international fashion centres of Paris, Milan, and New York grew and prospered, so did Toronto. MacKay observed that the convergence of "fashion, baby boomers, money, and narcissism" directed new attention to fashion brands, logos, and styles. *Flare*, another new women's fashion magazine, evolved from *Miss Chatelaine*, a teen version of the long-running Canadian women's magazine *Chatelaine*. Fulsang notes that although *Chatelaine* had historically covered fashion in its own pages, and fashion stories had been part of Canadian newspaper reporting since the 1890s, Canada did not have a national, monthly fashion magazine of any kind until *Flare* appeared in 1979.[59] The *Globe and Mail* began a weekly fashion column, penned by David Livingstone, on 15 April 1980, dedicated to reporting on "the fashion industry itself, with designers and other fashion figures contributing columns."[60] These new media outlets became integral to stories about Toronto, fashion, the cultural scene – and about M·A·C – as discourse bound these forms of practice together.

In 1985, Jeanne Beker's new television show, *FashionTelevision*, (also known as *FT*) premiered on CityTV, Toronto's independent television broadcaster. Beker was an entertainment reporter for CityTV news and had been the host of the popular and groundbreaking all-music magazine show *TheNewMusic*, as well as the Toronto correspondent for *Entertainment Tonight* since 1983. *FashionTelevision* had first been conceived as a fashion video show that would be hosted by a model; instead, it was Beker who took her interviewing skills and real-woman charm to the world of the fashion elite. Capitalizing on a moment when fashion advertising was blooming and image and excess were the norm, *FT*'s fashion journalism was heavily influenced by the music video genre, which had arisen in 1981 with the American *MTV* cable channel, and in Canada with the Toronto-based *MuchMusic* specialty channel in 1984. Beker covered fashion stories both locally and internationally. With *FT*, fashion reporting became visual, dynamic, and, most importantly, entertaining. Before this time, fashion reporting was considered trivial and light, with little dedicated coverage, or it was presented according to more formal journalistic conventions, epitomized by CNN's *Style with Elsa Klensch*, and there was nothing whatsoever about fashion in Canadian broadcasting. Beker brought the world of fashion to the masses through *FT* with a distinctly Canadian flavour. By de-emphasizing fashion's elite qualities (Bourdieu's "haute couture") without diminishing them, while accentuating its entertainment value, Beker further democratized fashion. She highlighted Canadian fashion designers, models, culture, and art, usually at the beginning of the half-hour show to capitalize on a captive audience, and she was a strong advocate for Canadian fashion. *FashionTelevision* deliberately aligned Toronto with the world's fashion capitals in its reporting, which discursively put Toronto on the fashion "map" even though the city certainly was not a fashion hub in the same way. The catchy theme song – the 1984 hit "Obsession" by Animotion – became instantly identified with the show (and remains so for many Torontonians). *FashionTelevision* ran for twenty-seven years, first on CityTV, and later on specialty cable, ending in 2012. It was joined by the CBC's *Fashion File*, hosted by Tim Blanks, in 1989.

The *Canadian Fashion Annual 1989* was a one-off book project that captured this historical moment. Donald Robertson, now a Festival of Canadian Fashion organizer as well as a frequent collaborator with Toskan at M·A·C, created the book concept, and journalist Nancy Jane Hastings wrote it "With Contributions by Marina Sturdza, Rita Zekas and David Livingstone," all Toronto-based fashion journalists of the day. Describing itself as offering a "wide-ranging overview of who's who and what's hot in Canadian Fashion," the *Annual* comprehensively surveyed the designers making waves in Canadian fashion in 1988. David Livingstone's "Reflections on Canadian Fashion" defined the characteristics of the Canadian fashion industry: a lack of identity; a small and scattered market across a vast landscape; and typical Canadian modesty. He noted "a number of [Canadian] fashion designers reflecting a more confident sense of self. They still have to confront enough obstacles to keep them from smugness, but at the same time, they seem to recognize that it is pointless and provincial to worry unduly about where you come from." He contended that creativity and a sense of empowerment were finally coming to the forefront in Canadian fashion to showcase a "raw, diverse, unconventional, we've-got-nothing-to lose spirit."[61] Marina Sturdza promoted the book, which was released the second week of September 1988, in her column in the *Globe and Mail*.[62]

As both fashion discourse and cultural artefact, an example of the production and reproduction of Toronto's fashion scene in action, the *Annual* offers a particularly illuminating and legitimizing picture of Toronto fashion, highlighting its structure, agents, and practices and their relative positions in the field in the late 1980s. The twenty-five Toronto designers outnumbered Montreal's seven and Vancouver's two. Included were the internationally recognized Roots, Alfred Sung, and Wayne Clark, alongside nationally known labels Hilary Radley, Ports International, Tu Ly, and Clotheslines, and less well-known but beloved Toronto talents including Comrags, Emily Zarb, Loucas, Zapata, and Price Roman. The *Annual* also made official M·A·C's reputation, or symbolic capital, within the Toronto fashion field. Taking up a full page, M·A·C was featured in the "EXCESSories" section as the sole Canadian cosmetics brand. Beside a shot of a single red lipstick (most likely Russian Red), Canada's "M.A.C.nificent make-up company" was "redHOT." Frank Toskan unabashedly stated that "M.A.C is a new face for the fashionably inclined," and the *Annual* noted that M·A·C was "painting the continent red" in Toronto, New York, and Los Angeles, a nod to M·A·C's recent expansion to Henri Bendel and Nordstrom in the United States.[63] The book serves as compelling evidence of the structurally self-reproducing nature of the field, for it was created and written by those in the field who had a stake in maintaining the dynamics of that field – a key feature of cultural production. The *Annual* also implicitly revealed how other agents in the Toronto fashion field, such as the designers, photographers, journalists, models, and fashion news editors, were influential in establishing M·A·C's position within that field. They told M·A·C's early history both to outsiders and to one another, including within the *Annual*. The *Annual*'s writers, particularly Livingstone and Hastings, were also newspaper journalists, and each wrote at length about M·A·C in their newspapers, the *Globe and Mail* and the *Toronto Star*, respectively.

All of this activity is similar to the ways that Paris has been represented materially, discursively, and symbolically through various media as the fashion capital of the world. Fashion scholar Agnès Rocamora's analysis of Paris in *Fashioning the City: Paris, Fashion and the Media* demonstrates how the symbolic construction of, and "belief" in, Paris as the fashion centre of the world has taken place through fashion discourses as practices, operating alongside its cultural production: "Discourses of symbolic production are discourses not simply about fashion commodities but also about practices, individual agents such as designers and celebrities, and collective agents such as companies and also cities."[64] Rocamora notes that the fashion stories in magazines, newspapers, and various other media all serve to construct this discourse. Toronto's field of fashion was similarly constructed through its media. Toronto never rose to the same status as Paris or New York; even so, artefacts like the *Canadian Fashion Annual 1989* demonstrate that those inside that field of cultural production attempted to produce and reproduce the Toronto fashion scene.

M·A·C generated most of its exposure through word-of-mouth, celebrity endorsements and testimonials, and newspaper coverage. It did not receive any credit in one particular corner of the Canadian fashion media: fashion magazines. This seems unusual, considering the brand's popularity and prominent place in the Toronto fashion industry. Indeed, Toskan certainly wanted to work with the magazines. He did one editorial for *Essence* (the cover and inside pages), but he found it a lot of work without much pay-off, and he would not work for free. Toskan went to another magazine with his portfolio and was told he was "not high profile enough," an observation that seems particularly disingenuous. The real reason – largely unspoken – why M·A·C and Toskan did not receive any editorial or magazine coverage was that M·A·C did not advertise. This had always been one of Toskan's personal and ideological "rules," setting aside the fact that advertising was too expensive for the Franks' small, start-up company in its early years. Toskan knew that someone eventually had to pay for advertising, and it was usually the customer, and this structure offended him. The Franks had no intention of downloading that expense onto their customers. Mostly, though, Toskan considered advertising to be ethically dubious and refused to participate. Furthermore, Toskan never sent M·A·C products to beauty editors to review; he would send written blurbs about launches but never free products, because he thought the products and the brand would lose value if he did. So, even though M·A·C was being used extensively by make-up artists for editorial work and fashion magazine covers, the fact that M·A·C did not provide advertising revenue to these publications disinclined editors to giving the brand its rightful acknowledgment in their pages. The Franks understood that traditional advertising and promotional tactics were the formula for media attention, but they were not prepared to play by those rules.

It was only much later, in a profile on M·A·C in *Toronto Life Fashion* in January 1995, that M·A·C's exclusion from fashion coverage in Canadian magazines was explicitly addressed. Journalist Serena French observed that by the mid-1990s, M·A·C "has received more editorial coverage in the United States and England than it has at home. In one case, a local publisher sought to have the mention of M·A·C product stricken from a celebrity interview; in another, a story on cosmetics packaging that would have seen M·A·C in a positive light was killed. In yet another, a completed profile of M·A·C never made it to press." Make-up artist Frances Hathaway confirmed in this article that the reason for this was the Franks' decision not to advertise M·A·C. For her, these repercussions were more personal. She acknowledged the political economy of Canada's media industry during M·A·C's early years; in the mid-1980s, "I was using M·A·C, and I always had that political problem whenever I worked for magazines. Because M·A·C didn't advertise, the magazine couldn't give them credit, which I think personally is unfair and also deceiving the public. We understand that without the advertisers, the magazines wouldn't exist, but I don't think every single credit should go to the advertisers. Because truth be known, most of those makeup people were using

M·A·C." As Hathaway later said, there was a certain amount of "pushback" from the Canadian media, which, she speculated, viewed M·A·C's "business model," such as it was, as a threat to the magazines' very existence. But the consistent lack of editorial credit was also hurting Hathaway professionally, and she ultimately left Toronto, unable to obtain the necessary credits in Toronto to build her portfolio and her own professional reputation. European fashion, she said, emphasized and valued artistry much more, and Hathaway built a thriving career there, using M·A·C products freely. The *Toronto Life* profile also speculated that this media silence was one reason relatively few people in Canada, outside of the Toronto fashion scene, knew about M·A·C during the 1980s.[65] Donald Robertson concurs: "You can't find any editorial on M·A·C in Canada at that time." This situation also explains why most of the (relatively few) media accounts of M·A·C in the 1980s and early 1990s appeared in newspapers.

Unlike the Canadian press, the American media were excited about this new "discovery." Donald Robertson recalls this enthusiasm, compared to Canada's: "The American press is the opposite [of the Canadian press]. They're like, are you new? Are you new? Oh my god, you're new. Oh my god, we're writing about you."[66] This situation would begin to change to some degree by the mid-1990s. Suzanne Boyd, by then editor-in-chief at *Flare* (from 1996 to 2004), gave M·A·C a great deal of press: "I personally wrote tons of stories about M·A·C and credited them," she notes. "It was always such a great Canadian story to tell ... I was personally happy to cover them as much as possible."[67] Nonetheless, despite this silence by the Canadian magazines in the 1980s and early 1990s, M·A·C generated all the publicity it needed (and could handle) through its professional fashion network, customer goodwill, and fashion events, and through discourses emerging from the field of fashion by newspaper journalists like Bernadette Morra, Nancy Hastings, Marina Sturdza, and David Livingstone. Indeed, M·A·C's lack of advertising, and the aura this "silence" created around the brand, would later serve it well.

Jeanne Beker asserts that Toronto's fashion industry generally remained supportive and proud of M·A·C's success: "It just felt like it was really one of our own that had come up through the ranks and was starting to make noise in New York very early on, before many Torontonians, or Canadians, for that matter, were really going down there and making any kind of difference."[68] As in many other fields, however, success was not substantial until it happened in the United States. These were the consequences of the Franks' business, artistic, and ethical practices, but they hardly mattered: M·A·C's social capital within the field of fashion was assured, despite or, increasingly, *because* it consciously opposed the commercial logic inherent in the conventional advertising arrangement. M·A·C's founders competed for their position in the fashion field as much as everyone else and successfully established their own and M·A·C's distinctive creative reputation and social capital. As well, the general democratization of fashion that influenced the inclusive nature of those in Toronto defined the field in uniquely Canadian ways. The history of the field of fashion in Toronto emerged through this series of struggles by all of its agents – designers, models, stylists, make-up artists, and hairstylists, as well as journalists, photographers, and editors – in a particular time and place, and many of those struggles were captured in these media accounts. As such, Toronto's fashion field came into being and could be discerned by this index of lives and actions. But one particular struggle affected the field more than others at this time, and it would have devastating repercussions on these dynamics within the fashion industry: the AIDS epidemic.

AIDS in Fashion

As M·A·C was moving forward with its creative products and gaining more recognition in Toronto (and, increasingly, south of the Canada–US border), the Toronto fashion industry was building its own momentum. It was an exciting and unparalleled moment, but at the same time, the fashion and design communities sensed a strong but silent spectre. Lawrence K. Altman wrote an early story published in the *New York Times* on 3 July 1981 about a "Rare Cancer Seen in 41 Homosexuals." This seemingly new illness was striking urban gay communities the hardest, and it had already been written about in independent gay publications, such as *The Body Politic* in Toronto and the *New York Native* in New York City, but the *Times* article is generally accepted as the first story about AIDS in the mainstream media. The earliest AIDS cases in the United States were called GRID (gay-related immune deficiency) and were often associated with Kaposi's sarcoma, a rare and disfiguring skin cancer, and pneumocystis pneumonia (PCP), both of which were fatal. The first four GRID cases in Canada were reported in the *Globe and Mail* on 21 July 1982. GRID was renamed AIDS (acquired immunodeficiency syndrome) in September 1984. The virus that leads to AIDS, the human immunodeficiency virus (HIV), was identified in 1984 by Dr Luc Montagnier in Paris and subsequently by Dr Robert Gallo in the United States in 1986, although there is some debate about who could legitimately claim that discovery.[69]

AIDS, like many epidemics that preceded it, was viewed as reflecting a decay of the social order and as striking those on the margins of social responsibility and respectability.[70] From the beginning, AIDS was prone to metaphorical descriptions and explanations. Communications and gender scholar Paula Treichler famously called AIDS "an epidemic of signification" for the way it took on both simultaneous and contradictory meanings, depending on who was talking about AIDS and what was at stake. Allusions to earlier plagues, condemnations of "immoral" sexual conduct, contentious and ongoing disagreement about HIV's origins, and numerous conspiracy theories were part of the early discourse surrounding AIDS, which was initially positioned as occurring in "guilty" victims and associated with punishment for behaviour that included not only all forms of gay sex but also sex work and drug use.[71] This ideological categorizing obfuscated how HIV and AIDS affected all members of society, including women. Later, once AIDS began appearing among "innocent" victims (heterosexuals, children, women) as it spread to "the general public" (instead of being confined to society's "undesirables"), the disease was likened to a war. This war was described as a general threat to the (heterosexual) social body as well as to the physical body.[72] The paradoxes surrounding AIDS – that it infected those who ought to be punished for their deviance but also infected the innocent, especially children – were maintained, as essayist Susan Sontag wrote in *AIDS and Its Metaphors* in 1988, through the power of metaphor, which opened spaces for these slippery meanings and connotations regarding what was, in essence, a strictly medical condition.[73]

The first year that AIDS deaths were recorded in the province of Ontario was 1987, but these numbers were not accurately captured, because of inadequate reporting measures and because in the early days the actual cause of death was often obfuscated or misrepresented by doctors or families. Yet it was clear from the beginning of official record keeping that the majority of HIV and AIDS diagnoses in Canada were in Ontario and that most of the Ontario cases were in Toronto. AIDS cases roughly doubled each year in Toronto and consistently represented between 62 and 66 per cent of all the AIDS cases in Ontario during the 1980s.[74] Statistics on AIDS cases by profession were not kept, but people in the fashion industry felt the epidemic's effects first-hand. As Phillip Ing remembers,

> [AIDS] affected you at that time because we worked in fashion, and because of the fear it prompted ... It affected every fashion person who was sexually active, but it doesn't mean that only the fashion industry people were dying from it. Some of them were. The impact was that that fear spread through almost every member of – just like it spread through every gay man alive eventually. In the early 80s, I think a lot of people were still pretty naïve. *Extra* magazine always listed people who had passed away, almost on a weekly basis. That fear was real.[75]

This fear surrounding AIDS, and the ensuing panic, were devastating to the community.

In major urban centres across North America – and Toronto was no exception – the onset of AIDS during the 1980s profoundly affected the field of fashion as well as other creative industries including theatre, design, and dance. *FashionTelevision* host Jeanne Beker recalled:

Fashion and AIDS: The two seemed to go together hand-in-hand 20 years ago, when the first season [1985] of FT (Fashion Television) hit the airwaves. The disease was ravaging our industry, and there wasn't a soul working in fashion that hadn't, in some way, been touched by AIDS. Friends, lovers, collaborators and muses were falling like flies. We wanted to pierce the heavens with our screams of injustice – so much talent and inspiration was being taken from us.[76]

The creative fields have traditionally attracted gay men, for they are places where difference is more generally accepted and indeed celebrated. Bernadette Morra points to the convergence and concentration of the creative and media industries in Toronto as one reason the effects of AIDS were experienced so intensely in the city: "If Toronto were not a centre of publishing and did not have these magazines, you wouldn't have had that closeness between the photographers, the designers, the hair and the make-up people who were getting sick. People were getting sick – designers, hairstylists, make-up artists – and these were all people who worked together producing fashion shoots, producing fashion magazines, producing advertisements."[77] In the end, however, accounts about AIDS deaths in Toronto's fashion industry, and the impact they had, are largely anecdotal. Stylist Susie Sheffman recalls: "I would say I probably knew about 20 people myself that I dealt with, from the hairdressers and make-up artists. There were obviously more, but I'm just talking about within my own warm circle ... Certainly people got sick but they didn't necessarily die in the 80s, they died in the 90s – you know, later."[78]

From the start, the fashion industry in New York City was reticent about confronting AIDS. The thinking was that if the public were to associate fashion with AIDS, or with a particular fashion brand, sales would plummet. It was also thought that the presumed link between AIDS and homosexuality could perpetuate hurtful gay stereotypes, which would then extend to tarnishing a brand's reputation and value. Furthermore, fashion is preoccupied with image, beauty, and creativity, which did not fit with media images depicting the illness and the embodied reality of living with AIDS (Kaposi's sarcoma, for example, left disfiguring sores). The fashion industry wanted to distance itself from these associations. Many well-known New York fashion names, brands, and labels generally refrained from participating in AIDS-related events during the early to mid-1980s. The co-chair of Fashion Affair '84, Pauline Trigère, said that the "big designers were almost nowhere to be seen" at a November fashion show and auction in support of the AIDS Medical Foundation. These designers had given money to the cause and lent clothes for the show, but they did not appear at the event in person.[79]

A front-page article in the US trade journal *Women's Wear Daily* in May 1985 titled "AIDS: It's Everyone's Business" highlighted precisely how the New York fashion industry was maintaining this silence and had not adequately responded to a disease that was affecting so many of its own members. Author Mort Sheinman interviewed Dr Alvin Friedman-Kien of the New York University Medical School, who pointed to the effects of Kaposi's sarcoma and the high prevalence of AIDS in the New York fashion industry.[80] Indeed, AIDS was striking a wide variety of fashion insiders, including fashion assistants, showroom salesmen, shipping clerks, retail executives, fashion show choreographers, bridalwear designers, eveningwear designers, and sportswear designers. Two years later, Carol Hymowitz observed in the *Wall Street Journal* that fashion and other arts fields were cautious about responding to the crisis: "AIDS is devastating all of the arts, interior design and architecture. But, oddly, the fashion industry has been the slowest to acknowledge the decimation in its ranks and to raise money for research and care."[81]

The physical and emotional strain caused by repeatedly visiting and caring for sick friends, dealing with their deaths, mourning, and grieving were taking a toll on people in the industry, besides decimating businesses, partnerships, and creative practices. It was becoming much more obvious that fashion collections lacked their former creative edge, that people were vanishing, and that their replacements, already difficult to find, were disappearing as well. The impact of their loss was being felt throughout the fashion system, trickling down from the top in New York, into mass fashion, and finally into the malls. By late 1987, the New York fashion industry had lost designers Perry Ellis, Chester Weinberg, Willi Smith, and Tracy Mills to complications from AIDS. Other deaths within the New York field included display artists Larry Bartscher and Robert Benzio; fashion illustrator Antonio Lopez; make-up artist Way Bandy; models Michael Hanshaw, Brice Holman, Joe Macdonald, and Gia Carangi; fashion photographer William King; and fashion retail executives Pasquale Pagano, Steve Maxfield, and Carl Erickson, as well as other less well-known but locally successful designers and fashion people, whose names and businesses died with them. Lester Gribetz, executive vice-president of Bloomingdale's, said in 1987 that "along with the terrible loss of life, we're losing creativity, which is this industry's foundation ... You lose a brilliant display artist or designer, and his vision, talent, ability to create a style is gone forever – and can't be replaced."[82] AIDS was disrupting the field's natural evolution by displacing and too often eliminating players completely outside of the normal struggles or "rules" of the game.

Toronto reacted to the AIDS crisis in some unique ways, for several reasons. The fashion and design communities in Toronto were much smaller than in New York, so their participants were much more closely intertwined. Susie Sheffman explains:

> What was different about Toronto was that we had a very tight community – *very* tight community: fashion, art, music; exceptionally tight and exceptionally close knit, interdependent on each other from a friendship standpoint and a business standpoint. Because it was such a close-knit community, we really felt the loss so acutely. Because we were small – if you're thousands of people and you lose ten, it's not as shocking or as impactful as if you're fifty people and you lose ten. I think the size of the fashion and art community here, and the fact that people were just literally dropping like flies, made it a very impactful moment.[83]

Frank Toskan and Frank Angelo, M·A·C's employees, and their colleagues in the Toronto fashion industry had the same direct experience of AIDS. As Toskan notes, "whatever happened there to one person was very quickly understood" by others in the industry. Many insiders emphasized that what was distinctly Torontonian was, as Toskan characterizes it,

> the family kind of intimacy that the industry experienced. We all knew each other here. When we went to New York, it was such a big thing. You were lost; you were this little drop of water. In New York it was much harder to get that message out. As a community, I think Toronto was very supportive of each other. We had an incredible strength within that small community because we were connected.[84]

Within this cultural, social, and creative milieu, responding to AIDS also became an essential, and creative, expression of the Toronto fashion industry's – and M·A·C's – most deeply held values.

CHAPTER 3

Caring Is Never Out of Fashion

A number of forces were propelling the AIDS epidemic in Canada, and Toronto's fashion industry reacted to these dynamics. From the start, the stigma associated with AIDS, or with being HIV positive, coupled with already existing homophobia and discrimination, raised substantial barriers to effective action against AIDS, inside and outside the field of fashion. In both the United States and Canada, homosexuality had been pathologized and AIDS had been moralized by the medical establishment. Support for AIDS awareness and for people living with HIV/AIDS was a controversial and indeed often forbidden topic for governments to publicly address. As one example, Jake Epp, Canada's federal health minister from 1984 to 1989, dodged the issue of AIDS as much as possible and avoided actually saying the word "AIDS" for several years.[1] Likewise, US president Ronald Reagan notoriously refused to speak about AIDS. The death of actor Rock Hudson in 1985 brought AIDS into more mainstream conversation, yet even after that, government malaise about HIV/AIDS research, prevention, and treatment in North America was the norm, and homophobia saturated much of the early discourse surrounding AIDS and HIV. Discrimination delayed the appropriate governmental and medical responses to this frightening disease, with the result that those affected by HIV and AIDS faced many struggles and encountered numerous obstacles in terms of receiving support, education, and effective medicines. The metaphorical and moral understandings of AIDS impeded research into the virus and potential drug treatments. As a result, formal AIDS activism was initiated by those living with complications of AIDS or who were HIV-positive. These people consistently and strategically challenged the traditional top-down administrative style of health regulation and care, recognizing that the fight against AIDS was inextricably linked to the fight for gay rights and against discrimination and homophobia.[2]

AIDS activists fought for patients' rights, home care, increased access to affordable experimental drug treatments, and less rigid design in drug testing. These issues were not necessarily AIDS-specific; they suggested a broader critique of health agencies' management style. Grassroots activist organizations contested health professionals' deeply held view that only the medical profession could, and should, manage health care and disease. Activist groups argued instead that the people who were directly affected by HIV and AIDS should have a strong voice in their own health care – a position reinforced by the fact that most activists were speaking from personal experience, as many of them were dealing with AIDS or were HIV-positive themselves. Activists continually resisted adapting to state policy agendas and launched new, community-based models of health care, support, and education. AIDS activism pushed government institutions such as the Health Protection Branch, located within the federal Health and Welfare Department, to change their traditional models of response to disease. Once the focus was shifted to those living with HIV/AIDS, a precedent was set for directly representing patients' interests and experiences in disease research, drug testing, and treatment.[3] As management scholars Steve Maguire, Cynthia Hardy, and Thomas B. Lawrence note, "[t]he reaction of the gay community to this situation [AIDS] not only introduced a new form of activism regarding disease treatment, but also led to new forms of organization (PWA organizations and ASOs) and completely changed traditional notions of the 'patient.'"[4] Activist groups maintained their autonomy even as they eventually learned to work with the government agencies that could assist them. In Toronto, activist groups were largely rooted in the politics surrounding gay identity, liberation, and sexuality – issues that the AIDS crisis now highlighted. Activists who had recently organized around these and other relevant issues drew upon their experience and channelled it into the new AIDS activism. In Toronto, these individuals capitalized on a strong sense of community, one that had already forged its own networks and alliances. This support was particularly strong following the gay bathhouse raids of 1981, in the course of which the Toronto police arrested three hundred men. Three types of organizations subsequently developed in response to AIDS, all of which were generally local and coordinated from within the major urban gay communities in Toronto, Montreal, and Vancouver.[5]

The first type of AIDS organization to emerge was the most common one: the multipurpose AIDS service organization (ASO), which provided counselling, education, and emotional support to the community.[6] Gays in Health Care (GHC) was formed in Toronto in 1980 by psychiatrist-in-training Stephen Atkinson to deal with sexually transmitted diseases, addiction, gay mental health, and coming out. It initially comprised medical doctors and later included other health care professionals. On 5 April 1983, GHC sponsored a public meeting at Ryerson Polytechnical Institute to discuss the AIDS crisis. From this, five working groups on AIDS-related issues were formed around community education, patient support, fundraising, medical liaison, and media and public relations. These groups became the basis for Toronto's first and primary ASO, the AIDS Committee of Toronto (ACT). The founding of ACT, which was led by local activists, including University of Toronto academic Michael Lynch and *The Body Politic* editor Ed Jackson, was announced at a press conference on 19 July 1983.[7] Toronto Public Health assisted with the AIDS crisis, but much of the day-to-day work fell to ACT, since its mandate was not just education but also the provision of health care, counselling, support, and other resources for those living with HIV and AIDS.

New organizations and projects subsequently coalesced in Toronto. Several AIDS groups, including ACT, joined forces in 1985 to form the Ontario AIDS Network (OAN). ACT announced at a press conference on 21 January 1986 that plans were under way for Casey House, the first free-standing AIDS hospice in Canada, an occasion also noted in major media outlets including the *Toronto Star* and the *Globe and Mail*, as well as *The Body Politic*.[8] Casey House represented "a symbolic place which embodies the gay community's defiance against AIDS and its empowerment to deal with an issue hitherto marginalized by the state." Geographers Quentin P. Chiotti and Alun P. Joseph observe that Casey House served as a prime example of how community organizing around AIDS defied the top-down dictates of institutionalized medicine, becoming "a statement against society's homophobia and AIDS hysteria."[9] In 1986, the second annual Canadian AIDS conference in Toronto facilitated the formation of the Canadian AIDS Society (CAS). The following year, the Toronto People with AIDS Foundation was established to supplement ACT's work; the year after that, it changed its name to the PWA Foundation.

The second type of AIDS organization focused on specific health-related concerns about AIDS, generally arising from those directly affected by HIV and AIDS, and advocated for greater medical intervention. In New York, playwright Larry Kramer had founded the Gay Men's Health Crisis (GMHC) in 1981 (he wrote the AIDS-themed play *The Normal Heart* during this time). In Toronto, organizing around health care and patients' rights was also a priority. The long-standing Hassle Free Clinic, a community-based health clinic dedicated to sexual health, had been Toronto's largest health care provider to gay men since 1973. The clinic tried to address the immediate health concerns of its urban clients affected by HIV and AIDS but was vastly unprepared. Since it was generally recognized that the AIDS epidemic in New York and San Francisco was about two years ahead of Toronto, those in Toronto closely monitored events south of the border to anticipate what was coming at them in the way of health-related patterns.

The third type of AIDS organization expressed a more radical critique of state policy and a stronger commitment to action. In Toronto, AIDS Action Now! (AAN!) formed in early 1988, loosely based on New York's ACT UP (AIDS Coalition to Unleash Power). AAN! developed as a treatment activist group to carry out the work that ACT, a government-funded not-for-profit organization, could not. A notice for the 1988 annual general meeting described how the organization's objective was "to fight politically to improve the care and treatment people living with AIDS (PLWAs) receive from the health care system," zeroing in on the lack of effective drug treatments.[10] There were still no drugs that cured AIDS or halted its symptoms, although many experimental drugs, including AZT, and other potential drug therapies were available in the United States. The large pharmaceutical companies were bound by strict Canadian regulations, and the small Canadian market offered little incentive for research and development. Many of ACT's founding members, such as academic and *The Body Politic* writer Michael Lynch, were part of AAN!'s core group. AAN! was especially successful in making its voice heard in government bureaucracy and in the media. Despite strategic differences among all of these AIDS organizations, they largely cooperated with one another.

Political scientists David M. Rayside and Evert A. Lindquist emphasize that a productive working attitude positively affected organization around AIDS in Toronto. They observe that Toronto's various tactical approaches were partly "the product of a broader pattern in Canadian progressive activism, and partly the product of circumstances unique to Toronto and Ontario."[11] In Quebec, the reductions in social spending on health care, the English/French divide, and Quebec's cultural diversity created additional tensions that hindered cooperation among groups in that province. In Ontario, there were still obstacles at the provincial level, even with a Liberal government elected in 1985 that espoused a reformist agenda. Local tactics did find some support in pockets of local government. Progressive shifts in local leadership helped, epitomized by Toronto city councillor Jack Layton, whose downtown ward had a large gay population and who was also the chair of the Toronto Health Board. As Rayside and Lindquist note, "the willingness to accommodate differences within and between AIDS organizations may well be part of a more general pattern in progressive Canadian organizing."[12] Thus, Toronto proved to be an especially positive political environment in which to engage in AIDS activism, a circumstance that perhaps had a knock-on impact on other facets of social and cultural life in the city.[13]

In August 1985, *Globe and Mail* fashion journalist David Livingstone related how proceeds from an upcoming men's fashion show produced by Cynthia Korpan, titled Leonardo, would be donated to the AIDS Committee of Toronto. Livingstone called attention to these "less than conservative" activities within Toronto's fashion community, alluding to the fact that publicly associating with AIDS was a risky and even subversive act.[14] In New York, more public responses to AIDS began to develop around 1986. In May of that year, designer Calvin Klein underwrote an AIDS benefit show at the Jacob K. Javits Convention Center in New York City, marking "the first time the fashion, cosmetic and fragrance industries combined forces to raise money to fight acquired immunodeficiency syndrome." The event promised to be "a place to see just about anybody who's anybody in fashion, as well as Elizabeth Taylor," who co-hosted the event with Klein and would soon become a highly regarded ally and advocate for AIDS awareness and fundraising.[15] In November, a major social event and fundraiser held at the National Building Museum in Washington, D.C., further aligned AIDS philanthropy with the New York fashion industry. This fundraiser supported the AIDS Research Program of the Cancer Institute at the National Institutes of Health, as well as the Washington Fashion Group's Scholarship Fund. Change was in the air, and the following year, the Toronto fashion industry collectively mounted its own response to AIDS.

Fashion wholesaler Syd Beder, whom Festival of Canadian Fashion organizer Steven Levy jokingly called "the Pope of Queen Street," represented several of Toronto's burgeoning designers, including Emily Zarb, Comrags, Babel, and Franco Mirabelli, and a number of commercial lines at his Power Clothes Works showroom on Queen Street West (what was then *very* west, at Portland Street). Beder's boutique WOW on the Queen West shopping strip also carried these young designers' products, and Rick Mugford managed the store. Beder had also participated in the Festival, having selected some of its talent, besides producing other local fashion shows. Beder recalls that when he was visiting his mother in Florida around 1986, it seemed that all he heard on the American news was reports about this new health crisis called AIDS. When he returned to Toronto, he educated himself about HIV and AIDS and decided that something needed to be done in his own city.[16] Around that time, Beder had launched the Toronto arrival of the British fashion and culture magazine *i.d.* with a fashion show, and he had read in that magazine about an early AIDS fundraising event held in London, England, in 1985. That event had been organized by the

UK fashion public-relations specialist Lynne Franks and was called "Fashion Cares." It consisted of two items for sale: a T-shirt signed by forty-eight top European designers, including Karl Lagerfeld, Vivienne Westwood, Azzedine Alaïa, and Jean Paul Gaultier, and an off-shape heart pin. Both items were sold in London fashion stores, with the funds raised going to the Terrence Higgins Trust, the first charity in the UK (founded in 1982) to respond to the HIV/AIDS epidemic. *i.d.* fashion editor Caryn Franklin had helped Lynne Franks organize that event. Beder came back from London with some of the Fashion Cares T-shirts and an idea.

Beder suggested to Steven Levy that an AIDS fundraiser be held during the Festival of Canadian Fashion. Levy was unable to comply because the Festival already had an official charitable partner, so he suggested a separate event. Through Franklin, Mugford asked for permission to "borrow" the artwork and organize a similar Fashion Cares event in Toronto. The impetus for Toronto's Fashion Cares was clear: just as in London and New York, HIV and AIDS were hitting Toronto's fashion industry hard. As Beder noted at the time, "AIDS is the scourge of Seventh Avenue in New York ... We want to help stop it from becoming the scourge of Spadina."[17] Beder later recalled that this fashion show came into being by drawing on "some of the ideas that I'd gleaned from the Festival; and I kind of made a marriage and decided I was going to attempt this and a lot of the people who worked on the Festival in those days were co-opted into working with me – Phillip [Ing], Jann [Coppen], etc. so it was a great bunch of people who helped that first year."[18] Indeed, it just made sense for Beder to turn to the same people for this new project. Beder was the inspiration behind the entire event; he "led the charge," Levy remembers.[19] Beder turned to Rick Mugford for help, and they started organizing.

Mugford began by calling the local Toronto designers with whom he and Beder did business. He showed them the *i.d.* magazine spread and asked them to participate. If people did not call him back, Shelley Wickabrod from the Clotheslines design team intervened. Since Mugford did not know everybody in the industry, he relied on Beder's and Wickabrod's clout, or social capital, to reach the more established designers. Those designers who did agree to participate did so because they knew Mugford or they knew

Beder and they understood the event was more about helping others out than offering any commercial advantage. Designers were told that all funds generated by this Toronto version of Fashion Cares would be donated to the AIDS Committee of Toronto. Both Mugford and Beder felt that ACT was the best venue for providing education and that financially supporting ACT would offer the most direct benefit to those living with HIV/AIDS. ACT was also chosen because Mugford and Beder felt it would attract broader support from designers. Not everyone who was asked agreed to participate, and likewise, others who might have participated were not asked; some of the very biggest names in Canadian fashion ultimately said no, while others did not have the opportunity to say yes.

Writer and journalist Ann Silversides recounts how the AIDS Committee of Toronto had initially been funded by a $62,415 federal grant back in June 1983, administered through the Employment Development Program and supplemented by private fundraising. In June 1984, ACT received, somewhat clandestinely, another $30,000 from what was publicly identified only as the "provincial government." The sources of this funding, the Ministry of Health and the Ministry of Citizenship and Culture, did not want to be credited by name. The ministries' desire for secrecy underscored how the stigma attached to AIDS was so strong that even government officials did not want to be publicly associated with the disease. ACT had charitable status, which meant that federal law prohibited it from engaging in political advocacy or strong activist efforts, and doing so would have jeopardized its government funding. But as ACT broadened its range of essential services, the government began to recognize ACT's importance. By 1985, funding from the municipal, provincial, and federal levels of government was in place. ACT was given a grant of $179,400 from the federal government under the Special Employment Initiatives Program. The terms of the grant required ACT to raise $40,000 on its own. ACT also received interim funding of $40,000 from the Metropolitan Toronto Council and periodically received money raised by local arts groups, which would now include the funds raised by Fashion Cares.[20] Beder and Mugford decided to produce a fundraising T-shirt (as the British event had done), and to hold a science-fiction-themed fashion show to coincide with ACT's AIDS Awareness Week, running from 5 to 14 June 1987.

Fashion Cares was scheduled for Wednesday, 10 June 1987, at the Diamond Club, a small underground dance club on Sherbourne Street in Toronto. The Festival of Canadian Fashion's Phillip Ing took over from friend Sam Turkis when she got a European modelling job, and he directed the show, despite being on crutches, having infamously broken his ankle running after dancer Robert Desrosiers at the Festival earlier that year. The *Toronto Star*'s Nancy Hastings enthusiastically noted on 30 April that "there's a consciousness-raising effort afoot in Toronto's fashion community in support of AIDS relief."[21] In the 7–13 May 1987 edition of *NOW*, a Toronto weekly independent newspaper, the show was listed as part of Fashion Vignettes, a regular event held on Wednesday nights at the Diamond Club. These weekly fashion nights featured local fashion talent and retailers and were venues where, as *NOW* stated, "fashion fans and fashion people head down to dance, mingle, drink and view the latest in fashion within the confines of the perennial party atmosphere of the Diamond."[22] A month later, in the 4–10 June 1987 edition of *NOW*, Loretta Chin and Juliet Warkentin promoted Fashion Cares in the fashion news. In this same issue, an ad placed by the AIDS Committee of Toronto described Fashion Cares simply as "A Benefit for ACT" to be held in tandem with other activist and education events during AIDS Awareness week later in June.[23] ACT confirmed in its own 5–14 June 1987 newsletter that all proceeds from Fashion Cares would help fund "education programmes, counselling support groups and financial assistance for people with AIDS."[24] David Livingstone wrote enthusiastically about the event in the *Globe and Mail*'s "Style Notes," as did Nancy Hastings in the *Toronto Star*.[25] The people who attended the Diamond Club's Fashion Vignettes were a built-in fashionable audience for Fashion Cares. This characterization of Fashion Cares as "underground" reinforced its identity as an event that was accessible mainly to fashion insiders, all of whom possessed the required forms of capital for entry, in contrast to the very public Festival of Canadian Fashion, which was open to fashion insiders *and* outsiders.

The word "AIDS," however, was conspicuously absent from any of the event's promotional communications. Designed by Paula

Munck of Reactor Design, the Fashion Cares poster was published in *NOW* in the 4–10 June 1987 edition. It read:

> FASHION CARES. What it wears to the most **most** fashionable party of the year. Yes Toronto, the most fashionable party in the world playing at the Diamond Club on Wednesday June 10 at 8:00 p.m. SHARP. Mingle with top fashion designers, modern models, stars, video, entertainers, real trendy people and their friends, rich people, debutantes, the jetsons & dance relentlessly, nuf nuf entertainment, the hottest dee jays; people from the emerald city, at The Diamond Club, 410 Sherbourne Street, General Admission $10 NO GUEST LIST Tickets available at BASS and other fashionable outlets. Produced by Power Clothes Works, for info phone 863-1818.[26]

The Diamond Club agreed to host the event on the condition that the word "AIDS" not be used in any promotional materials, posters, or advertising in which the Diamond Club's name also appeared. Even the show's beneficiary, ACT, could not be identified on the poster because it had "AIDS" in its name. ACT volunteer David Clark remembered that "you couldn't even say the word AIDS without freaking people out. It had such terrible stigma at that time."[27] Outside support for the event, particularly in the form of corporate sponsorship, was difficult if not impossible to obtain, said Beder, who has steadfastly never named names. Instead, the promotional communications focused on how the show would be "the most fashionable party in the world." Because of their social capital and positions in the industry, however, fashion insiders already knew that Fashion Cares was an AIDS fundraiser, and immediately it was a hot ticket. Suzanne Boyd clearly remembers sitting on the people-watching patio of the Black Bull, a well-known bar on Queen West, when Beder came by with the T-shirts and the $10 tickets; no one gets in for free, Beder had said.[28] As he repeatedly stated, Fashion Cares was a fundraiser.

The Fashion Cares show exhibited the creative qualities of the people involved to their fullest extent. According to its producer, Phillip Ing, each designer produced only one or two outfits for a show that would run more "like a parade" than a traditional fashion show. The designers and organizers had to make do with the materials they could scrounge up, whether donated, repurposed, or reimagined – another example of the creative resourcefulness that characterized the event. Models appeared on the "catwalk" only once, to allow more time for the stylists to create the hair and make-up designs. The show's science-fiction theme was brought to life with a space-age set, and the models were painted green, like "Martian-monster people," Ing later joked. As Ing recalls, this theme was, despite being fantasy, actually an AIDS allegory: "It was part metaphor, part tongue and cheek – we just knew it [AIDS] was this horrible thing amongst us."[29] M·A·C Cosmetics played an integral role at Fashion Cares: the Franks donated all of the M·A·C cosmetics used in the fashion show, and Frank Toskan and Frank Angelo, with a small M·A·C make-up artist team, applied the make-up on the more than thirty models in the Diamond Club's cramped backstage area. The Franks, along with Vidal Sassoon hair stylists, also created some of the hair looks, a time-consuming – and dangerous – process consisting of applying mud and shards of glass to each model's hair. The designers who participated in Fashion Cares exhibited a creative spirit despite, or perhaps because of, the seriousness of AIDS. Everyone involved in Fashion Cares, in whatever capacity, channelled their fear and frustration about AIDS into making the show as creative and exciting as possible.

David Livingstone, who attended the event, wrote in the *Globe and Mail* on 16 June that the show "was a showcase for all the good things that fashion can be: artful, gregarious, pertinent, humorous, and spirited."[30] There was a great deal of (mostly male) nudity. The garment that both opened and closed the show was a dress created by Dean and Dan Caten under their Dean and Dan label. This black rubber "safe sex" dress was long-sleeved, short-skirted, and fit very close to model Trudy's body. The dress had the words "Rubberize" across the bust and "Play Safe" on the back across Trudy's derrière. Dean and Dan recognized safe sex as an important issue in preventing HIV transmission, most obviously by directly referencing the colloquial word for condoms, "rubbers," on the front of the dress. The dress, ostensibly a woman's garment, also spoke to the need to make the safe sex message inclusive – men and women, gay and straight. In retrospect, the "Rubberize" dress represented "a desperately needed message in 1987, when awareness about the AIDS epidemic was limited."[31] Dean and Dan's cultural capital within the Canadian fashion industry, their skill as women's wear designers, and their perspective as gay men living and working in Toronto were all on display with this dress. The highest-selling garment of the night, the dress sold for $1,500 in the silent auction after the fashion show, which was hosted by Toronto personalities including *MuchMusic* VJ Erica Ehm and singers Lisa Dal Bello, Petula Clark (who just happened to be in Toronto performing that night), and even Murray McLauchlan, who came onstage briefly. Syd Beder recalls that the dress epitomized the whole point of the event: "The fact that it was done in rubber, and it was so suggestive – it kind of summed up the whole notion of what we were trying to say, which was play safe and educate yourself."[32] Ticket sales for the event raised more than $13,000. The show's designs yielded $10,000 in the celebrity auction, and T-shirt sales another $3,000. Additional T-shirt sales after the event brought the overall total to around $40,000. This $40,000 represented a very significant material contribution to the AIDS Committee of Toronto's education programs, marking the event a success in that regard.

But not everyone appreciated the irreverent nature of Fashion Cares, in light of the fact that it was a fundraiser for a deadly disease. Rick Mugford, along with many others in the industry, remembers when "the papers came out and one writer thought it was terrible and crass and too tongue-in-cheek and not serious enough for the seriousness of the event."[33] He was referring to Nancy Hastings, whose article, "Fashion Cares AIDS Benefit Raises Eyebrows – and Funds," was published in the *Toronto Star* the following week. She implied that Fashion Cares was frivolous. Designer brand Hoax Couture had created a suit with a clear-plastic, fully delineated derrière for the show that was, according to Hastings, "off color and counterproductive in light of the evening's theme." More to her liking, it seemed, was Roots' decidedly conventional and clean-cut black-and-white leather rugby jacket, which sold for $700 in the auction.[34] Hastings also criticized the event's lack of a guest list (and thus her inability to enter as a VIP) as seemingly disregarding fashion industry etiquette and protocol, as well as a slight to her own symbolic and social capital, and implicitly her status as a fashion insider. Hastings was an early and vocal supporter of the event, yet she appears not to have grasped that Fashion Cares did not have a guest list specifically *because* it was a fundraiser and everyone was expected to pay the entry fee, just as Syd Beder had promised. Hastings's article seems to have created a great deal of long-lasting hurt within the closely knit Toronto fashion community; many people felt confused and angered by Hastings's unexpected comments.

But the consensus was that Fashion Cares had succeeded both as a fashion event and as a fundraiser. Rick Mugford recalled that access to the first Fashion Cares show was tightly restricted and highly coveted: "The first event was the coolest fashion event I had ever been to in the city. Everyone was clamouring to go; nobody could get tickets."[35] Bernadette Morra agrees: "I remember the first Fashion Cares being the most fun fashion event I'd ever been to. And the calibre of what was on the runway was really great."[36] Frank Toskan sums it up: "We were all on the same team trying to win the same game."[37] AIDS presented a new challenge for the fashion field and its agents, and they were united around this cause; the competition inherent in the "rules of the game" had been set aside in order to collectively challenge this new and threatening presence.

Almost all of the participants in this first Fashion Cares had taken part in the Festival of Canadian Fashion and would soon appear among the "who's who" in the *Canadian Fashion Annual 1989*. As Entwistle and Rocamora note, the traditional fashion show "materializes" or "reifies" fashion as a field by making visible the boundaries of the field as well as its agents, relational positions, *habitus*, and forms of capital. Entwistle and Rocamora argue that the fashion show's function is "to produce, reproduce and legitimate the field of fashion and the positions of those players within it," including the people who organize the show, the designers and participants in it, the production and output of the show, and the conditions in which it takes place. They state that this activity is visible at fashion shows primarily through external boundaries such as physical barriers, gates, gatekeepers, and ticketholders, which establish who can and cannot enter the show. Those who participated in Fashion Cares had their social and symbolic capital – what Entwistle and Rocamora call "fashion capital" – guaranteed by their participation in the show.[38]

Furthermore, Toronto's field of fashion and its fashion capital were reified not just in the fashion show, but in the Fashion Cares fundraising T-shirt. The T-shirt figured prominently in the fashion show and was worn by the models as a fashionable designer garment itself worthy of the catwalk. A number of forms of capital converged around this T-shirt. For instance, social and symbolic capital were symbolized by, and materially manifested in, this T-shirt. Like the original British Fashion Cares T-shirt, with its designers' signatures, the Toronto T-shirt had "Fashion Cares" printed on the front and the signatures of thirty-seven Canadian designers on the back, most of them from Toronto.[39] The small maple leaf on the front of the T-shirt, just below and to the left of the Fashion Cares logo, cemented the event's Canadian identity. The dimensions of the fashion field were thereby materialized in the T-shirt as represented by these signatures. At the same time, and perhaps just as importantly, as Phillip Ing asserts, the "T-shirt stood out because it was a sign of solidarity. All those names went on that T-shirt. It was a solidarity that was very new. It was like a political stance."[40]

From its very inception, Fashion Cares was guided by the same logic of the field of fashion that was more formally represented in the Festival of Canadian Fashion. The events were similar in that both relied on the same community, or field, of players, given that Beder "called in favours" when he pulled the Festival people into Fashion Cares. It was only natural that they would be the same people; Suzanne Boyd points out that "it's such a small community, they'd have to be, right? Of course, that would obviously be happening. This is Toronto."[41] However, Fashion Cares was unlike the Festival in a number of significant ways. One crucial difference was the commercial incentive. The Festival was explicitly designed to build trade and commerce, heighten brand identity for the designers, and strengthen the fashion industry professionally; it was a promotional event. Fashion Cares, as a charitable fundraiser for the AIDS Committee of Toronto, was definitely not a commercial venture. If the AIDS crisis influenced the cultural output of the

Toronto field of fashion, then Fashion Cares manifested how the field creatively translated AIDS into a cultural product, a complex synthesis of an external event and the internal field dynamics of this close-knit community. Fashion Cares became, like the Festival of Canadian Fashion, a crucial space in which the Toronto field of fashion was reified, but with the core value of AIDS advocacy as a defining feature. The next challenge was whether Fashion Cares could be replicated, or whether it would be a one-off event like its British counterpart.

Fashion Blooms

The first event having been a success, a second Fashion Cares was immediately initiated, reprised as Fashion SCares and scheduled for 29 October 1987 at the dance club RPM on Toronto's waterfront. It was billed as a "'Mask'erade only for the terrifyingly trendy" and had an entrance fee of $20. Like the earlier Fashion Cares event, it had no guest list. The poster and ad were designed using the same font and style as the ad for the Fashion Cares event at the Diamond Club, but this time the word "AIDS" did appear on it. This ad is noteworthy for another reason: alongside the logos for RPM, ACT, and Ticketmaster, at the bottom left corner of the ad the M·A·C brand logo could be seen, placed above ACT's. Certainly, the association between Fashion SCares and M·A·C was consistent with a Halloween fundraiser, which presumably would involve costumes, a "Mask'erade," and, almost certainly, heavy use of cosmetics. Unlike Fashion Cares, Fashion SCares was co-managed by ACT, and this new arrangement was represented by the logos displayed in the *NOW* ad. Instead of models, dancers from the Toronto Dance Theatre modelled in the fashion show, wearing elaborate masks instead of designer clothing.[42]

This event was, however, much less successful than the earlier Fashion Cares, leading Nancy Hastings to chide the fashion crowd in the *Toronto Star* that they had missed a show featuring "designer masks and drag performances that was one of the most entertaining, creative club-land productions ever on the Toronto fashion scene." She speculated that perhaps "fashion doesn't care" after all. Hastings expressed surprise that members of the fashion community and the gay community were absent, with only five hundred people attending.[43] However, David Livingstone had predicted as early as 15 September that there would be a lower turnout. Designers, he wrote in the *Globe and Mail*, had been asked to create a special outfit for Fashion SCares. Many had complained that they were inundated with requests to design clothing for fundraising events and were opting out this time. Livingstone wrote: "Quite happily they would do anything, but not that. So it will be a show of masks."[44] More likely, the show took place too soon after the Diamond Club event, and perhaps it just did not appeal to the sensibility of the fashion crowd in quite the same way. The following year marked a return to the event's fashionable origins, but with a more "elite," even "haute couture" edge and with fewer of the subcultural qualities that marked the first 1987 show.

When Fashion Blooms was planned in 1988, its identity as a noteworthy Toronto fashion event, even a social occasion, was an explicit part of the publicity strategy. In contrast to the first Fashion Cares show, this time a group composed of Toronto's fashion "elite" took on AIDS and explicitly sought to make AIDS a *fashionable* cause. This idea did not sit well with many of the fashion insiders who had participated in Fashion Cares the year before. Fashion Blooms was structurally similar to the 1987 Fashion Cares event – a fashion show with the show's designs auctioned off afterwards – but now there would also be a dinner. Fashion Blooms was held on 17 May 1988 in the old North Building of the St Lawrence Market in downtown Toronto, a much larger venue than the Diamond Club. Sandra Matteson was the Fashion Cares group chairman. The fashion and beauty editor at *Homemaker's*, a Canadian women's lifestyle magazine that had published nine times a year since 1966, and a freelance writer for the *Toronto Star* (she had written an early profile on Donald Robertson in 1986), Matteson was also the executive director of the Council of Fashion Designers of Canada. Matteson had experience as a special events co-ordinator, including with The Chanel Ball for the Fashion Group of Toronto.[45] A committee comprising fashion industry key figures was formed that included Sharon Balsys, Syd Beder, Jeanne Beker, Gail Campbell, Lucy Chapman, Melanie Diamond,

Sydney Krelstein, Richard La Prairie, Lloyd Perlmutter, Heather Reid, Ronnie Richman, Morris Saffer, Carrie Sager, and Elsa Young, collectively known as "The Fashion Cares Group for the AIDS Committee of Toronto." ACT's development co-ordinator, Lorraine Manley, and its head of fundraising, Denny Young, both assisted Matteson. The press release for the event indicated that proceeds from Fashion Blooms would go to ACT, "a non-profit organization focusing on public health and counseling."[46] Like Fashion SCares, Fashion Blooms was part of ACT's official fundraising arm, although the event was clearly identified in press releases as a "fashion industry sponsored fund-raiser."[47]

But Fashion Blooms was a very different event than Fashion Cares. For one thing, Fashion Blooms was much broader in scope than Fashion Cares had been. Tickets were $100, much more expensive than the previous year's $10, and only twenty tickets were available at "MAC Hair" at M·A·C's Carlton Street store. There were 1,035 Fashion Blooms T-shirts produced that year, available at twenty-one local fashion retailers, although inexplicably only 934 could be accounted for – 101 of the T-shirts seemingly had gone missing. The T-shirts were designed by Donald Robertson and sold for $20. They were available at the downtown Simpsons store, at WOW on Queen West, and at other trendy downtown locations.[48] The word "AIDS" itself was not mentioned on the event's promotional poster, also illustrated by Robertson, but "AIDS Committee of Toronto" was front and centre, a change from the previous year's ban on any mention of AIDS whatsoever.[49] This event was expected to draw six hundred to eight hundred people. A press release on 22 April 1988 revealed that food would be donated and prepared by six top Toronto restaurants – Centro, CIBO, La Fenice, Noodles, Orso, and Prego – and served before the fashion show.[50] It went on to state that Alayne Kato and Peter Laurence would be producing the fashion show, with the fundraising silent auction and a dance to follow.[51] The Fashion Blooms invitation read: "Come join Toronto's fashion elite in a garden of earthly delights for an evening that promises to be everything but garden variety."[52] This emphasis on Toronto's fashion "elite" marked the event as having a different flavour than the previous year's subcultural party; one can only speculate whether Matteson's more institutionalized place in the media industry influenced her ideas about what kind of event Fashion Blooms should be.

Matteson and Manley approached fashion designers, corporate sponsors, politicians, and government officials, soliciting financial support for the event, asking that they "[b]e part of the fashion community's effort to fight AIDS!"[53] A letter of solicitation to Michael Walton, promotions manager at the *Toronto Star*, taunted him "Everyone will be there!" and listed the better-known fashion people and fashion brands taking part, including Roots, Alfred Sung, and Wayne Clark.[54] Apparently, Walton agreed to participate in some way, since handwritten with great enthusiasm on the internal copy of the letter was "Holy Cow he said yes!"[55] Matteson's correspondence to Bonnie Bickell, president of B.B. Bargoon's, a fabric retailer, promised: "Every top professional in the fashion and interior design industry is involved in this event. Jeannie Becker [sic] is one of our committee members and is dedicated to promoting everyone involved." Such egregious errors in spelling Jeanne Beker's name – she was a very well-known figure in Toronto's media and fashion circles (and a fellow committee member) – perhaps undermined Matteson's credibility and fashion capital. Matteson also stated that the event "could be an exciting promotional advantage to your company." Sponsorship, which had not existed the first year, now came at a price.[56] Another letter, addressed to "Ms. Travis," outlined the various levels of financial sponsorship available: becoming a sponsor for the fashion show would cost between $5,000 and $10,000; a corporate supporter with a table was $3,000; and a regular table went for $1,000.[57]

The event was talked about in the Toronto fashion trade press as well as in local newspapers. Fashion industry writer Audrey Gostlin wrote about Fashion Blooms in her trade newsletter *Inside Fashion: The People, Places and Events Inside the Fashion Business* on 8 February 1988, highlighting that Fashion Blooms was "a fashion industry gala fundraiser."[58] In the same issue, Gostlin discussed industry business, contemplating how the terms of the North American Free Trade Agreement (NAFTA) could affect the Canadian apparel industry. There appeared to be some debate about how the Canadian government defined "designer" and "design sector," and this lack of clarity influenced whether textiles could be imported duty-free. Gostlin mentioned Fashion Blooms again in the 2 May edition with more details on the date and how to buy tickets.[59] Nancy Hastings promoted the show in the *Toronto Star* on 21 April: "Fashion Expected to 'Bloom' at AIDS Fundraising Gala."[60] Such media discourses from within the industry further shaped how the show was positioned as a legitimate fashion industry event but equally as a social occasion.

The government's commitment to Fashion Blooms, like its commitment to AIDS generally, continued to be uneven. Letters requesting financial support were sent to Ontario's health minister, Elinor Caplan, and culture and communications minister, Lily Munro, and to Toronto Mayor Art Eggleton. The form letter read: "Last year, Fashion Cares was an event to remember! Besides raising money for The AIDS Committee of Toronto, the show did a great deal of good to the Canadian Fashion industry and put several young designers on the map."[61] That statement seems naive considering that most of the designers participating in Fashion Cares were already involved in the Festival of Canadian Fashion and were thus already "on the map." Furthermore, the first Fashion Cares had by no means been a commercial event, and such imperatives were non-existent in the creative response to AIDS that the 1987 Fashion Cares embodied. Clearly, Matteson and Manley were using Fashion Blooms' identity as a "fashion industry" event to capitalize on Toronto's bureaucratic mission to boost cultural production. Indeed, Matteson had promoted Fashion Blooms to Toronto Ward 6 Alderman Dale Martin. Martin, on behalf of the City of Toronto's Fashion Liaison Committee, apparently verbally offered financial support of $5,000 to Fashion Blooms. The Fashion Liaison Committee was a City of Toronto initiative begun in 1984 to support Canadian-owned fashion businesses in Toronto. Comprising representatives from manufacturing, fashion schools, trade associations, unions, and design, its mandate was to promote and strengthen the city's fashion district and preserve and develop employment. However, the Fashion Liaison Committee never came through on its financial promise. This offer was either withdrawn or forgotten, with no explanation provided. Even so, the city's name appeared on the invitations, much to Matteson's chagrin, since the Fashion Liaison Committee reneged on the promised $5,000 too late in the game for the program to be amended.[62]

Fashion Blooms was, as its name suggested, organized around a floral theme. Sandra Matteson related how the idea for the floral theme came from her travels to the Paris fashion shows in October 1987, where the designers had all used floral fabric for their designs.[63] Matteson was able to secure hundreds of yards of floral fabric from local supplier Greeff Fabrics, which she distributed to participating designers for the fashion show ensembles. The Fashion Blooms show consequently featured forty-seven outfits and one bridal gown, all in the themed floral fabric that Matteson had procured. The runway was a series of small platforms with staircases interspersed between them, flanked by potted trees and urns filled with flowers. As each model finished her turn on the runway, she positioned herself around its perimeter, allowing the audience more time to view the garment. The show's designs were, compared to the previous year's "Rubberize" dress and derrière trousers, conventionally feminine, consisting mostly of dresses. Each female model carried an identical small, round purse with the number of her garment on it, identifying it for the silent auction to follow. Each walked slowly and solemnly, in a style referencing the more formal Paris haute couture shows. It was a very different presentation from the energetic dancing and green-painted models on the catwalk the previous year, lacking the vital energy of a subcultural, even avant-garde fashion community willing to push boundaries when responding to AIDS and the health crisis. This show was, instead, meant to be a "high culture" event. The models' hair was styled by Denis Bouchard, Ray Civello, La Corte, Robert Gage, Paul King, Le Shoppe, Monroe, Reinhart McMillan, Vidal Sassoon, and Tuxedo. Once again, M·A·C donated all the cosmetics used in the fashion show, and a M·A·C team created the make-up designs for the models, although the show's video credits rather unfortunately attributed the make-up to "MAC Codmetics."[64] This typo seems symbolic of the larger inattention to the backstage workings of the event. Phillip Ing recalls that Frank Angelo was very angry after Fashion Blooms: the organizers had not thought about the needs of the backstage people and offered only a small cramped room for all of the make-up artists, hairdressers, and stylists. Angelo felt deliberately slighted by the inattention to the backstage in favour of the runway, and while Ing facetiously termed Angelo's reaction as "bitchy fashion mad," Angelo's assessment reveals how the less visible but integral drivers of the fashion industry felt relegated to second-class standing by those who ought to have known better, in favour of the perceived status of the designers onstage and the guests who attended.

Indeed, the crowd attending this event was very fashionable, much less underground and subcultural than the previous year's Wednesday night Fashion Vignettes club-goers. The *Globe and Mail*'s David Livingstone described the fashionable crowd's outfits in great detail, articulating the cultural and symbolic capital of those who belonged to it:

> Beverly Creed wore Lacroix; Toronto Life Fashion publisher Debbie Gibson wore "Lacroix" via Victor Costa. Sublime's Paula Holgate wore a strapless pink satin sheath by Diane Pernet; she covered her shoulders with a black chiffon scarf and her ears with flowers. Ruth Lockhart, from Atomic Age, wore "a mixed metaphor" of Zapata, Marc Jacobs and Martha Sturdy's daisy earrings. Alayne Kato (who, with Peter Laurence, directed the runway show at just the right quick pace) combined a Wayne Clark bustier with a skirt she made herself from a quick pattern. Milliner Su Downey had made herself a matching ensemble of hat, dress and bag. Mannikin Monika Schnarre, who is working on a book to come out next year, sported a tailored jacket over a green brassiere of wetsuit material.

Livingstone observed that it was not just the women who dressed with flair; the men were equally fashionable:

> Men in the crowd were dressed with equal invention and flair. Alan Goouch wore a tie of Liberty lawn with a white jacket bearing hand-painted blooms. Photographer John Phillips wore a shirt designed by Peter DeFrietas that featured a rolled-back collar and clear buttons. Charles Puma, of Classica Uomo, mixed a Gaultier jacket, Venturi shirt and a scarf tied at the neck. Also sporting a dandified scarf was Sublime's Anthony Ohordnyk in a Morisane tie-belted suit. Beaver Canoe's

Lloyd Perlmutter wore black and white check trousers, a black vest, floral bowtie, and a jacket of pink cashmere.[65]

Such cultural capital in the field of fashion is readily apparent when objectified, becoming evident in what one wears, taking the form of designer-branded clothes and accessories, which also indicate one's economic capital. What one wears, including make-up – which, like clothing, is worn on the body – is integral to one's place within the field. Livingstone's detailed descriptions of guests' outfits displayed his own social capital as an insider, observer, and fashion writer. He also demonstrated his cultural capital: he personally knew many of the guests and could identify their clothing brands, and he likely could comfortably approach them to ask them about their outfits.[66] This observation was confirmed by Bernadette Morra: "Of the 800 guests who paid $100 each for the dinner, dance and fashion show, many were familiar faces from Toronto's restaurant, fashion and interior design world, including the owners of Prego and Centro restaurants, and Noakes-Cohen interior design, who donated their talents to the event."[67] Likewise, the guests exhibited their own embodied cultural capital in their clothing choices, branded or otherwise. Yet according to Phillip Ing, who did not direct or attend this show, Fashion Blooms was not considered as successful as the 1987 event.

The effects of commercialism and status in relation to how the Toronto field responded to AIDS are also worth mentioning. Several fashion insiders suggested that those in Toronto were generally less concerned about making money. This quality made associating with AIDS an act with fewer economic repercussions. Donald Robertson is clear on this point:

> I just think at that time it [AIDS] was just something that was so insanely dangerous for business. I don't know one person in Canada, when we were setting up, who talked about getting rich. Nobody was doing it for money. We were all just doing it because we wanted to be cool and we loved what we were doing and we were into it. Can you imagine? Oh my god. You could just do the right thing and it wasn't even really a conversation.[68]

In other words, the creative ethos and the *habitus* of those in the field responded to the health crisis without concern for gaining economic capital. It is also useful to think about Toronto's relationship to New York in this regard. In the larger, international field of fashion, Toronto was, as many have noted, so completely dominated by New York culture, fashion, and music that it hardly mattered what the Toronto fashion industry did, despite its aspirations for greater prominence as a fashion capital. Toronto could thus be considered as engaged in more autonomous cultural production within the international fashion industry, whereas New York was involved in more heteronomous production; this more or less reflects the poles of small-scale and large-scale production that constitute the field. So the New York fashion industry had a clear economic stake in avoiding a public association with AIDS, realizing the damage this would most likely do to brand image. The Toronto fashion scene's relative autonomy from New York, and from any other fashion capital, for that matter (despite its aspirations), permitted its participants to respond with creativity – even be avant-garde – with less concern for the financial consequences. This is not to say that economic considerations did not exist; there were definitely some (unnamed) Canadian designers who did not want to participate in Fashion Cares; clearly, they were concerned about the monetary impact of being associated in any way with AIDS. Even so, the Toronto fashion scene had less to lose, and thus also much more to gain, from taking the risk in publicly supporting AIDS fundraising.

Historical accounts of the AIDS epidemic and activism in Toronto generally do not acknowledge how important Fashion Cares was to ACT or to AIDS awareness and fundraising in the city. There is still relatively little historical work on the history of AIDS in Canada; Ann Silversides's biography of Toronto activist Michael Lynch, *AIDS Activist: Michael Lynch and the Politics of Community*, is one notable exception.[69] Silversides's monumental work on Lynch also offers a comprehensive history of AIDS activism in Toronto, since Lynch was at the forefront of much of it. Lynch was involved in, and indeed founded, many of the most prominent AIDS activist organizations in Toronto, and besides being a scholar of nineteenth-century American literature, he was a prolific writer on gay issues. As a scholar, he appreciated the value of archives and kept detailed diaries, and his story as articulated by Silversides captures the spirit, the sadness, and the joy of AIDS activism and of Lynch himself, who died of complications from AIDS in 1993. Silversides mentions Fashion Cares only once, when one of Lynch's friends attended the 1987 event.[70] Perhaps these omissions occur because Fashion Cares sidestepped the types of formal activism described in these accounts, which were more overtly political in design and intent.

Another explanation is that the origins of Fashion Cares are to be found within a different cultural frame. Fashion Cares was both a source and a product of the field of Toronto fashion during a historical moment when AIDS and fashion converged. Fashion Cares manifested, materialized, produced, and reproduced Toronto's field of fashion, just as the Festival of Canadian Fashion did, but with one key addition: it highlighted how important the AIDS cause had become to the Toronto fashion industry's core values. The same energy generated by, and for, the Festival was routed into the first Fashion Cares. Indeed, the same people were involved, from the designers to the hair stylists to the make-up artists, so it was natural for everyone to direct their professional knowledge, energy, and creative practices into Fashion Cares. Importantly, the shows became a space to reconcile death within the fashion community with a celebration of its creativity. "I think it's the coming together of creative people and the whole kind of rallying around the idea that we're not going to let anything get to us," said Susie Sheffman. "We're bigger than this and we'll rise above and we'll rise together. It was very powerful messaging: that the fashion industry won't be taken down by this."[71] Phillip Ing concurs: "We were all young enough to have this 'fuck you' attitude about it ... You made a creative statement out of a fight, which is why I think Fashion Cares lasted longer than a lot of other charities because it always had that side to it ... It was a really ugly disease and I think we made it – I don't know if we made it *understandable*, but, for lack of a better word, we kind of made it *palatable*."[72] Just as importantly, fashion gave disenfranchised people – such as M·A·C's "underdogs" – a place to speak and act through creative practice. Jeanne Beker agrees; fashion, she says, is "so uplifting. It's all about celebration of self. And that's something that's really important. Fashion is all about identity. That's something that's really important when you're thinking of an issue like AIDS. Fashion is all about putting a face on something. Fashion is all about jubilation through sartorial expression. Especially for a lot of those people, fashion gave them a voice."[73] For Syd Beder, Fashion Cares was born "out of naivety" and represented a grassroots or intuitive response: "It was a pinnacle moment of the 80s when everything came together."[74]

Fashion Cares became a crucial forum where the Franks' practices within the field of fashion could develop. AIDS advocacy and fundraising, through the fashion show, became firmly embedded and embodied in the Franks' and their artists' practices and routines and soon began extending into M·A·C's brand identity. M·A·C's attention to AIDS came into focus as the company moved into the new decade; all the while, it became clearer that M·A·C's reputation and "fashion capital" were expanding beyond Toronto and Canada, moving through the international field of fashion, through culture, and through entertainment in unexpected ways.

PART II
Creative Activism

CHAPTER 4

Put Your Money Where Your Mouth Is

AIDS continued to hit hard within the fashion industry into the new decade. By 1990, the American fashion trade journal *Women's Wear Daily* had begun to publish news of AIDS deaths, and the mainstream media were more upfront about discussing AIDS. In the early 1990s, American journalist Joyce Saenz Harris wrote that "relatively few of fashion's deaths involve names prominent enough to make the industry papers' obituaries. The real count would include the many others who have died – the fashion retailers, buyers, art and display directors, sales people, models, makeup artists, hair stylists and fledgling designers."[1] A *New York Times* article titled "AIDS and the Fashion World: Industry Fears for Its Health" underscored this reality.[2] Holly Brubach, fashion writer for the *New Yorker*, was quoted in a 1990 *People* magazine article lamenting the industry's loss: "There's a finite fund of talent in any generation ... There is an assumption that if a great designer dies, someone else will step in to replace him. But if AIDS keeps up as it has, we are going to be living in impoverished times. Each time a person of great talent dies, the landscape gets a little more drab." In the same *People* article, Vincent Larouche, an American designer based in Paris, said that "[i]t's not just a question of numbers. Even if just one person dies in a company, it's a broken link in the chain that the whole creative process depends on. It's tragic. It has a terrible effect on everyone."[3] The death of American fashion designer Halston in 1990 attracted more mainstream attention and marked a turning point for an industry that could no longer ignore the obvious. The fashion field found itself in constant flux as many holding key positions disappeared and those who followed lacked the social and cultural capital – and the creativity – to fully replace them. In Toronto, Clotheslines designer Shelley Wickabrod noted: "These are our friends. We spend once a week ticking off names."[4] An unexpected outcome of the epidemic was that female-led design firms now experienced a surge in financial support, since women were thought to be largely immune from HIV infection – another example of ideology, rather than science, informing the popular understanding of HIV/AIDS. One positive change in the new decade was that the impact of AIDS on the fashion industry was being discussed more openly in the mainstream press. Thus, the need for events like Fashion Cares did not end with the 1980s. In New York, the first 7th on Sale event was organized by the Council of Fashion Designers of America (CFDA) and *Vogue* magazine; it took place from 29 November to 2 December 1990. Proceeds from the sale of donated designer and celebrity-owned garments went to local AIDS charities.

Slowly and steadily, the Franks cultivated M·A·C's connections to cultural events, movements, and figures, all the while contemplating a more public stance on social issues that were important to them and to their employees, including HIV/AIDS. In 1988, fashion journalist Nancy Hastings had written that "M.A.C wins kudos as one of the most progressive of Canadian fashion companies."[5] Now, as the new decade began, this position was solidified. In January 1990, Madonna was photographed wearing a "M·A·C Cruelty Free Beauty" T-shirt while jogging on Central Park West in New York City. This photo was published in *People* magazine, bringing more attention to M·A·C and strengthening the brand's celebrity connections. That T-shirt, created by Donald Robertson, was available by mail order for $20 directly from the M·A·C store on Carlton Street, with proceeds going to the Johns Hopkins University Institute for Alternative Testing Methods (PLATE 13 and PLATE 14). M·A·C had always been against animal testing and had long ago established its own recycling program (PLATE 15 and PLATE 16); the idea that M·A·C was an ethical company besides being a "hot" insider brand was now planted in the public's mind through the power of celebrity culture. Yet M·A·C remained at the forefront of new and subcultural fashion directions and trends. Its fall 1990 colour collection received a great deal of attention in local newspapers as it captured the 1960s aesthetic that was currently influencing fashion and music, a testament to Toskan's cultural and fashion capital.[6] This 1960s-style revival was epitomized by the New York DJ band Deee-Lite and its ubiquitous hit "Groove Is in the Heart," which was featured in a number of fashion runway shows that season. Fittingly, M·A·C launched its make-up collection in August at Toronto's downtown Simpsons store with a troupe of go-go dancers. By then, the company was no longer confined to its second-floor corner. The lipstick colours were named after the iconic 1960s models "Twiggy," "Veruschka," and "Shrimpton," with "Mod" and "Carnaby" matte eye shadows and "Bardot" blush (although later Toskan changed "Twiggy" to "Twig" after Twiggy's management complained).

When Canadian supermodel Linda Evangelista declared that she used M·A·C's Spice lip liner, a neutral reddish-brown shade that suited all skin tones, a stampede to the M·A·C counter ensued, much like the one inspired by Madonna's confession that she wore Russian Red lipstick. Princess Diana had loved M·A·C's products ever since Toronto make-up artist Frances Hathaway introduced them to her in the mid-1980s. Even Cher had been spotted at a M·A·C counter, in Ogilvy's in Montreal, where she spent several hundred dollars.[7] The Franks decided the time was now right to open an American stand-alone M·A·C store similar to their Carlton Street boutique. They unveiled it at the corner of Christopher and Gay streets in Greenwich Village in June 1991. People thought Toskan was foolish for opening a location downtown – Henri Bendel was in the more upscale midtown – but Toskan insisted that he wanted to cater to the creative, underground crowd and that was where those people lived, and he was correct. The store was immediately popular with the downtown fashion crowd and celebrities. Jane Mussett wrote in the *Toronto Star* in July that "rumor has it, the who's who of the entertainment and fashion industries are shopping. Though Toskan says he sells to many makeup artists and entertainers who like the line because it's long wearing and stands up well under strong artificial lighting, he won't name names. But the U.S. press has sighted Cher, Madonna and model Naomi Campbell on the premises."[8]

Toskan designed the New York store largely on his own, employing Donald Robertson's keen eye. One evening before it opened, Toskan and Robertson stayed up all night gluing powder compact mirrors all over the wall and ceiling into a reflective collage. They installed a ground-metal counter with sloping legs, a new look designed especially for the New York store. Eschewing traditional showcases and drawers, they placed the merchandise on open shelves, directly accessible to customers. Toskan wanted to be part of everything in that store and to leave his personal mark on it for as long as possible, so he bought an apartment nearby on Christopher Street. Characteristically, he spent a great deal of time working alongside his new make-up artists in the New York store. Kim Myers-Robertson, Donald Robertson's wife, was the store's first manager (PLATE 17).

Within a couple of months, the New York store had generated utter mayhem. People were looking for something different, and they swarmed it, which raised new and unexpected concerns regarding M·A·C's style of "management," such as it was. Donald Robertson remembers how he and Kim Myers-Robertson and the Franks collectively decided that they had to "hire a bodyguard because we literally need[ed] somebody at the door to make people stop pushing and to control the crowd. Imagine!" And these crowds required a decidedly different type of supervision. Robertson continues: "So my wife is like, 'oh my god, I know who we should get: we should get RuPaul. First of all, he'll do it; he needs the money, and he's hilarious.' And Frank doesn't want a police officer; he says that's too scary. So RuPaul and Lady Bunny became the 'doormen.' And they would show up in full drag and they would yell at people and it was the best." Watched over by this fierce duo, a revolving door of customers, models, musicians, and celebrities, including Lady Miss Kier of Deee-Lite, Michael Jackson and his sister Janet, and Linda Evangelista, shopped at the New York store. Robertson reminisces about how the store's staff were a vivacious bunch, but as much as M·A·C allowed ultimate creative freedom in its staff, there had to be limits:

> There were days when Kim had to sit down with people and say, "you have to wear a shirt *or* pants, you have to pick one or the other, you

can't just wear a leather diaper. It's just not going to work. You're doing make-up, for Christ's sake." And this guy would be standing there, with pierced nipples in a leather diaper. Obviously, he'd been out all night, and had walked into work and was starting to do make-up. And we couldn't send him home because there were too many people in the store. *That* was our HR problem.[9]

M·A·C's New York store offered another space where staff and customers alike could unleash their creative impulses and practices.

Business was booming. M·A·C's soaring status within the international field of fashion got another lift in August 1991 when the brand received a promotional boost from renowned American make-up artist Kevyn Aucoin in the Canadian newsmagazine *Maclean's*. Aucoin famously used neutral colours and matte textures like M·A·C's in his own work to great effect, and his make-up style and unique practices significantly influenced make-up trends, beauty editorials, and fashion photography. Aucoin admitted that it was "a dream come true" when he discovered Linda Evangelista's M·A·C Spice lip liner. He used it on her for the May cover of Italian *Vogue* (considered the premiere edition), declaring that "[e]veryone in the business considers M·A·C to be the cutting edge."[10] Aucoin's statement epitomizes how those in the field decide among themselves the standards of authenticity in cultural production. In any event, his endorsement was highly influential.[11] The *Maclean's* article's title, "The M·A·C Attack: A Canadian Firm Takes on the Cosmetics Giants," emphasized the seemingly antagonistic nature of the cosmetic industry. It positioned M·A·C as the defiant, risk-taking newcomer challenging the established cosmetics players, suggesting that the game was not just about power but also about nationality. Yet the Franks did not really care whether M·A·C threatened the cosmetics industry; they were more comfortable staying "close to our instincts," Toskan said in an interview a short time later.[12] As further evidence of those instincts, or fashion capital, M·A·C's fall 1991 collection, called Ice X.T.C., was described as a "nineties Barbarella look." Its colours included "Chill," "Lazer Blue," and "Grafite." In the *Globe and Mail*, Toskan described the collection as "futuristic. We mix frosts with mat makeup. It's made with professional [make-up] artists in mind."[13] But M·A·C continued to price its products very competitively: lipstick was $10, higher than mass-market lipsticks such as Max Factor ($4.29) and Revlon ($5.95), but much lower than prestige brands Christian Dior ($16.50) and Elizabeth Arden ($18).[14] It is possible that in making a specialized cosmetics line that was accessible to the mainstream consumer, the Franks facilitated "the M·A·C attack" themselves – that is, if customers could actually get their hands on the products, since they were always selling out.

"A New Way of Marketing"

Frank Angelo hired Valerie MacKenzie (then Valerie Hay), a self-confessed "make-up freak," in 1991 as M·A·C's first marketing assistant, even though there was no real "marketing" department at M·A·C – the title seems to have been conjured up mostly as a recognizable descriptor in the help-wanted ad that Angelo placed in the *Toronto Star*. MacKenzie, now vice-president of product innovation at M·A·C, remembers that she and make-up artists Philippe Chansel and Gordon Espinet, now in corporate creative product development and innovation at Estée Lauder and Senior Vice-President of Makeup Artistry at M·A·C, respectively, all started at M·A·C on the same day and were trained by Jane McKay. The company was growing so quickly (by then it had tripled in size) that the Franks needed someone devoted to the tasks that fell, roughly, within the area usually considered to be marketing. For instance, by 1992 M·A·C had fifty counters across North America, and one of MacKenzie's tasks was to duly purchase fifty copies of all the magazines that contained any M·A·C coverage and laminate tear sheets to send to each counter's press book, which was left out for customers to peruse. MacKenzie quickly became the official liaison between M·A·C and the celebrities, their make-up artists, the press, and the retail counters; she also handled the growing number of external inquiries. M·A·C was receiving a great deal of editorial coverage and publicity because more and more celebrities were wearing M·A·C. Its products were featured, sometimes prominently, in popular shows like *Beverly Hills 90210* and *Melrose Place*, and they were being used by musical groups like Wilson Phillips. MacKenzie took calls from make-up artist superstars Kevyn Aucoin and Bobbi Brown, the make-up artists to singers Madonna, Prince, and Gloria Estefan, and make-up artists working in television and film. Sometimes, MacKenzie said, without naming names, the make-up artists used M·A·C "under the radar," especially when the models had contracts with other cosmetics brands. Furthermore, M·A·C products were frequently used in photo shoots, but since M·A·C still would not advertise, its products remained unnamed and uncredited. Instead, the products of another cosmetics brand that did advertise were substituted in the media credits.[15] By default, MacKenzie established M·A·C's customer service department, handling all the customer requests, orders, and complaints herself for the rapidly expanding company.

Because M·A·C was a private company, its financial details were not publicly available, although Toskan and Angelo often talked numbers in media interviews. M·A·C's North American sales in 1990 had been $15 million, and the Franks projected that 1992 sales would be more than $25 million.[16] They would be wrong: M·A·C's 1992 sales were *$43 million*, almost triple those of 1990. Compared to, for instance, Revlon's $1.63 billion in sales in 1992, M·A·C's sales numbers were small; nonetheless, they represented substantial yearly growth.[17] Much of this growth was due to increased production capacity, overseen by Toskan's now brother-in-law Victor Casale. Production had moved to a 5,000-square-foot facility in Markham, Ontario, northeast of Toronto, where more innovation could take place and production could be expanded. New products included M·A·C's updated skincare line, with a pH-balanced cleanser, Phyto-Astringent, and a moisturizing lotion, products that Toskan himself used. Early in the decade, Toskan and Casale developed M·A·C into one of the first "cosmeceutical" brands on the market, one that offered skincare benefits such as being oil-free and containing vitamins and sunscreen. "Cosmeceutical" is the term for cosmetics that have pharmaceutical benefits but are not, strictly speaking, drugs. Toskan and Casale correctly predicted that cosmeceuticals would dominate make-up and skincare products into the 1990s.[18]

Victor Casale was integral to realizing Toskan's creative vision and managing M·A·C's vast production facilities. The skincare line reflected Casale's working practice of investigating and using of-the-moment ingredients in M·A·C products. Casale had never tested M·A·C's products on animals and used only cruelty-free hairs for its make-up brushes, a fact broadcast more widely when Madonna wore the "M·A·C Cruelty Free Beauty" T-shirt. In mid-1992, Casale brought in-vitro efficacy and safety testing to M·A·C to investigate potential skin sensitivity issues. Casale had visited a California bioengineering lab that had developed skin grafting technology. As a side business, that skin could be used for other types of testing. Casale worked with this supplier to improve the technology, then brought it to M·A·C in Canada. The safety of skincare and cosmetics products typically relies on three approaches: using GRAS (generally recognized as safe) products and ingredients that have been trusted in the industry for a long time; conducting leading-edge safety testing in petri dishes on regenerated skin cells; and having dermatologists conduct repeated-insult patch testing (RIPT), where human volunteers are recruited (and paid) to wear the products. With this last approach, the product is applied to arms and covered, a process repeated over a week to determine sensitivity outcomes. When the skin is irritated, it releases histamine, the output of which can be measured to determine possible cosmetic irritations and sensitivities. Casale used Lee Graff's Toronto dermatology clinic for M·A·C's safety testing. Graff was a corrective make-up artist who worked at Sunnybrook and Women's College Health Sciences Centre in Toronto with patients who had severe skin conditions such as burns and vitiligo. Soon, Graff was sending her patients to Casale at the M·A·C factory. Often too self-conscious to go shopping at the make-up counter in the department store, these patients were invited to the factory after hours, when Casale could work with them privately to help develop new and individual cosmetic products to treat their very specific skin conditions and colour needs. It was very impactful and meaningful work, Casale said, and he also received immediate feedback about these clients' very special requirements.[19] As well, it became a company practice to bring the M·A·C artists to the Markham factory and educate and train them about ingredients and production processes. For three days, the artists would observe and then work in groups within each department to make a product. The quality assurance department would inspect each group's "production," usually dismissing the results as unacceptable. By the last day, the artists had a better understanding of how M·A·C's products were made and the people who made them; this augmented their product knowledge, which improved their selling practices at the counter.[20]

A new product, Studio Fix, was released in 1992, which combined the coverage of a cream foundation with the ease of a powder compressed into a portable compact. Casale remembers that he and Toskan spent a great deal of time working on this innovation. The product had to work both dry and wet while still providing varying intensities of coverage. Casale launched a new, systematic shade name system to correspond to Studio Fix. Instead of colours or names that related to often-subjective (and sometimes implicitly racist) definitions of "Ivory" or "Tan" skin tones, this new system was based on two factors: skin undertones, which are cool (blue-based), warm (yellow-based), or neutral; and colour intensity, meaning light (10) through to dark (50). Thus, a customer could purchase Studio Fix for a specific skin undertone and colour depth such as "NC15," designating a neutral-cool, lighter-intensity skin tone. Casale's system has since become an informal industry measurement that consumers still use to describe their skin tone and cosmetics choices, even when they are not using M·A·C products. Studio Fix was an industry-wide innovation; at one point, Casale had to outsource some of its production because the Markham factory could not keep up with customer demand. The product spawned endless imitations by other brands and remains an industry leader in this category.

Corporate Involvement

Phillip Ing had assumed that new people would take the helm of Fashion Cares. Ing did not participate in the 1988 Fashion Blooms event as he had been in a serious car accident; he remembers how its organizers "tried to make it into more of a social event" than the 1987 show, which had arisen "organically from what was happening."[21] In 1989, Fashion Cares acquired a new organizer in Ronnie Richman, an experienced fundraiser for the Sunnybrook Hospital Ball and the Opera Ball. Ing returned to direct the show, and Fashion Cares resumed its former name and spirit.[22] Jann Coppen was its new production manager, and she and Ing would remain involved in Fashion Cares for several years (Coppen had met Ing in 1986). Fashion Cares An Evening of Sheer Drama was held on 9 May 1989 at the Terrace Roller Rink, a decrepit downtown Toronto venue slated for immediate demolition. The show resumed its focus on creativity, extreme looks, and spectacle. On its roster were fifty-four designers, including the familiar names Alfred Sung, Bent Boys, Brian Bailey, Comrags, Dean and Dan, and Wayne Clark. Another T-shirt featuring these fashion brands was produced, this time designed by Stephen Bailey. Seven hair salons, including Denis Bouchard, Ray Civello, and Vidal Sassoon, donated hairstyling services. Richman told David Livingstone in an interview that trying to get corporate sponsorship for the event was "the hardest thing I've ever had to do," adding that one corporation wanted to know if the waiters would be wearing gloves.[23] There were only three corporate advertisements in the event program, placed by local establishments Group Four Consultants, Body Alive gym, and The Richman Group and Michael Lorne Cooper.[24] As in the previous two years, M·A·C provided the cosmetics and the make-up artists.

Richman's hard work in 1989 paid off: the Toronto fashion community, including M·A·C, successfully established Fashion Cares as a yearly tradition into the new decade. It was increasingly apparent to organizers that corporate sponsorship was desirable, indeed necessary if the event was to be an ongoing financial success. Implicit in corporate sponsorship was the acceptance of AIDS as a worthy, not frightening, social cause to support. However, finding corporate sponsors was still a challenge because of the strong stigma attached to the disease and the general homophobia that characterized the sluggish responses to AIDS from all sectors. Yet corporate support grew each year. Fashion Cares The Crystal Ball was held on 25 April 1990 at the St Lawrence Centre. The night would be long remembered, just as much for the citywide power outage that presented logistical dilemmas all round, including for stylists, who created hair and make-up looks on the models by candlelight, even using lighters, an alarming proposition considering how much hairspray was in use. The organizers proclaimed in the program: "[N]ever before have so many designers, sponsors, supporters, and volunteers joined together in one creative effort. Each year more doors open to us. Each year more individuals accept a personal responsibility for fighting AIDS." They were not wrong. The upscale fashion retailer Holt Renfrew ran a full-page ad in the program that read: "Caring is never out of fashion." The major event sponsors were H. Halpern Esq., a Toronto men's retailer, and the Labatt Brewing Company, both of which also took out full-page ads. The H. Halpern Esq. ad read: "Thank you for joining us. In the fall of 1989, H. Halpern Esq. became the first mens [sic] specialty retailer to donate time and money to the cause of Aids [sic] awareness. We would like to take this opportunity to salute our peers in the mens [sic] fashion retailing community who are now following suit." The program presented ads for the Versace boutique, menswear retailer Harry Rosen, the Toronto brand Clotheslines, the Robert Gage hair salon, Simpsons, and Sporting Life sports store, indicating growing support. As the program proudly revealed, there were around 160 small businesses and corporate sponsors, patrons, and benefactors that year, a huge increase from the previous year.[25] David Livingstone acknowledged forty-three of these in his follow-up piece in the *Globe and Mail* on 10 May, perhaps as a public challenge for even more corporate participation in the future.[26]

The following year, M·A·C again provided all the cosmetics and a make-up artist team for Fashion Cares Red Hot & Blue, held at the Masonic Temple on 24 April 1991. The event's theme was "30's nightclub – steamy, dark, sizzling, crowded, smoky," inspired by an unrelated Cole Porter tribute album of the same name released in 1990, the first of a series of American musical compilations by well-known artists, with the proceeds directed to AIDS research. Local singers included Molly Johnson, Liberty Silver, and Meryn Cadell. The event was becoming more expensive – tickets now cost $150, $40 just for the after-show dance – but the higher price also raised more money for ACT, to the tune of $75,000.[27] Jane McKay,

M·A·C's director of technical training and a senior M·A·C artist, was interviewed while working backstage, and she described the fashion show as "avant-garde. The designers, the hair, the make-up, everything is probably pushed a little bit to the edge. You're definitely seeing avant-garde hair, clothing, and make-up and it's everything that's ultra-current. It's showing and showcasing things that are happening today. Not necessarily mainstream. But it's definitely out there." Hairstylist Bill Angst had a similar view: "I think that it [Fashion Cares] opens people's minds to creativity and I think that it gives all of the fashion people, stylists, make-up artists, an opportunity to explore everything other than the commercialism involved in the industry. It gives them a chance to be themselves and just let loose."[28] Both comments exemplify Bourdieu's "anti-economic" stance of "art for art's sake," with its commercially disinterested quality.[29] Unlike the trade-driven Festival of Canadian Fashion, Fashion Cares primarily offered a creative space for artistic exploration, experimentation, and cultural production outside of profit; indeed, people actively resisted such commercialization at Fashion Cares in their pursuit of artistic expression for its own sake. And while Fashion Cares was focused on AIDS fundraising, it was also vital for producing and reproducing the Toronto fashion industry and its ideals. However, this perspective is simultaneously at odds with how a certain type of commercialism was, in fact, highly desirable for the event as a whole, for the purposes of fundraising and sponsorship and for conferring legitimacy on the AIDS cause, which was necessary if Fashion Cares and ACT's work were both to continue.

Commercialism, in the form of corporate presence, was much more pronounced at Fashion Cares in 1991. For the organizers, this was good news. Grocery retailer Loblaw and its house brand President's Choice, along with McDonald's, donated food for the hundreds of event volunteers. Decor chair Nicholas Pinney recalled: "That was the year I got Holt Renfrew on as one of the sponsors. They were one of the first big retail sponsors to come on board. It was very hard to get sponsors in those days for AIDS benefits; people didn't want to know about it."[30] Holt Renfrew and fashion retailer Club Monaco did much to decorate the event space. Labatt Brewing Company, a long-time sponsor, remained attached to the event, although its participation likely had as much to do with maintaining the brand loyalty of the event's alcohol-consuming, club-going crowd.[31] ACT needed this heightened corporate buy-in in order to raise the event to the next level of visibility, legitimacy, and financial success. This recognizable corporate presence signalled a big step up from the original 1987 event, which could not even print the word "AIDS" on its poster. For a charity fundraiser, such corporate sponsorship suggested a more enlightened attitude towards AIDS, but there was still much to be done in getting corporations on board.

It was now particularly necessary to maintain creative productivity in Toronto's fashion industry. The Festival of Canadian Fashion was suspended after the 1990 run due to a lack of interest among the trade, and ultimately it was cancelled. Attendance at the 1989 Festival had been much lower, and as the number of fashion shows fell to seventeen (from twenty-seven in 1987), it appeared that interest was waning. Later that year, Toronto City Council created a not-for-profit organization to run the Festival, but 1990 turned out to be its final year. It is also clear that Fashion Cares did not replace the Festival in either purpose or function. According to Suzanne Boyd, the two events had very different and unrelated goals: the Festival was a commercial event, whereas Fashion Cares was a creative fundraiser. Jeanne Beker agrees that the Festival and Fashion Cares were very different events: "Fashion Cares had nothing to do with commercial fashion. Fashion Cares was all about unbridled creativity ... it went so far beyond business. It really had nothing to do with the business of fashion. It had to do with the art of fashion."[32] Toronto's fashion industry had been building in other ways, and perhaps corporations and brands were turning to Fashion Cares as a viable promotional opportunity. However, insiders agree that the AIDS fundraiser did not replace the overtly commercial and promotional paradigm that the Festival had briefly, but significantly, offered to the Toronto fashion industry.

In the midst of these changes, Frank Toskan devised a new project that spoke to M·A·C's ethos of inclusivity and acceptance, now directed specifically towards the AIDS epidemic. M·A·C retail counters began selling a new fundraising T-shirt. On the front, in Donald Robertson's signature style, the new design depicted gay, straight, and lesbian couples kissing. The back read: "make up, make out, play safe." Toskan can be seen wearing the T-shirt in a postcard, photographed by Toronto director Floria Sigismondi, promoting an upcoming personal appearance at Nordstrom (PLATE 18). The T-shirt went on sale on 9 September 1991, with proceeds donated to the American organization Design Industries Foundation Fighting AIDS (DIFFA) and to the Canadian AIDS Society (CAS). In an interview in the *Globe and Mail* just before its launch, Toskan described the T-shirt as "a little controversial but those are the chances we take," adding that this initiative represented "a new way of marketing: sharing our concerns and life experiences with customers."[33] Toskan felt the message "had a little bit of everything: it was a little bit hard, a little bit soft, it related to make-up, it offered a lot of hope, and it made people aware that we have to be careful and we can overcome. It was a powerful message."[34] To be sure, this message also spoke to the long-standing safe sex messages integral to contemporary AIDS discourses, which included calls for condom use. This facet was reminiscent of Dean and Dan's "Rubberize" dress at the 1987 Fashion Cares, which had a similar message, "Play Safe," emblazoned on it. M·A·C's T-shirt also had some similarities to an earlier activist art project produced in 1989 by the ACT UP art collective Gran Fury for "Art Against AIDS on the Road." Created under the auspices of the American Foundation for AIDS Research, Gran Fury's piece implicitly referenced a 1980s United Colors of Benetton advertisement in its visual style. It depicted three stylish couples kissing, but only one couple was heterosexual. The caption read: KISSING DOESN'T KILL: GREED AND INDIFFERENCE DO." This image was a reference to kiss-ins held by AIDS activists to demonstrate that HIV was not transmitted through casual contact, and it highlighted the homophobia, racism, and ignorance surrounding HIV/AIDS. Gran Fury's piece served as a direct comment on consumer culture and capitalism while addressing myths and misinformation about AIDS, particularly the idea that HIV was spread orally.

M·A·C's new T-shirt similarly referenced discourses of AIDS circulating at the time but made them relevant to M·A·C's own creative practices by incorporating cosmetics. The "make up, make out, play safe" T-shirt challenged the many myths about AIDS that were still being spread despite local public health education campaigns that promoted factual knowledge about HIV, AIDS, sexuality, and safer sex. M·A·C's message was a different one, of education and hope, with a creative edge. In line with M·A·C's values, the T-shirt also called attention to the generalized homophobia and misinformation associated with AIDS that had exacerbated the social ostracism experienced by people living with HIV and AIDS.[35] The Franks wanted their message to be both humorous and serious. Toskan later conceded that sometimes,

> the humour and the sickness don't go well together. But I think it's important to remember that the *living* have to live. It's not only about the dying; the living *have* to live, and be healthy, and be supportive of the people that are ailing. So I think that message was appropriate for that moment. It was appropriate. It was very well understood by a younger audience, and they, in turn, made that message strong and successful and they, I think, interpreted it to their parents and the older consumer.[36]

This limited edition T-shirt was M·A·C's first independent consumer-based initiative in raising AIDS awareness, and for M·A·C it really did represent "a new way of marketing," since it was not really marketing at all; instead, the T-shirt promoted education and compassion about HIV and AIDS through creative practices and discourses.

M·A·C's staff and the Franks certainly had first-hand experience with AIDS. The idea that touch and contact could be deadly was planted early in Toskan. He had been aware of AIDS from the beginning of the epidemic in Canada. His first boyfriend in high school, John, was the first person he had lost to AIDS. This was in the early 1980s, when AIDS did not yet even have a name and no one knew how HIV was transmitted. It was suspected that it could happen from touching someone, or drinking from the same cup, or even being in the same room as an infected person. John's friends and family were told that he possibly had an immune disorder, or septic shock, or perhaps tuberculosis, but they did not really know for sure what his ailment was. Toskan was called to the hospital and was given gloves, a mask, and a gown and told to stand back six feet and not get close to the bed. He was actually afraid to enter the room, although in the end he did. John's illness and death had a profound effect on Toskan, but he did not initially know what to do about it. He began researching AIDS and educating himself, because he felt that AIDS would eventually affect him. The gay community was scared to death and could not understand what was happening. By the time M·A·C created its "make up, make out, play safe" T-shirt, more information about HIV transmission and the science and epidemiology of AIDS was available, but rumours and myths persisted and a cure was not yet in sight.[37] For M·A·C, the T-shirt became the starting point for M·A·C's public stance on AIDS, one that embodied the professional, creative, and social contexts in which they had all been living and working in Toronto for years. Toskan recalls, "[w]hat we felt at that time took years for people to understand outside. It was like being at ground zero"; fashion was "where we found our strength because that was the core audience that we had. We lived it. We didn't manufacture anything. We lived it day to day. People were sick; people were dying around us." Responding to AIDS "was not a calculated thing. It just was what it was. It was what was happening around us." And some of those people "dying around us" were also M·A·C employees. Friends and colleagues affected by HIV/AIDS included M·A·C artist Tony de Freitas, and Pier Tetro, a make-up artist with the Shiseido brand. "They were people who were our friends, our family," said Toskan. "What could we do? We couldn't turn our back on them."[38]

As a company, M·A·C was not involved in formal AIDS activist projects or initiatives beyond its T-shirt and Fashion Cares. Any other activities were conducted one-on-one, at a grassroots level, as individual acts by individual people, and this included coming out. Few public figures had come out at that time. Toskan realized he was fortunate to have always had a loving, accepting family and supportive friends: "I was an out gay person in high school. I was never bullied. I don't know; maybe I was a lucky one. I had friends, straight friends, throughout my youth. I never had a problem being closeted, and neither did many of my friends."[39] Toskan said he never felt discriminated against in Toronto and that he found the city to be a relatively more progressive and perhaps less fearful place. Despite Toskan's own personal comfort, acceptance was by no means the most common reaction to others who came out. He had friends in other places who were not out or who faced harsh discrimination if they were. This aspect was poignantly evident in the Franks' own relationship: Frank Angelo had never come out to his own family. As a result, the fact that the Franks were a romantic couple, and not merely business "partners" or just "friends," was not disclosed in contemporaneous media accounts, even though it was "loud and clear" during interviews that the Franks were together romantically. Toskan and Angelo never tried to hide anything about themselves, although many people described them as a very private couple. Everyone in the fashion community knew they were together – after all, they were "the Franks." Journalists, many of whom were firmly established in the same local fashion field as the Franks, certainly obfuscated this fact, sometimes because it was not directly relevant to their story, and other times because they were cognizant of their more mainstream and conservative readers' sensibilities, but mostly, it seems, out of consideration for the Franks' privacy. Toskan later said that "[t]he most difficult thing for me, in terms of dealing with Frank, was not being able to share with his family the fact that we had so much together. It was such a loss for him; it was a loss for me, and I can't image the struggles that went on inside of him. Those are pretty major struggles. I can't imagine not being out to my parents."[40] In the hundreds of contemporaneous media accounts, interviews, and business reports spanning almost two decades, only a very few – perhaps just two or three – presented the Franks as a romantic couple. This injects a striking contradiction and an uncomfortable tension into the stance that M·A·C took as a company in promoting acceptance and countering homophobia – perhaps it partly motivated that stance – besides serving as a testimonial to the times in which the Franks were together.

Put Your Money Where Your Mouth Is!

In 1992, the Franks decided to formalize M·A·C's commitment to AIDS. Toskan created a vibrant new red lipstick based on M·A·C's original and best-selling Russian Red, in a shade he called VIVA

GLAM. Toskan went on to describe how this new lipstick originated in his own creative practices: "Being in this business, as a company we feel a certain sense of responsibility. As a company, we wanted to do something to raise money for this cause. I thought: what am I going to do? Obviously, I'm in the make-up business so I'm going to make the most incredible lip colour I've ever made. From the sales of this lipstick every penny goes to AIDS."[41] Toskan's "outspoken" deep-red shade meant "long live glamour," a sentiment that he felt defied the death constantly accompanying AIDS. VIVA GLAM's bold red was designed to suit all skin tones so that most people could wear it and look good, thus maximizing sales. The Franks were also very clear about VIVA GLAM's purpose: 100 per cent of VIVA GLAM's entire selling price – not just the profit margin – would be donated to local AIDS organizations. M·A·C covered all production, distribution, and sales costs associated with the $10 lipstick. M·A·C did not make any profit whatsoever on the product; in fact, M·A·C technically lost money. "We pay for the lipstick," Toskan said at the time, "we pay for the tube, we pay for the box, we pay for the shipping, and we demand that the department store doesn't take anything on it – that way we get a clear contribution from the customer."[42] The VIVA GLAM initiative was intended to be very transparent to consumers.

Disseminating knowledge about VIVA GLAM's function took place at the retail counters. M·A·C's artists were encouraged to talk about VIVA GLAM and its fundraising purpose with receptive customers at the point of sale, thereby incorporating a unique form of "activism" into the artists' routine creative sales practices at work. Toskan gave his staff information about HIV and AIDS that he obtained from Casey House, the Toronto AIDS hospice, and characteristically, he entrusted his staff to tailor this information in their own style to suit their customers. Toskan wanted his staff

> to soft sell; we wanted them to sell information first, we wanted them to talk about the cause, to educate as much as possible, and they had to feel comfortable about where they could go. We had to, because there were people we couldn't get into it [with] too much, so we had to be careful, and we had to try and understand what that customer was; would they be offended? A lot of people were offended.

Also, VIVA GLAM was sold with a condom very early on, "for those who want it. We don't force it," said Toskan, re-emphasizing the AIDS safe sex message. For many customers, the VIVA GLAM message hit home. One artist had a customer who bought twenty-four VIVA GLAM lipsticks in one sale. Toskan remembers another time when one of his artists excitedly called him to say she had just sold sixty VIVA GLAM lipsticks to a single customer who was planning to give them to her friends as gifts.[43]

The visual presentation for VIVA GLAM at the retail counter comprised, in typical M·A·C style, a small postcard display with a personal message to customers written by Toskan. Donald Robertson helped Toskan create the postcard concept, which they printed, DIY-style, at a local print shop. The postcard's design was like many things at M·A·C: the result of a happy accident. On the front, the lipstick colour was, ironically, blue, which Toskan said was to make the image stand out; red was "ordinary" and "expected" but blue was neither of these (PLATE 19). What actually happened was that when Tom Burton created the graphics with Stephen Stanish, a jewellery designer, the colour separation came out a bit odd. Toskan loved it anyway. The handwritten-style copy on the front proclaimed: "Put your money where your mouth is! VIVA GLAM by Frank Toskan." The back stated:

> The crisis is not over!
> AIDS continues to rob us of precious friends, lovers and family.
> I am proud to introduce M.A.C. VIVA GLAM Lipstick, one of the best matte lip colours I've ever created, and my way of raising millions of dollars to fight AIDS.
> Every cent raised from the sale of VIVA GLAM will be donated to fund AIDS education, support and prevention.
> Please buy, wear and enjoy M.A.C. VIVA GLAM Lipstick, while you help raise AIDS awareness and much needed money.
> Thank you. Play safer. Frank Toskan.

The fine print informed customers that funds raised would, like the "make up, make out, play safe" T-shirt, be directed to the Design Industries Foundation Fighting AIDS (DIFFA), to the Canadian AIDS Society, and to various local AIDS support groups. A small red square on the side of the postcard cheekily showed the "Actual VIVA GLAM colour." As well, the "make up, make out, play safe" T-shirt graphic appeared on the back of the postcard (PLATE 20). To promote his new initiative, Toskan took VIVA GLAM on a Canadian fundraising tour in late 1992. M·A·C's quiet association with AIDS did not diminish business: by January 1993, sales of the $11 VIVA GLAM lipstick, and thus donations, had yielded $100,000 for these AIDS organizations.

M·A·C took part in an unusual event in early 1993. The animal rights organization People for the Ethical Treatment of Animals (PETA) staged its second annual "Fur Is a Drag" fashion show on 2 February at the Hard Rock Cafe in New York City. The M·A·C-sponsored show was an outright parody of a high-fashion runway show and featured cross-dressing men wearing paint-splattered fur garments. Celebrity participants included Canadian singer and animal rights activist k.d. lang, dressed in her "Miss Chatelaine" video "drag" garb.[44] lang's song and sartorial presentation appeared to gently mock a previous honour bestowed on the singer by the Canadian women's magazine *Chatelaine*, which, in January 1988, had proclaimed lang "Woman of the Year," a more contemporary version of the magazine's yearly "Miss Chatelaine" contest. M·A·C's authoritative position and its fashion capital allowed it to challenge, even subvert, a vital fashion tradition like the fashion show, even while it had enthusiastically and earnestly participated in the more "legitimate" Festival of Canadian Fashion in the previous decade. Like Fashion Cares, the "make up, make out, play safe" T-shirt, and now VIVA GLAM, this PETA fashion show further advanced M·A·C's alignment with social advocacy. In his column about the PETA fashion show in the *Globe and Mail* the following week, David Livingstone directly connected M·A·C's sponsorship of the PETA show to the VIVA GLAM fundraising initiative, which had by now raised $300,000. Livingstone implied that M·A·C was becoming invested in unconventional – at least for a cosmetics company – projects that now reached beyond Fashion Cares.[45]

A couple of months later, however, the reception of Fashion Cares was mixed. Fashion Cares Arcouture took place on 8 May 1993 at BCE Place in the heart of Toronto's financial district. The event's name was a blend of "art" and "couture," fitting for an event that took fashion design to elevated artistic heights. However, there was a perceived contradiction between the deadly reality of AIDS and the celebration of life and creativity, a big difference from the year before. That event, Fashion Cares Rags 2 Riches, had been held on 29 April 1992 at Showline Studios in Toronto's film district and presented benefactors with the opportunity to support "one of the most worthwhile causes of the 20th century."[46] The fashion show's creative requirement that year had been for twelve specially selected artists and designers to interpret the "dreamcoat" for the 1990s, a theme no doubt influenced by the coinciding Toronto production of *Joseph and the Amazing Technicolour Dreamcoat* at the Elgin Theatre on Yonge Street, starring Donny Osmond. The Fashion Cares musical line-up included Infidels and The Nylons, both popular local bands, and, in an astute instance of cross-promotion, the *Joseph and the Amazing Technicolor Dreamcoat* Children's Choir. Sixty-five local designers participated, and tickets were a cool $150. M·A·C remained the sole cosmetics brand used at the growing event, with M·A·C artists creating all of the make-up designs. That year, the dinner table centrepieces, made by florist Richard Hayter out of twisted tree branches decorated with moss, caught fire, another incident that would live on in Fashion Cares infamy.[47]

But now, in 1993, Fashion Cares' notoriety was of a different kind. Kate Fillion reviewed the show in the *Globe and Mail* on 13 May under the headline "Overshadowing the AIDS Message" – an indication of what she thought of the show's artistic vision. Fillion highlighted how the seeming frivolity of Fashion Cares obscured just how severe AIDS was, producing mixed messages. In a nod to the continued impact of AIDS on the field of fashion, she noted: "Now, the fashion community, both here and in other countries, has been hit hard by AIDS. So many talented designers, hairdressers, models and makeup artists have died or are dying that it is not surprising that the industry as a whole has been one of the leading fund-raisers for AIDS charities." But, said Fillion, some of the male participants portrayed people with AIDS as deathly saints, martyrs, and skeletal depictions of everlasting life in death. Meanwhile, the thin fashion models adhered to the contemporary fashion and beauty ideal, one that especially depicted the malnourished "waif look" body types that were currently in style. There was a contradiction in these juxtaposed representations of fashion and AIDS: "And yet, no one commented on the obvious irony: two skin-and-bones male models telegraph a message about AIDS and evoke pity, two skin-and-bones female models telegraph a message about glamour and evoke envy," wrote Fillion.[48] The reality of AIDS had collided uncomfortably with its creative, fashionable translation into art. Bernadette Morra, writing in the *Toronto Star* on the same day, concurred on a number of these points in her review, as evident by its title, "AIDS Gala Scores Hits and Misses."[49]

Fashion Cares Arcouture was noteworthy for another reason. The poster announced that Sebastian International, an American hair care company, would be the event's official corporate sponsor.[50] Sebastian had donated $25,000 in cash and $20,000 in hair care products for the event. Canadian singer Alannah Myles, then at the peak of her international fame, was flown to Toronto from Los Angeles to introduce this new corporate partner who had made it possible for the Fashion Cares Committee to realize its maximum fundraising potential. Myles earnestly described how Sebastian's corporate support extended to other projects, including a fundraising program called Club Unite that benefited the Ontario AIDS Network. Sebastian executive Scott Cox accepted Fashion Cares' thanks (and an event poster) with a telling but slightly naive speech at the event: "Corporate America must take a stand and get involved with fighting this disease we call AIDS."[51] Cox seemed to have forgotten which country and community Fashion Cares was serving that night; even so, his speech acknowledged the increasing corporate support and attention to AIDS that Fashion Cares now commanded.

The year 1994 marked a sea change in corporate and financial support for Fashion Cares and for AIDS advocacy in Canada. Sebastian, having received accolades from Fashion Cares organizers just the year before, was now nowhere to be seen, and a new corporate sponsor was announced: M·A·C Cosmetics. Phillip Ing had approached Frank Angelo and The Bay's (formerly Simpsons') Rod Ulmer, explained how difficult it was to keep Fashion Cares afloat, and asked for money.[52] M·A·C and The Bay (albeit as a more silent partner) both contributed to keep Fashion Cares running. The event was officially renamed, and rebranded, as M·A·C VIVA GLAM Fashion Cares, an extension of the successful VIVA GLAM initiative. Financial stability for the event and for ACT was now more certain. Many corporations had donated money and goods to Fashion Cares and ACT in various capacities over the years or advertised in the event programs. M·A·C, however, was the first company to stake its entire corporate identity on a clear and permanent affiliation with the AIDS fundraiser. Almost in the same moment, Angelo asked Ing to formally join M·A·C, which he did (and never left – he is now a consultant for M·A·C, after years of being an executive).

That year, Fashion Cares host Bryan Levy-Young emphasized in his welcome speech that M·A·C was "behind us in a very big way; in fact, behind the whole AIDS charity movement. They have a year-round commitment to it, not just on an evening like this." Levy-Young revealed that M·A·C had contributed $125,000 to the 1994 event, setting a record for the largest single Canadian corporate donation to an AIDS event to date. ACT chair Bill Flanagan then praised M·A·C in his speech for showing "exceptional leadership and commitment."[53] Other corporate sponsors that year included Holt Renfrew, Eaton's, and The Bay. The event took place on 7 May 1994 at Toronto Island Airport's Shell Aerocentre. The theme, "Wings of Life," highlighted 1930s Art Deco style with an emphasis on wings of all kinds, perhaps in homage to Tony Kushner's *Angels in America*, the AIDS-themed play that had won the Pulitzer Prize the previous year.[54] As always, there was some drama: torrential rainstorms in Toronto that night flooded the tents and dressing rooms. Later in the evening, thousands of guests were stranded on Toronto Island because the only ferry running could not transport everyone back to the mainland in one trip.[55] Nonetheless, M·A·C VIVA GLAM Fashion Cares Wings of Life raised $350,000 for ACT in 1994, which, when M·A·C's donation was included, made the total more than twice that of the 1993 event.[56]

In light of VIVA GLAM's success, both at the counter and now at Fashion Cares, the Franks incorporated a new charity, the M·A·C AIDS Fund, on 30 September 1994, to formally distribute the funds among various AIDS organizations, including ACT, that

VIVA GLAM sales had generated.[57] Augmenting VIVA GLAM was the smaller initiative "Kids Helping Kids," a yearly holiday greeting card program in which cards designed by children living with HIV and AIDS were sold at the counter; funds raised went to purchasing supplies such as diapers, social services, and care for children in need. The new M·A·C AIDS Fund board of directors comprised the Franks, Bruce Hunter from Toronto, Michael Locke from Montreal, lawyer Ian Ness, and accountant Allan Shimmerman. Toskan described the early recipients of M·A·C AIDS Fund grants as the "grassroots" organizations that were most in need, such as Toronto's Casey House AIDS Hospice and children's AIDS hospices. Toskan gave funds to every charity in Toronto that had a connection to HIV and AIDS. For instance, Casey House once needed a special bathtub and asked the M·A·C AIDS Fund for money to purchase one. If the money was raised in a certain community (i.e., where VIVA GLAM was sold), the funds went back to that same community, because Toskan felt that was the fairest distribution method. Toskan kept a close eye on those disbursements: "We knew exactly what we were getting. Again, it's part of being frugal. I wanted to make sure that every cent was well spent. So we were very in touch, and very hands-on, and very connected."[58] Once the word got out, the M·A·C AIDS Fund was inundated with applications. In the beginning, Toskan sorted through all of these applications himself. Bruce Hunter would also go through them. They then determined which organizations were most in need, and those were the requests to which they responded first.

The M·A·C AIDS Fund followed through on its charitable gifts, with the Franks and the board members regularly conducting site visits, often unannounced. Recipients of funds in 1995 (which already totalled $2,404,263 from VIVA GLAM sales and $146,984 from Kids Helping Kids by February 1995) included ACT, Toronto People with AIDS, and the Canadian AIDS Society in Canada; in the United States, God's Love We Deliver, DIFFA, and AIDS Project, LA; and the Children with AIDS Charity at St Mary's Hospital in the UK.[59] Also, the Franks wanted their staff to stay in contact with those who had received assistance from the M·A·C AIDS Fund, money generated by the VIVA GLAM lipsticks they sold. For instance, in Vancouver, the staff visited various AIDS charities, and the staff became involved in that community and experienced the charity's work first-hand. It was important to the Franks that their staff not merely stand at the counter and talk about something they knew nothing about; they needed to personally experience how money raised from VIVA GLAM lipsticks sales was being put to good use.[60]

The First Face of M·A·C Cosmetics

There was one final piece to put into place. It was a big one, and it marked a huge departure for the Franks in a number of ways. Frank Toskan decided that they needed someone to promote VIVA GLAM beyond the staff talking about it at the retail counter, to bring even more attention to the M·A·C AIDS Fund. However, given Toskan's long-standing dismissal of beauty advertising, and the generic beauty standard that the cosmetics industry usually promoted in advertising, Toskan had a dilemma: Who *could* actually represent M·A·C in this capacity? Donald Robertson recalls that deciding on a spokesperson for VIVA GLAM was difficult, given both the co-founders' ideological position against advertising and the difficulty of choosing only one person to represent a brand that promoted diversity so strongly. Up until then, the unofficial "face" of M·A·C Cosmetics had always been Toskan himself, who had appeared in the numerous articles, interviews, and photos about M·A·C over the years. M·A·C was for everyone: all ages, all races, all sexes. It would be impossible to find one person who could embody this stance yet still show M·A·C make-up advantageously *and* be seen as an authentic representative of AIDS awareness as the first chairperson of the M·A·C AIDS Fund. The solution was so outlandish that no one saw it coming.

Back in 1991, Toskan and Robertson had attended Wigstock, the yearly drag festival held in New York City. The drag superstar RuPaul had performed there and left a big impression on both of them.[61] RuPaul Charles, better known simply as RuPaul, was the twenty-four-year-old black, New York–based drag queen and singer whose hit song "Supermodel (You Better Work)" had topped the Billboard charts in 1992.[62] Toskan thought that RuPaul's drag make-up was phenomenal. And of course, they already knew Ru-Paul because he had been the "doorman" at the New York City M·A·C store with Lady Bunny when it had first opened. Toskan and Robertson started talking, tentatively, about RuPaul as the M·A·C spokesperson. The idea of asking RuPaul to represent M·A·C was outrageous but also very appealing and made sense in many ways, mostly because RuPaul was "who we were," said Toskan. And Toskan had always known that, should M·A·C ever have a spokesperson, it would never be a traditional "face." RuPaul's glamorous and extraordinary appearance and performances made him a "natural" choice for M·A·C, said Toskan, who said at the time that he had long considered using a man to represent M·A·C: "We couldn't find anyone who wore more makeup and had so much fun doing it ... I've always thought it would be impossible to put a face to MAC because of what we stand for – all sexes, all races, all ages. But RuPaul is male, he's female, and he's ageless. He fits the bill."[63] The Franks also knew that they would not have to teach RuPaul anything about AIDS awareness and advocacy; he would be able to go onstage and talk with authenticity about the M·A·C AIDS Fund and its message. RuPaul had worked for many AIDS shelters, had raised money doing drag shows in clubs, and was in a position to speak knowledgably about the positive outcome of raising money for AIDS hospices and organizations. Ultimately, choosing RuPaul as M·A·C's first face and as chairperson of the M·A·C AIDS Fund was a collaborative decision between the Franks and Robertson. The official launch of RuPaul in his new role as spokesperson for the M·A·C AIDS Fund was held on 1 March 1995 at Henri Bendel in New York, the location of M·A·C's first American retail counter. A few days before the launch party, Toskan and Robertson tacked up posters around New York City that teasingly asked, "Who is the M·A·C Girl?" Guests at the Bendel party were treated to "?" shaped cookies. As evidence of M·A·C's fashion capital and national loyalty, *FashionTelevision* personality Jeanne Beker hosted the launch party, and Phillip Ing and Frances Hathaway were prominent guests. The answer to the question was now clear: RuPaul proudly proclaimed: "I am the M·A·C Girl."

As if choosing a spokesperson was not surprising enough, Toskan and Robertson created M·A·C's first print ad for VIVA GLAM featuring RuPaul. Given Toskan's distaste for advertising, the ad appeared to indicate a fundamental shift in M·A·C's practices. The company had, of course, maintained a "no advertising" policy for ten years, claiming that advertising was too expensive for the entrepreneurial, start-up company. Since the brand had always been heavily promoted by word-of-mouth within the fashion industry and received free publicity in the media, it had not needed much additional promotion. But this would be no ordinary beauty advertising campaign. Like VIVA GLAM, the Franks paid for this advertising out of their own pockets rather than from M·A·C's operating budget, suggesting that the ads served a different and decidedly more personal purpose. Shot by Albert Sanchez, the image showed RuPaul clad in a red bustier, red thigh-high stiletto boots, and a long blonde wig, with his body spelling out each of the letters V-I-V-A G-L-A-M. While this action did not appear, at first blush, to be particularly shocking, a closer inspection of the "M" revealed RuPaul's legs wide open, his genital area provocatively presented to the viewer (PLATE 21). Not everyone liked this image. The department stores were particularly unwilling to display it, so Toskan, characteristically, had a small postcard printed up to distribute at the retail counters. Ultimately, the image did exactly what any good ad does: it offered information, it created buzz, and it sold more VIVA GLAM lipsticks.

The "Cruelty Free Beauty" and "make up, make out, play safe" T-shirts, and now VIVA GLAM lipstick, were, like the fashion show, both a source and an outcome of creative practices of the field of cultural production; the result was a particular type of creative activism. For the Franks, VIVA GLAM was just another example of their own instinctual business practices. Indeed, the Canadian company had never seemed more at odds with the global cosmetics industry in which it played. Valerie MacKenzie remembers how, when M·A·C installed its 1-800 number, customers were always taken aback that they were calling Toronto, surprised that M·A·C was a Canadian company. Customers thought the company was American. They were partly right.

CHAPTER 5

Selling Out

M·A·C was "wired." Serena French described how for Fall 1993, "wired" included "lingerie and underwear, tattoos and pierced private parts, telephone and modem sex lines, the industrial look – black boots, studded biker jackets, crewcuts, work socks – MAC Cosmetics – they're so wired they have extended stores out of the country."[1] M·A·C was now a signifier for a particular type of taste, imbuing status and fashion capital on those who knew about the brand and used it. M·A·C's core users had always been professional make-up artists, whose kits were full of M·A·C products. Now, the "ordinary" consumer too, someone who did not work or create in the field of fashion but nonetheless wanted the distinction of being an insider, just like the artists, the models, and the celebrities – of being "wired" – was buying M·A·C. Toskan welcomed these consumers, who included women he felt had been fed lies and false hope through conventional beauty advertising and wanted something more. Yet this increasing attention presented a new set of problems. In 1993, M·A·C had grossed $60 million, a number beyond anyone's expectations.[2] The Franks now faced a supply and demand issue that could not be ignored.

M·A·C had inadvertently created a new desire for something that had not existed for decades: the professional make-up artist line. By the mid-1990s, other professional "make-up artist" lines were entering the market and competing with M·A·C. M·A·C's niche position was being threatened by an influx of other professional brands entering the cosmetics market, such as François Nars, Trish McEvoy, and Bobbi Brown, who had once been an enthusiastic M·A·C customer herself. These lines offered similarly rich, intense pigments, colour products that suited many skin tones, professional grade brushes, and sleek and innovative packaging, and they too did little or no advertising. Importantly, they relied on the same cool aura surrounding the make-up artist, a job within fashion that had new cultural – indeed, fashion – capital now. These companies vied for the position that M·A·C had originally carved out for itself within the cosmetics industry.

But the most immediate concern for the Franks was the quantity of M·A·C products being sold on the "grey" market in Asia. In this regard, the Franks were under imminent threat of losing control over their products and the M·A·C brand name and trademark. Consumers were purchasing M·A·C products in the United States and shipping them to Asia, where they were being illegally resold. In fact, when Toskan travelled to Hong Kong, he saw "M·A·C" products sold on the street and on the sidewalk. Some of these items actually were M·A·C products, but many were fake. Counterfeiting was a new issue. Toskan visited a store that said "M·A·C" on the outside but was obviously not a M·A·C store because the Franks did not operate in Asia. At one point, there were three "M·A·C stores" in Hong Kong. Inside these stores were display pieces that once stood on real M·A·C counters. People were coming from Japan and Hong Kong and cleaning out the stand-alone stores in North America. This demand for M·A·C had been created in magazine editorials, so naturally someone was going to respond, legally or not. But it would take years for M·A·C to legally operate in Asia, since the Franks simply did not have the infrastructure and knowledge to put the necessary distribution channels in place. M·A·C would also have to undertake new ingredients testing, create new packaging, and contend with language issues. Even so, the Franks were given only one year by various levels of government to set up M·A·C legally in Asia; if they did not succeed, the Franks would lose all rights to the M·A·C trademark in these Asian countries.[3] The Franks tried to control this activity by placing a limit on quantities of products sold to any one customer in the stand-alone M·A·C stores, a new practice Toskan deplored but now felt was necessary.[4]

Discouraged, and fearful of losing control of their business, the Franks sought a tangible solution for these difficulties, and found it, unexpectedly, at the Estée Lauder Companies Inc. in New York. M·A·C's acquaintance with Estée Lauder actually had its origins in Formula K, the Gladys Knight hair care line. Back in the late 1980s, Toskan had found it very difficult to break into the US market, mostly because, he later surmised, he had tried to position the line as appropriate for everyone; the market had just not been amenable to a product line that had no clear consumer. Toskan had been doing the trade shows alone in all the major cities in the United States, but the Franks knew they needed a major distributor to really market the products effectively. Despite a 1989 relaunch, the Franks never got the mileage from Formula K they wanted.[5] In 1992, the Franks had approached the New York–based cosmetics giant about distributing Formula K. The Franks had thought such a partnership would be mutually beneficial, but CEO Leonard Lauder was not interested in the Formula K business plan. Instead, Lauder said, "I love what I see with M·A·C." The Franks had not been remotely interested in a partnership between M·A·C and Lauder at that time. But now, the situation was very different, and increasingly dire. The Franks called Leonard Lauder again and said, "We've got a problem."[6]

The Franks and Leonard Lauder had an immediate connection and an excellent professional and personal working relationship right from the start. Estée Lauder had operated in Asia for years. Its distribution networks could start shipping M·A·C overseas almost immediately, and M·A·C clearly needed Estée Lauder to help them get M·A·C legally into the Asian market. Lauder responded to the Franks' call with an offer: a partnership between Estée Lauder and the Canadian company. The Franks agreed this was the best solution. In December 1994, the Estée Lauder Companies Inc. bought 51 per cent of M·A·C for $38 million. M·A·C was Lauder's first acquisition of a competitor. In this partnership, Lauder sought to maintain M·A·C's unique identity and its niche market while expanding the brand across a global marketplace, a strategy in line with broader movements within the cosmetics industry. Usually, Lauder left each of its divisions to manage itself, which created a type of "internal competition."[7] Lauder had always created its own brands in-house, but Leonard Lauder astutely recognized that it could not duplicate M·A·C's artistic aura and specialized brand identity. He realized that it was not possible to create or engineer a brand like M·A·C from a marketing strategy, in the same way that Lauder had done with the Prescriptives brand, for instance, which had been specifically built as a custom-colour concept. The Lauder executives acknowledged that M·A·C was filling a market that Lauder had never filled, nor could it ever do so, and that made M·A·C a very attractive addition to the company's brand roster.

This partnership/purchase provided M·A·C with the means for global distribution through Lauder's sophisticated logistical channels, but it was a difficult personal process for Toskan, who felt like he was "giving up his baby"; he wanted to keep M·A·C exactly the same as it had always been, and he wanted to protect it. But he realized that M·A·C, just like a child, had to develop a life of its own. The Franks themselves were being stretched more and more, and they realized that they had to let others in to do some of the work. Toskan also immediately appreciated that even though Leonard Lauder loved the brand's identity and the M·A·C AIDS Fund, he did not (and could not) really understand M·A·C's unique culture, and thus dared not interfere in its operations. This gave Toskan a wide berth to maintain creative control over his products and manage his staff. Toskan did not like to think about sales and business matters, nor did he need to; he left that to Frank Angelo. For his part, Angelo, always the business mind, enjoyed dealing with Lauder's management; Toskan said that Angelo "liked playing with the big guys," and he saw this new partnership as enabling him to get his foot in the door for other business ideas.

This deal, however, presented substantial inconsistencies in its "optics" to industry pundits, consumers, and employees alike. The Franks were certainly cognizant of the apparent contradiction in M·A·C, the creative, small-scale Canadian producer of a relatively niche product, joining forces with the $2.5 billion American cosmetics behemoth. The Franks clearly anticipated a backlash once others learned about the partnership. So they did something very uncharacteristic: they deliberately obfuscated the exact nature of the Lauder relationship by not disclosing that it was actually a purchase, stating only that it was a "partnership." That it was in fact a purchase would not be revealed until a year later.[8] Press releases and other communications in the media about the Lauder/M·A·C relationship throughout 1995 discussed Lauder's ability to offer its global distribution network and retail resources to M·A·C in a "joint venture." The *New York Times* reported on 10 February 1995 that Lauder would "distribute M·A·C products in Europe, Asia, and other markets outside North America."[9] But as Cyndee Miller noted in *Marketing News* on 11 September 1995, "Toskan admits that one of the biggest challenges will be expanding without selling out."[10] This piece, like other media accounts, expressed a general scepticism about whether M·A·C's authenticity could remain intact now that M·A·C had "sold out" to the type of company it had always distanced itself from.[11]

And there was no question that this new partnership greatly troubled M·A·C's employees. Jane McKay remembers that when she heard about the Lauder deal, it was "shocking to my core."[12] The Franks had been very forthright with their staff and had regular meetings with them to explain their growing pains and the problems M·A·C was experiencing with supplying the demand, but M·A·C's staff were not comfortable with this new arrangement at all; there was a lot of fear and uncertainty. Valerie MacKenzie remembers that when Frank Toskan pulled the staff together and told them about Lauder, "I felt almost like a bullet was put through my heart." MacKenzie, who had more of an insider's perspective, understood the business rationale behind the Lauder purchase, but the make-up artists did not. She remembers travelling to Atlanta in late October 1995 and consoling the make-up artists, some of whom were in tears wondering what would happen to M·A·C with Lauder looking over their shoulder. She assured them that, to the best of her knowledge, M·A·C would stay the same. There were people at M·A·C who felt betrayed, however, saying to the Franks, "What are you doing, you're selling us out for money." In retrospect, MacKenzie notes that "Lauder was really smart about not changing anything." Several things did have to change from a regulatory standpoint, especially with certain ingredients, and some of the staff had to be let go because of redundancies, but for the most part, M·A·C remained unchanged. "But it was terrifying at the time," she recalls, and for some, bad feelings lingered.[13] The "secret" was finally revealed in December 1995, and only inadvertently, after Lauder, a formerly private company, filed an initial public offering in October 1995.[14] Lauder was required to disclose its financials for the IPO, and this exposed Lauder's controlling ownership of M·A·C. Lauder vice-president William Lauder was personally troubled by the Franks' desire for secrecy, but for a different reason: "It would have been nice if they were able to position [the acquisition] in such a way that we were not seen as a big corporate monster who was likely to change M·A·C."[15] Complicating this situation, another troubling detail emerged: the deal specified an option for Lauder to assume the remaining 49 per cent of M·A·C, in two stages, by 1999.

Certainly, Lauder's corporate culture was very different, and it was not easy for M·A·C's staff to adjust. Toskan knew that his staff could not understand M·A·C's growth pressures or envision the future. He felt that ultimately, the transition to Lauder's stewardship would ensure that M·A·C's staff could have thriving careers and secure futures, and despite their trepidation, this turned out to be the case for many of the original M·A·C artists including Jane McKay, Philippe Chansel, and Gordon Espinet, who became senior M·A·C artists, and Valerie MacKenzie and Phillip Ing remained with M·A·C in executive roles. The Lauder deal had the potential to offer them the types of opportunities that were part of a global operation. All the while, Toskan assured his staff that M·A·C's autonomous management style would be maintained and that Lauder would take a "hands-off" approach, and this appears to have been the case. Having obscured the full details of the deal during that first year, Toskan was now in a position to "prove" to his staff that Lauder had no intention of interfering with M·A·C's creativity or decision-making or with the M·A·C AIDS Fund. This purchase satisfied all the stakeholders: Frank Toskan retained complete creative control; Frank Angelo oversaw the complex business details related to M·A·C's global expansion; managing partners Victor Casale and Julie Toskan-Casale continued in their roles in R&D and innovation, and public relations, respectively; and Lauder acquired the hottest brand in town. It was the best of all worlds for the Franks, who genuinely could sustain both creativity and commerce under this arrangement while continuing to protect and nurture their staff. However, the initial deception by the Franks indicated their discomfort with, and clear understanding of, the idea of M·A·C "selling out." With the Lauder purchase, M·A·C had become a new type of player within the fashion and cosmetics industries.

One crucial source of M·A·C's creative power was its freestanding stores, autonomous spaces where the Franks could continue to do whatever they wanted without being subject to the same rules as the department stores or under Lauder's direction. Its people could be who they were and allow whomever they wanted through the front door. That freedom was important, recalls Toskan, and it was from this creative space that the Franks continued to fashion the M·A·C brand. A department store setting made a brand subject to someone else's environment and rules, as well as being overly sensitive to risk or controversy, all of which could water down a brand's identity. In the M·A·C stores, creative ideas could be worked out, no matter how outlandish, and staff could remain themselves, not constricted by another organization's practices. In their own stores, the Franks and their staff could explore new ways to learn about different urban centres and build new relationships with their customers. There were definitely differences in clientele from place to place; for instance, Toronto was where everything about M·A·C was born and it was the melting pot of ideas that would percolate. In New York, it was more about the street. The Franks learned in their stores about the kind of person they would subsequently service in the department store setting, a type of informal market research based on the same practices in which they had always engaged. In turn, the relationship with the department store was more assured. With this knowledge, the Franks had more confidence moving forward.

The Franks had always sought to keep M·A·C small. They avoided producing too much product or growing their company too big too fast, and they deliberately catered to those who really wanted M·A·C products. Toskan felt a need to maintain this creative, non-commercial approach to his business – to keep the "art" in Make-up Art Cosmetics. This had always been the most authentic, genuine, and effective practice for the Franks with M·A·C. Toskan and Angelo wanted the desire for M·A·C's products to remain within that smaller, professional word-of-mouth network that appreciated M·A·C and used the products in creative work. Although M·A·C was a business, the Franks, particularly Toskan, avoided obvious commercial practices. Now, however, it was difficult to ignore the fact that M·A·C *was* a commercial enterprise – a very, very successful and profitable one with a strong brand identity within the cosmetics industry. A *Financial Post* profile on M·A·C in 1993, "Facing up to the M·A·C Attack," noted that "Toskan firmly believes that the unavailability of M·A·C is an integral part of its mystique," but that "despite his intentions, M·A·C is now the rage. Toskan and Angelo seem alternately flattered and flustered by their company's swelling brand-name appeal." Bob Peter, president of The Bay, M·A·C's principal outlet in Canada, remarked that the Franks offered "a unique product and they cater to a distinct niche. We'd like them to grow faster but they've been very selective in their hiring and growth."[16] The Franks were nervous about quick expansion because they feared losing control over M·A·C's image and product integrity. Whatever they had intended, M·A·C's street credibility in the fashion world now extended beyond the professional sphere and into the general consumer landscape. M·A·C by this point was a mass cultural and commercial phenomenon. All of this resulted in a fraught balance between the cultural and the economic; consumer demand had become uncontrollable, an issue complicated by the partnership with Lauder that now facilitated global distribution.

Valerie MacKenzie, who was still in charge of the customer service phone line, fielded many questions and concerns from customers about the Lauder deal. At first, she maintained that M·A·C was privately owned and "still a proud Canadian company." However, she soon began receiving numerous phone calls – she estimates several hundred – that accused M·A·C of "selling out." One caller even threatened to post a complaint on "the World Wide Web."[17] Other inquiries were related to lack of availability, or to why M·A·C was in so few global markets, and MacKenzie explained that the Lauder deal would in fact help M·A·C reach consumers. Meanwhile, there were tense internal dynamics. In 1994, after twenty-five years, the Franks quietly ended their romantic relationship. Toskan's new partner worked in the M·A·C office as a designer, and this created additional stress and discomfort among the already confused and emotional staff. Frank Angelo moved to Miami, Florida, where he began exploring other business interests, especially in music. While M·A·C's day-to-day business continued, Frank Angelo and Frank Toskan now communicated mostly by phone and fax.

Frank Angelo addressed some of the concerns about M·A·C's management style when the Franks appeared in a television interview with CTV's Deirdre McMurdy on *Canada AM* on 22 April 1996:

> Frank and I are totally in charge of the corporation. We are the people that decide where we're going to open, what cities we're going to open in, how we're going to open, what the store's going to look like. We're completely in control of the company, in control of the staff. What we've really done is tapped into their [Lauder's] network of distribution for the Far East, for Europe, and we're utilizing the connection with Estée Lauder to help us with back-room management of the company – nothing in terms of the retail or marketing or image direction of our company.[18]

Statements like these were attempts to refute the notion that it was impossible to be both creatively and commercially successful. M·A·C was between worlds, being pulled in two directions. And since Lauder would not and could not assimilate into M·A·C's corporate culture, such as it was, it seemed inevitable that M·A·C would gradually fall into line with Lauder's organizational logic. Yet this did not happen, despite predictions otherwise. In 1995, *Canadian Business* had awarded the Franks "Entrepreneur of the Year in Marketing Excellence."[19] Fitting as that was, the Franks now found themselves confronted with the assumption that art and commerce were incompatible.

Also in 1995, to meet the growing demand for its products – which was now possible through the Lauder partnership – M·A·C opened a new production facility in Markham, Ontario. The company had expanded its production facilities seven times since its inception, gradually occupying more and more adjoining units at its Steelcase Avenue location. Victor Casale used to joke with his staff when setting up a new factory, "Don't tighten the bolts too much because we're going to be moving soon." Up until then, orders were still hand processed, packaged, and labelled by the factory's three hundred employees, who had to climb ladders and shelves to retrieve items. In the summer of 1995, the Franks moved the distribution centre into a separate 80,000-square-foot building. The new Pick-to-Light system, housed in a 55,000-square-foot facility on Bentley Street, was technologically light years ahead. Casale now needed a production director and distribution director to help him run the immense operation. By mid-1995, order turnaround time had decreased from six and a half hours to between thirty and forty-five minutes. Casale remembers that it took a bit of time to fine-tune the system; at times, he recalls humorously, it was like the classic *I Love Lucy* episode where Lucy and Ethel work in a chocolate factory, with the factory belt moving too quickly and the chocolates falling off – except here, it was lipsticks falling off.[20] In 1985, a day's work had been 2 kilograms, or about fifty lipsticks. Now, in one day Casale could make a 1,500 kilogram batch of M·A·C's bestselling "Twig" shade, which translated into 300,000 lipsticks.[21] The state-of-the-art plant, which was even featured in *Materials Management and Distribution* in November 1995, increased productivity by 200 per cent in two months. Orders could now be filled on time, which meant that M·A·C could carry out its global expansion plans.[22] Casale ran the entire manufacturing system, with the R&D facility housing seventy technical people and the manufacturing plant four hundred. His twenty-by-fifteen-foot white lab had come a long way. This was good news, because M·A·C's business was growing at an astonishing rate. By 1995, 75 per cent of M·A·C products were being sold in the United States and Britain.[23] The result was a staggering $150 million in sales that year.[24] There were now 110 outlets worldwide. M·A·C had been available in the United States at Henri Bendel and Nordstrom since 1989; now it was also selling its products at Marshall Field's and Saks Fifth Avenue. In 1993, M·A·C's first stand-alone store outside North America had opened, just off Carnaby Street in London (there was also a counter in the Knightsbridge store Harvey Nichols).

In November 1995, the first official and long-awaited Asian counter opened in Hong Kong's Seibu department store.[25] Under Lauder's umbrella, M·A·C's international business was booming.

One other aspect bears mentioning. Lauder had purchased M·A·C with the explicit goal of expanding the company globally. When opening in new markets, M·A·C had to develop new ingredients and new packaging, observe different regulatory policies, and heed cultural differences. All of this was time-consuming and expensive. In the years that followed Lauder's initial 51 per cent purchase, M·A·C expanded slowly and carefully; for instance, it opened one "door," or store, in Germany, one in Switzerland, one in Hong Kong, and two in Tokyo. The main benefit to this approach was that it allowed M·A·C to build secure logistics channels and ensure regulatory compliance. Had Estée Lauder wanted simply to maximize sales, open more doors across North America, or lift the embargo on purchases of multiple products, it would have easily achieved this. Instead, the Franks, Julie Toskan-Casale, and Victor Casale did what they thought was best overall for their family business, which was to ensure that legitimate M·A·C stores opened, not illegal distribution outlets. As a consequence, the family took somewhat of a financial loss, for this was the all-important "earnout" period before Lauder's final acquisition of the company. The earnout is a contractual provision stating that the seller of a business will obtain additional future compensation based on the business achieving certain future financial goals. These financial goals are usually stated as a percentage of gross sales or earnings based on EBITDA (earnings before interest, taxes, depreciation, and amortization). During this earnout period, the Toskan/Casale family chose not to maximize M·A·C's sales, focusing instead on building M·A·C's legacy.[26]

Who Does AIDS Belong To?

Community-based organizations are based in communities. It is here that I believe we get to the heart of the matter. The moral right to speak, be heard, give shape, and to hold accountable in regard to AIDS cannot belong securely to any individual or to any organization. Such claim to moral leadership is the proper business of communities: networks of mutual belonging, visible identity and common fate. In communities, individuals become persons and persons together build organizations.

I propose three criteria for assessing the claim of a community to moral leadership of the issues of AIDS and HIV infection. First, the people in these communities must be deeply affected by AIDS. Second, they must be deeply involved in confronting AIDS. And third, they must have the capacity to sustain an adequate response to AIDS in all its complexities. AIDS cannot belong to people for whom it is only a professional problem. It can only belong to those for whom it is an inescapable crisis.[27]

So stated Stephen P. Manning, executive director of the AIDS Committee of Toronto, when he asked "Who Does AIDS Belong To?" in his keynote address to the annual general meeting of the Canadian AIDS Association held in Winnipeg, Manitoba, in May 1990. Manning's response highlighted the rising tensions among the different groups who were claiming "ownership" of AIDS, as well as what was at stake. If, he suggested, AIDS belonged to the group with the most money, then that would be governments and pharmaceutical companies. If, he posited, AIDS belonged to the group with the highest credentials or status, or the most resources, then that would be the medical community and social services. For him, however, AIDS "belonged" to those who could rightly claim identity. For Manning, the groups with money, status, or credentials always demanded something in return. External supports and partnerships, especially corporate ones, raised concerns for Manning since they were often accompanied by conditions that resulted in power imbalances. Although Manning was discussing this issue in terms of ACT's governance, the question "Who does AIDS belong to?" was becoming increasingly relevant in the 1990s as the disease took on a more distinct commercial flavour and drew increasing corporate interest. M·A·C, because of the personal relationships it had developed and its location in a professional field of cultural production and practices, could rightly, and historically, claim to "own" AIDS in a way that other corporate players could not.

Just as M·A·C was entering into its business relationship with Estée Lauder, a broader debate about the commodification of social causes was taking hold that further complicated and threatened how others viewed M·A·C's authenticity, particularly its philanthropy around AIDS. M·A·C now stood as a corporate leader in advocating for AIDS, being the first cosmetics company with an AIDS charity, and sponsoring Fashion Cares; but it was actually not alone in developing corporate philanthropy around AIDS. The Kenneth Cole shoe company had produced one of the very first corporate-sponsored public service announcements for AIDS awareness back in 1986. Shot by celebrity photographer Annie Leibovitz, this PSA was developed by Cole and advertising agency Grace Kent Sage Inc. The image and copy avoided any suggestions of sexuality, gay or otherwise, and instead featured nine famous fashion models and eight (non-model) children. The copy read: "For the future of our children, support the American Foundation for AIDS Research. We do." Company head Kenneth Cole placed his AIDS PSA in the March 1986 issues of several major fashion magazines. The company contributed funds to the American Foundation for AIDS Research (amfAR), where Cole sat on the board of directors. While this ad was not cause marketing as such, since it did not present consumers with a fundraising component, the PSA established the company's long-lasting connection to AIDS within the New York fashion industry. Meanwhile, Cole continued his own personal and professional AIDS advocacy, and indeed expanded it to other areas. In line with his 1986 PSA for amfAR, Cole created a number of provocative advertising campaigns in the early 1990s for many social issues, such as gay marriage and abortion. The copy in one 1992 ad posed the question: "If we told you a shoe could help find a cure for AIDS, would you buy it?" The copy specified that all shoes were on sale for 15 per cent off and that 15 per cent of the reduced price would be donated to amfAR. This and many similar ads were clearly part of Cole's corporate social responsibility.[28]

Many other corporations and brands were partnering with social causes by the 1990s, breast cancer being one prominent focus. Estée Lauder was one of the first cosmetics companies to incorporate a breast cancer initiative into its general promotional strategy. In 1992, Evelyn Lauder, then senior corporate vice-president, created with the editors of the women's magazine *Self* a pink breast cancer ribbon, which was distributed at Lauder's cosmetic counters across the United States. This ribbon was a variation on an earlier, peach-coloured ribbon designed by a private citizen, Charlotte Haley, to promote breast cancer awareness and support.[29] Soon after, the Avon cosmetics company created a pink ribbon pin to signify awareness of, and support for, breast cancer. In 1993, an article in *Marketing News* noted this increasing tendency for corporations to align with social causes such as AIDS and breast cancer, but also rape and domestic violence. According to its author, Cyndee Miller, this trend was directed at a specifically female target market, as evidenced by companies such as Liz Claiborne and The Body Shop.[30]

But a deepening suspicion about these partnerships was forming. A backlash to brand-cause alliances also appeared in the fashion press. An October 1993 article in the Canadian fashion magazine *Flare* asked: "Is fashion's new philanthropy just another trend?" Journalist Diane Bracuk pointed out that AIDS had totally changed cause marketing and referred to the Toronto fashion community's response with Fashion Cares in this context. "Of course, we are living in a culture of commercialized caring," she postulated, "where being able to help save a loon, a lake, or part of a rain forest with an everyday purchase is the consumer norm. And so, for the cynics, the fashion industry's new earnestness could be viewed as nothing more than an exploitive attempt to sell more product." Bracuk rationalized this commercialism, however, by concluding that "having a cause to support through an everyday purchase is better than not having the choice at all."[31] Others were not always so forgiving. In 1993, the New York fashion industry had launched a project to create fashion panels for the NAMES Project AIDS Memorial Quilt. That quilt was a powerful symbol of memory, alliance, and solidarity, in which people who had lost a loved one to AIDS created a commemorative panel. When the quilt had first been displayed in 1992, there were already 20,000 individual panels.[32] New York's contribution was an additional seventy-nine panels commemorating friends and colleagues in the fashion community.[33] Now, however, this same fashion field found reason to criticize one of its own. AIDS Project Los Angeles had honoured New York-based designer Calvin Klein at its annual fashion benefit in June 1993. At issue was the fact that Klein received top billing in the show, implying that he had been a central figure in AIDS fundraising. Actually, according to an article in the *Advocate*, he had contributed very little. Klein's star power and brand value were being used as promotional tools to attract money and attention to the event. In an industry so affected by AIDS, AIDS Project Los Angeles's promotional strategy was perceived as particularly misleading, hypocritical, and egregious.[34]

The commodification of AIDS in particular added another layer of scepticism to cause marketing as a form of corporate philanthropy. Essayist and cultural critic Daniel Harris wrote a seminal piece in *Harpers Magazine* in July 1994 titled "Making Kitsch from AIDS: A Disease with a Gift Shop of Its Own."[35] He contemplated how AIDS "kitsch" – sympathy cards, T-shirts, teddy bears, tote bags, coffee table books – had overrun the AIDS landscape. Harris aligned AIDS kitsch with two distinct versions of the person with AIDS: it was someone who, as innocent, was angelic, seraphic, and surely heaven-bound, without having become a victim or passive agent in his or her life and death; or someone who was a sacrificial, heroic "soldier" who had lost the good fight but refused to surrender to the enemy. Such sentimentalizing replaced anger and urgency with pseudo-science, New Age religion, idealistic nostalgia, useless objects, celebrities, and superficial discourse, all packaged into "clichés." "The proliferation of AIDS kitsch," noted Harris, "can be linked to the unusual conditions under which activists were initially forced to raise money for research, treatment and education. It was at least in part because of the government's failure to act that AIDS has been heavily commercialized."[36] Harris suggested that AIDS was now commodified for mainstream consumption, which, aided by celebrity culture, obscured the disease's origins and meanings.

One such example of commercial intent, of which Harris was highly critical, was the United Colors of Benetton advertising campaign. One of Benetton's best-known advertising images depicted the dying AIDS activist David Kirby. Kirby, a white man, is shown as emaciated and powerless on his deathbed. His grieving family surrounds him, connoting Christian overtones of the death of Christ. This black-and-white image, shot by Therese Frare, originally appeared as a piece of photojournalism in *Life* magazine in

November 1990. The photo won a World Press Photo award after its publication.[37] Benetton's creative director, Oliviero Toscani, subsequently repurposed the image (with permission), transforming the black-and-white photo into a colour image for its notorious 1992 advertisement. Media scholar Marco Scalvini argues that Kirby's deathly presentation in a commercial ad was consistent with dominant images of gay men with AIDS being circulated at the time, even by AIDS activists.[38] This observation resonates with Harris's description of the images depicted in AIDS kitsch, as well as Kate Fillion's comments about the deathly male AIDS figures at 1993's Fashion Cares Arcouture and how their depiction as "fashionable" trivialized the seriousness of the epidemic.[39] Communication scholar Marita Sturken contends that while the Benetton ad might have perpetuated "phobic" notions of AIDS as a white man's disease, and of people with AIDS as passive victims, the ad also disrupted notions that people with AIDS were alone and without family or community around them – which could be regarded as a positive development.[40] Historian Paul Rutherford suggests that Benetton's AIDS ad is one of the best-known early examples of cause marketing.[41] But Benetton's ad did not offer links to not-for-profits or to charities associated with the social issue it depicted, facets that generally define contemporary cause marketing. Rather, Benetton's AIDS ad served as a branding tool that facilitated the larger process of commodifying social causes by placing them in the advertising space as part of a marketing and PR strategy.[42]

Unlike in the early years of Fashion Cares, when even saying AIDS out loud was verboten, by the mid-1990s social issues ran a real risk of becoming trivialized as a result of their links to fashion and promotional culture. While M·A·C received mostly accolades from its local fashion and business communities for publicly staking its brand identity on its affiliation with AIDS, others viewed such associations with scepticism and even contempt. Also, people were becoming bored with the AIDS red ribbon, which was often sported by celebrities, and this further trivialized the cause. Journalist Rachel Giese described in *This Magazine* in June 1994 how Canadian shoe retailer Aldo was one target of this type of criticism. Aldo's advertising, which featured a shoe and the AIDS red ribbon with copy reading "Aldo For Life," was misleading; the only money Aldo donated to AIDS organizations was from the sale of red ribbons, not from the sale of its shoes. Furthermore, Giese noted, while fashion shows like Fashion Cares had become one of the "hippest ways" to raise consciousness about and funds for AIDS, that attention could ultimately peter out due to cynicism, scepticism, and fatigue. AIDS risked being co-opted by capitalism and falling "out" of fashion.[43] Fully aware of this situation, and perhaps sensing this public sentiment, the AIDS Committee of Toronto found it necessary to take a clear – and official – anti-commercial stance in its operations and governance, maintaining an emphasis on community, action, and alliances rather than commerce. ACT stated in internal communications in 1994 that the organization "will not participate in cause-related marketing. Exceptions will be made when the sale of AIDS-related items like red ribbon pins [sic]. Cause related marketing being a situation where a product/service is sold and the agency would receive a percentage of the sale price [sic]. The focus of these situations is not the charity but creating an incentive for the consumer to purchase their product/service."[44] ACT's perspective was potentially awkward, since *Marketing Magazine* astutely noted in 1995 that Fashion Cares was "an important promotional vehicle" for M·A·C and the M·A·C AIDS Fund.[45] ACT evidently needed to turn a blind eye to the increasingly promotional nature of Fashion Cares, since the show remained one of its primary sources of funding.

VIVA GLAM's appearance coincided with these debates about corporate philanthropy and commercial motives. In a special edition of *FashionTelevision* devoted to M·A·C VIVA GLAM Fashion Cares Salute to Suburbia in 1995, host Jeanne Beker asked Frank Toskan, "Why is it so important for M·A·C to support something like this [AIDS] on this huge scale?" Toskan replied: "Jeanne, because, absolutely, we care. We've always cared. We want to give back. This industry has been affected tremendously by this disease and we want to do something about it. We want to get on the bandwagon and we hope other people join us. It's very important to us. We've got to make it happen."[46] People in the fashion field acknowledged that M·A·C's support of AIDS *was* positively influencing corporate opinion about AIDS and that this was an encouraging development. Fashion Cares co-chair Brian Gluckstein remembered that

> when you said the word AIDS, corporations had been slamming the door in your face, but it was getting easier ... MAC Cosmetics was the groundbreaker. Here was a well-respected company that was willing to show that not only did they care and donate money, but that they were quite vocal about being involved. They didn't want their name splashed all over it because they wanted the publicity; they wanted to show other companies that they should be proud of participating.[47]

Likewise, Jeanne Beker reflected in her autobiography, *Jeanne Unbottled*, that "in its [Fashion Cares'] first few years, there was a strong stigma associated with the cause and no one wanted anything to do with it. AIDS was a scary thing, and most corporations wanted to steer clear. But eventually, as the disease began to touch all our lives in some way, other corporations joined MAC in supporting Fashion Cares."[48] And in fact, other corporate sponsors did join M·A·C at Fashion Cares in 1995, including Smirnoff Canada and retailers Sears, Winners, and The Gap.[49] Even if corporations had been initially hesitant to get on M·A·C's "bandwagon," consumers were not: by July 1995, the M·A·C AIDS Fund had raised $2.5 million.[50]

Toronto Life observed that other cosmetics companies were now copying M·A·C, not just in products and packaging but also in charitable efforts. That article indicated a note of cynicism: "Lauder's president publicly acknowledges M·A·C's influence. And in October [1994] it [Lauder] launched a charity lipstick for sixteen dollars; six dollars of which went to breast-cancer research. Sound familiar? Revlon has a fund-raiser, too, but as one fashion pundit points out, 'The lipstick is $6.95. One dollar goes to breast cancer – what's a buck?'"[51] The debate about cause marketing often centred on the amount of money a company donated to the cause. A low or indeterminate amount implied that corporate profit was the primary concern and that the scheme was disingenuous. The VIVA GLAM campaign was transparent and could claim a 100 per cent donation model, unlike Aldo's or Kenneth Cole's campaigns, and this assuaged some consumer doubt. Indeed, as Angela N. Eikenberry, a scholar in public administration, notes, there can be immediate benefits and consequences from cause marketing arrangements for brands, not-for-profits, and consumers. For the brand, cause marketing can increase sales and profits, bolster reputation and publicity, improve brand image, expand markets, and boost employee morale; it can also distinguish the brand from others within the category or market. Eikenberry lists misalignment between the brand and cause, wasted resources, consumer scepticism, and a tainted image of the charity as the main consequences of cause marketing gone wrong. Since social causes must be compatible with the brand and add value to it, not-for-profit organizations or causes that are incompatible can end up being ignored. M·A·C mostly seemed to steer clear of these criticisms.[52]

But M·A·C was not completely immune from disapproval about its alliance with a social cause. Cyndee Miller, in her overview of the VIVA GLAM campaign in *Marketing News* in 1995, recounted a debate over M·A·C's motives. She noted that Gabriella Zuckerman of Gabriella Z. Ltd., a New York firm that specialized in the marketing of beauty products, ultimately "dismissed the RuPaul ads as a publicity ploy and said MAC should focus on establishing itself as 'the color authority,' playing up the line's unique and more fashionable hues" – an unusual comment, considering that M·A·C had already established itself as the leader in this area. Wendy Leibmann, president of WSL Marketing in New York, disagreed with Zuckerman: "I see them [M·A·C] as being much like the Body Shop, built up without a lot of advertising, relying primarily on PR. M.A.C has been very good at promoting the brand both through their philanthropic efforts and their use of celebrities who will be inevitably quoted about how very wonderful these products are."[53] However, as Christian Arthur Bain outlined in the *Advocate* in October 1995, some industry observers believed that VIVA GLAM was primarily a branding and marketing strategy, designed to augment the "halo effect" surrounding the M·A·C brand and to sell more M·A·C products along the way. He quoted *Vanity Fair* beauty director Patricia Foster, who clearly identified VIVA GLAM as "cause marketing," although she ultimately approved of the brand/cause fit: "Freedom and inclusion are what M·A·C emanates, and the message comes through with RuPaul's selection." Amy Astley, fashion editor at *Vogue*, also supported M·A·C: "I don't see how anyone who pays attention to the ads and to the company can fail to see how public-spirited they are, how generous M·A·C is."[54] This debate, as captured by Bain's piece in the *Advocate* in 1995, suggests that the VIVA GLAM campaign actually reinforced rather than undermined M·A·C's reputation as a socially conscious professional brand.

The Franks' authority as social advocates was buttressed by the fashion capital they and M·A·C had acquired over the preceding ten years and allowed M·A·C to generally avoid accusations of insincerity. Indeed, the *Advocate* gave M·A·C and the M·A·C AIDS Fund international exposure and a ringing endorsement in the article: "The man behind M.A.C. is pushing more than his latest shade of lipstick: try AIDS awareness, human rights, and RuPaul." Toskan explained that M·A·C's message was not that women should emulate RuPaul: "RuPaul's not here to sell product." Rather, he said, "the message is that people should be themselves." The auxiliary benefits to M·A·C's reputation and brand value were largely, and perhaps conveniently, left out of the discussion.

Corporate Involvement

Toskan continued to promote M·A·C's brand values when Canadian singer k.d. lang became the second VIVA GLAM spokesperson, as announced at a press conference following her performance at Toronto's O'Keefe Centre on 19 March 1996.[55] lang's new appointment was publicized again during New York fashion week in April, which Toskan used as an opportunity to reiterate M·A·C's philosophy:

> We're trying to break that myth of beauty ... With RuPaul, of course, he was pretty, so it showed what makeup could do, but the point wasn't necessarily to push product. I wanted to make sure the goal wasn't confused: it's about selling the awareness, the consciousness, the concern that we have, the whole philosophy of the company. MAC does many things – it's gone beyond being just about a product. So k.d., I think, is a very good choice.[56]

With this second spokesperson came a second VIVA GLAM ad, showcasing a new colour, VIVA GLAM II, a soft, muted mauve-pink colour that Toskan created especially for lang (PLATE 22). Toskan made it clear that the overarching commodity "for sale" was M·A·C's brand culture of acceptance, inclusivity, individuality, and, now, AIDS awareness.

However, Toskan still faced sceptics, especially regarding the Lauder deal. Jim Hicks, publisher of the Canadian cosmetics trade publication *Cosmetics*, had outright predicted in 1996 that M·A·C's cachet and clout would remain intact for only another few years under Lauder's oversight. After 1999, if or when Lauder completed its purchase, M·A·C's aura would disappear, Hicks contended.[57] While the tension between creativity and commerce was less fixed than it first appeared, critics like Hicks seemed to feel that M·A·C now presented a contradiction.

In 1996, at M·A·C VIVA GLAM Fashion Cares Future Perfect, Toskan expressed his altruism in a new way by extrapolating it to M·A·C's corporate identity and organizational structure. At the event, held on 11 May at the Moss Park Armoury, Toskan told Jeanne Beker, "we've certainly benefited as a corporation from being involved and I hope that other corporations look to, perhaps, to us as an example, and also get involved, because I think it takes the framework of an organization to bring all that energy and effort together to really make a difference."[58] In an interview with Bernadette Morra for the *Toronto Star* the following week, on 16 May, he asserted that the VIVA GLAM campaign "has brought our customers together, our staff together, and allows us to feel very good ... It has truly been a large part of our success because people come to us not just to buy a lipstick. They want to be involved with people who care."[59] Indeed, instead of being dismissive of corporate philanthropy, Toskan emphasized how M·A·C's corporate structure – one that now included Lauder – actually facilitated M·A·C's efforts around AIDS fundraising. For Toskan, corporate organization was integral to philanthropic success and did not jeopardize M·A·C's other brand values; indeed, it enhanced them.

Fashion Cares was now Canada's largest AIDS fundraiser, and 1996 marked the event's ten-year anniversary. There was a celebratory spirit; even so, the call went out to keep working until AIDS was just a "sad memory." In stark contrast to Fashion Blooms in 1988, this year's program indicated there was now a great deal of political support for the event. A message in the program from Toronto mayor Barbara Hall stated that "Fashion Cares is one of the most highly regarded affairs of its kind in the world and the largest AIDS fundraising event benefiting a single organization in Canada. It brings together dedicated people from all areas of Toronto's fashion, design, business and creative communities." There were similar messages in the program from Lieutenant-Governor of Ontario Henry N.R. Jackman, Councillor Alan Tonks, the chairman of Metropolitan City Council, and Ontario Premier Mike Harris. The chair of the ACT board of directors, Ron Rosenes, reminded attendees what was at stake: Fashion Cares secured the financial future of ACT. M·A·C's sponsorship amounted to $100,000 that year.[60] A video *in memoriam* called "Friends Remembered" featuring some of the key figures in the Toronto fashion industry who had died of complications from AIDS marked that year's event. Set to the tune of the hit song "Missing" by Everything But The Girl, the short video featured Andre Lafreniere, wig and hair stylist; Gregory Shaw Bennet, display and visual artist; Reg "Bang" Rose, display artist and Fashion Cares participant; Gary Brodeur, hair stylist; Neville Ying, display artist; Charles Christopher, hair and make-up artist; Richard Hayter, floral designer; Pier Tetro, hair and make-up artist; and Duncan Cowan, model booker. While this was a very subjective and edited list, it represented one of the few actual tallies of those in the Toronto fashion field who had died. Despite this, Fashion Cares remained fun and campy; RuPaul opened the show covering the Aerosmith song "Dude Looks Like a Lady."[61]

Toskan's practices for maintaining M·A·C's aura were discernible at another key public moment. In October 1996, M·A·C's first store in Paris, on the rue des Saints-Pères, opened. RuPaul wore a black velvet dress and k.d. lang wore a Prada suit. Frances Hathaway created the make-up looks for both spokespersons. The five-foot two-inch Hathaway remembers having to stand on a box to reach RuPaul properly. Toskan brought three employees from one of M·A·C's Quebec retail counters to illustrate the M·A·C "look" and train the local French staff in M·A·C's practices.[62] In an interview, Toskan noted that opening a store in Paris was an obvious next step in M·A·C's expansion: "We've been sought-after by makeup artists internationally and Paris is the centre of fashion" – a reminder to everyone that M·A·C was, first and foremost, a fashion-based brand. Indeed, in 1996, M·A·C was used backstage at the shows during New York fashion week for the first time, further enhancing M·A·C's fashion capital. At the same time, Toskan reiterated M·A·C's philanthropic platform: "It's not about makeup. It's about entertainment, culture and taking a stand ... kd and RuPaul give us a platform to talk about our company. They get us so much attention that we can then promote our corporate culture." For Toskan, aligning philanthropy with corporate goals was not an antithetical or contradictory move; indeed, it produced clear, tangible results: by the end of 1996, the M·A·C AIDS Fund had raised $5.5 million, more than double the previous year's amount.[63]

Certainly, as Phillip Ing, and those who were with M·A·C from its early days, testified, M·A·C's philanthropy had a "heart" that distinguished it from other corporate initiatives:

> It came from a pure place. Frank and Frank really were concerned about that disease. They really wanted to do something about it. Yes, they've got a brand. They wanted to do something that they could control. The whole idea that VIVA GLAM was going to be sold with 100 per cent of the proceeds going to AIDS research was an enormous idea. To this day, I don't know how many people do 100 per cent proceeds. A lot of the stores will never do it again.[64]

It is also quite probable that introducing RuPaul and presenting a beauty model so far outside advertising convention was the best strategy M·A·C could have deployed for maintaining its brand values of diversity, creativity, and acceptance and for deflecting consumer scepticism. The initial risks in using RuPaul for the ads ultimately appeared to work in M·A·C's favour. In 1995, Toskan shrugged off the idea of any threat to the brand:

> A lot of people said, "Don't do it, you'll turn customers off." But we stood our ground. And initially some of the retailers didn't like it. But if they didn't like it, too bad, we won't be there. I don't care. That's what

PLATE 1 A self-portrait of a young Frank Toskan, early 1980s. Frank Toskan personal collection.

PLATE 2 Frank Angelo, photographed by Frank Toskan, mid-1970s. Frank Toskan personal collection.

PLATE 3 The Make-up Art Centre counter in Simpsons, Queen Street, Toronto, upstairs and away from the main floor cosmetics department, early 1980s. The early prototypes of M·A·C packaging and visual presentation are visible, alongside The Hairdresser's Choice products and the Il-Makiage line. Note the chairs that allowed customers to sit down for consultations and make-up instruction. Image courtesy of M·A·C Cosmetics. Frank Toskan personal collection.

PLATE 4 The Haircutting Place in Simpsons, Queen Street, Toronto, often hosted special events with celebrity guests in the early 1980s. The Make-up Art Centre counter was frequently swarmed by fans. Image courtesy of M·A·C Cosmetics. Frank Toskan personal collection.

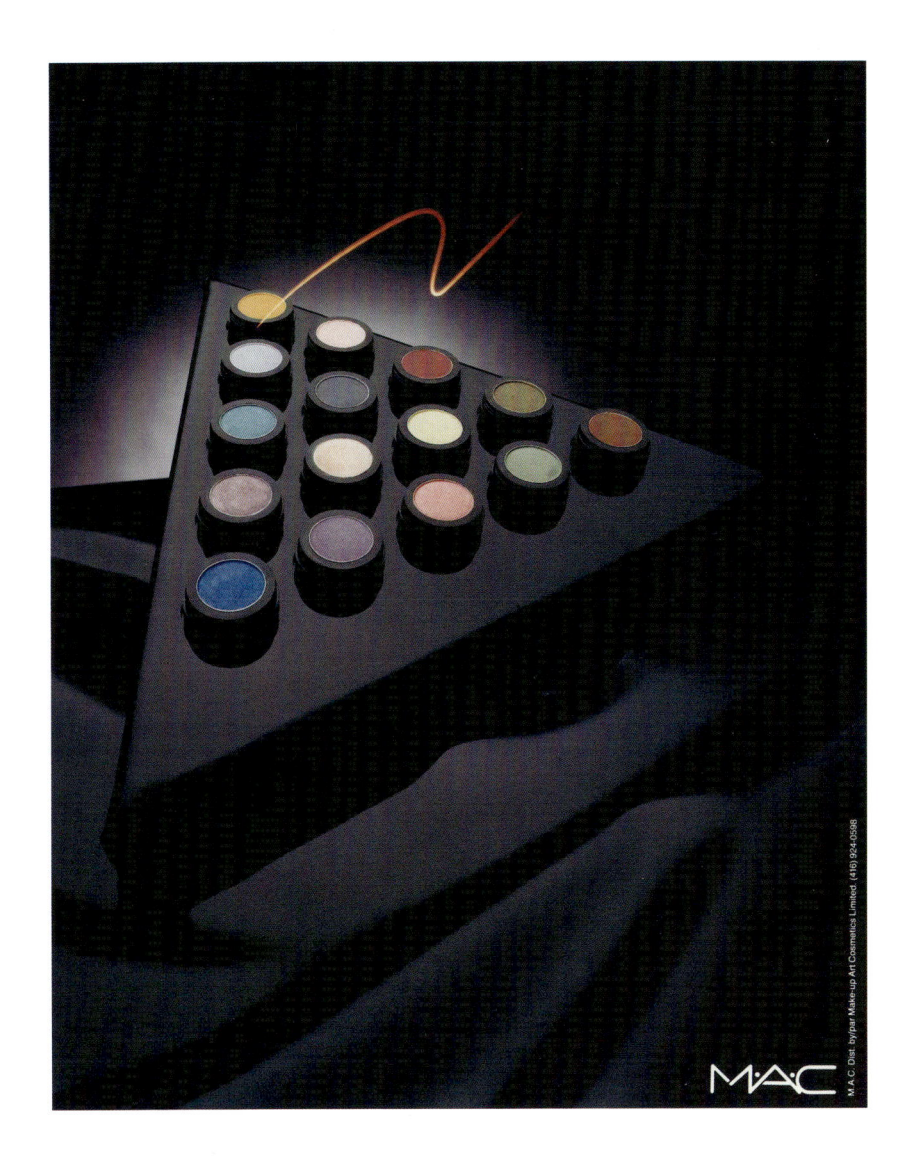

PLATE 5 M·A·C's products were individually packaged and displayed on-counter on plexiglass units that allowed customers to easily experiment with the colours, seen here in this early-1980s image. Image courtesy of M·A·C Cosmetics. Frank Toskan personal collection.

PLATE 6 Customers left the M·A·C counter in the mid-1980s with instructions for how to use their new cosmetics, sometimes recorded on a face chart such as this one illustrated by Donald Robertson (@drawbertson). Image courtesy of M·A·C Cosmetics. Frank Toskan personal collection.

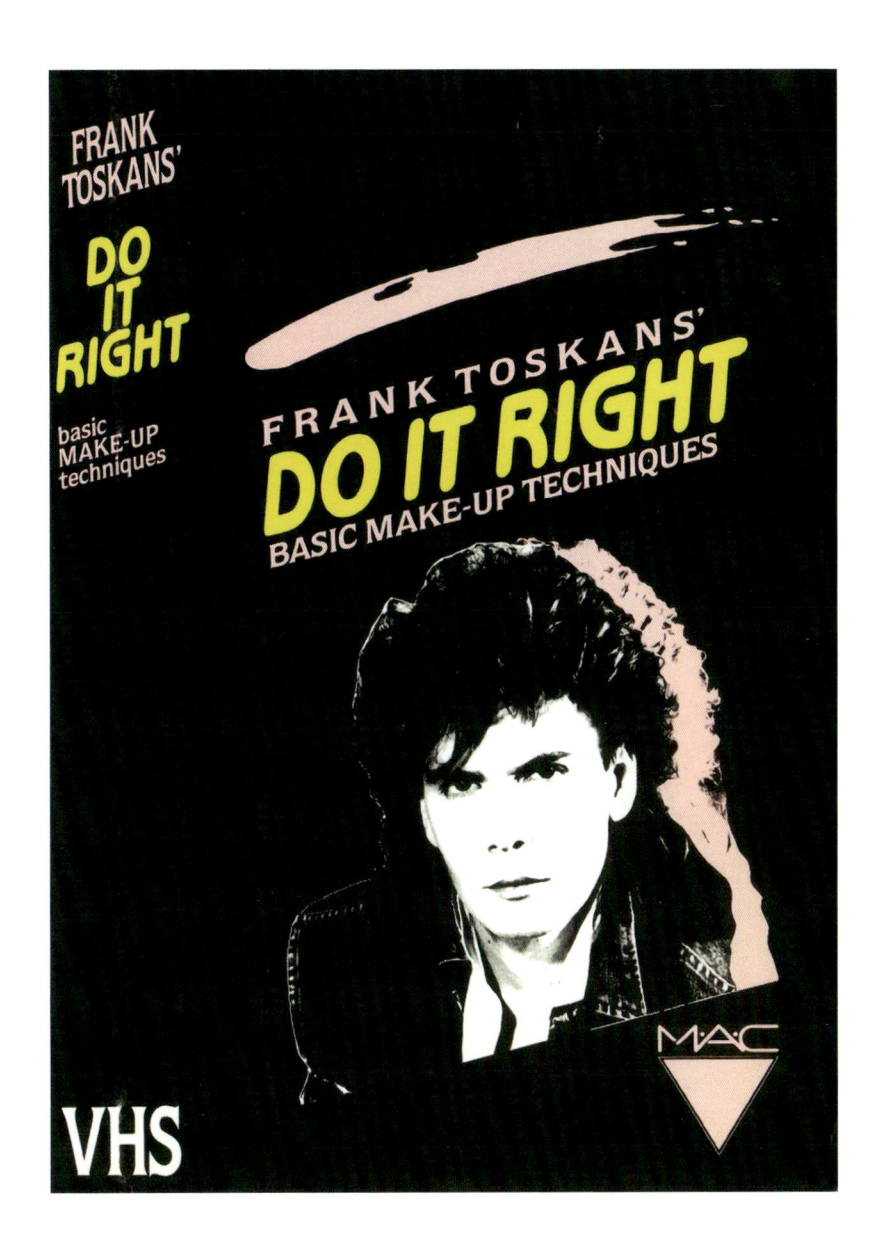

PLATE 7 The front sleeve of one of the instructional VHS videocassettes, mid-1980s, that Frank Toskan created and distributed to customers at the M·A·C counter and later at special events such as the Festival of Canadian Fashion. Image courtesy of M·A·C Cosmetics. Frank Toskan personal collection.

PLATE 8 An advertisement for make-up artist and M·A·C ambassador Frances Hathaway promoting her skills and M·A·C products (and ethos) in Toronto, mid-1980s, photographed by Walter Chin. Image courtesy of M·A·C Cosmetics. Frances Hathaway personal collection.

PLATE 9 An androgynous face, mid-1980s, characterized M·A·C as a brand that represented "all ages, all races, all sexes." Artwork by Donald Robertson (@drawbertson). Image courtesy of M·A·C Cosmetics. Frank Toskan personal collection.

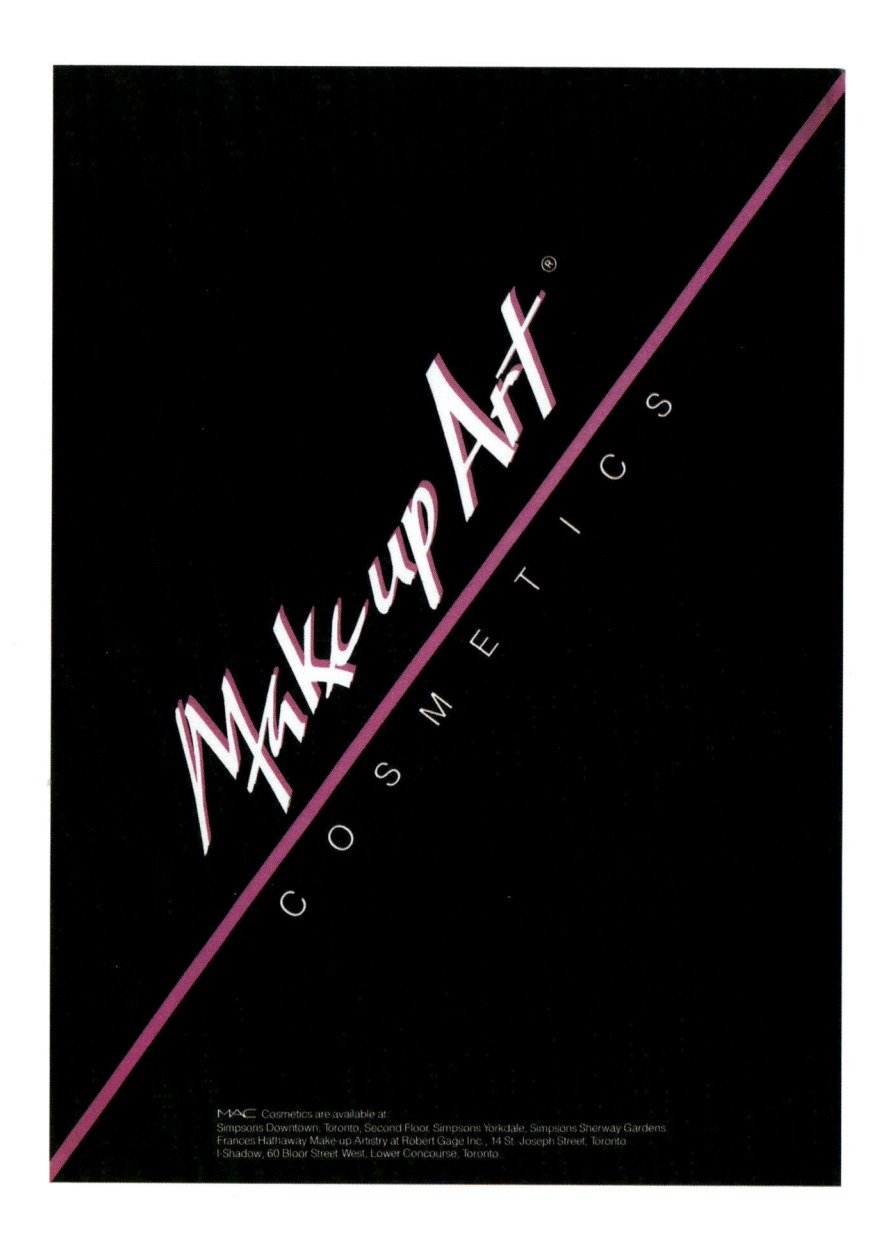

PLATE 10 Before the well-known logo was in use, M·A·C's visual identity was quite different in the early to mid-1980s. Image courtesy of M·A·C Cosmetics. Frank Toskan personal collection.

PLATE 11 Donald Robertson's illustrations were ubiquitous in fashion communications in Toronto in the 1980s, as featured here on the front cover of the 1987 Festival of Canadian Fashion program. Illustration by Donald Robertson (@drawbertson). Image courtesy of M·A·C Cosmetics. Frank Toskan personal collection.

PLATE 12 The Festival of Canadian Fashion held yearly in Toronto was an important venue for showcasing M·A·C's products and make-up artists. This story about M·A·C inside the 1987 program also featured this illustration of Frank Toskan by Donald Robertson (@drawbertson). Image courtesy of M·A·C Cosmetics. Frank Toskan personal collection.

PLATE 13 "Cruelty free beauty" postcard displayed at the M·A·C counter, early 1990s, illustrated by Donald Robertson (@drawbertson). Image courtesy of M·A·C Cosmetics. Frank Toskan personal collection.

Frank Toskan of MAC would like you to help him put an end to product testing on animals. MAC has never and will never test cosmetics on animals.

Which is why **Frank Toskan** has designed a series of T-shirts to promote CRUELTY FREE BEAUTY. MAC will donate all proceeds from the sale of these T-shirts to the search for alternative testing methods.

"Please help us with this worthwhile cause."

Thank You
Frank Toskan

MAC IS A REGISTERED TRADEMARK OF MAKE-UP ART COSMETICS LIMITED, TORONTO, ONTARIO M5A 2L2
(416) 924-0598. PRINTED IN CANADA ON RECYCLED FIBRE.

PLATE 14 M·A·C began communicating more broadly about its practices, including not testing cosmetics on animals and using ethical hairs for its brushes, described on the back of the "Cruelty free beauty" postcard. Image courtesy of M·A·C Cosmetics. Frank Toskan personal collection.

PLATE 15 M·A·C's practices of waste reduction, ethical production, and encouraging customer recycling became formalized in the Back 2 M·A·C program, seen in this postcard available at the M·A·C counter, late 1980s. Illustration by Donald Robertson (@drawbertson). Image courtesy of M·A·C Cosmetics. Frank Toskan personal collection.

BACK TO M·A·C

Because we share your concern about our environment, when you have finished using any plastic-packaged cosmetic item purchased from us, please bring the container **BACK TO M.A.C.**

We cannot reuse these containers for our products, but we can make sure that the material is recycled.

To give you credit for your good deed, each recycled container is worth one **BACK TO M.A.C.** sticker for this card. When you have accumulated six stickers, please select one lipstick as our gratis gift to you.

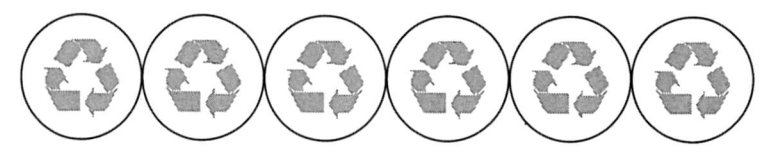

M.A.C. CRUELTY FREE BEAUTY

Proceeds from **BACK TO M.A.C.** T-Shirts and accessories will be donated in aid of the Environment.
• Offer valid at participating **M.A.C.** stores only

M·A·C IS A REGISTERED TRADEMARK OF MAKE-UP ART COSMETICS LIMITED, TORONTO, ONTARIO M5A 2L2. (416) 924-0598. PRINTED IN CANADA ON RECYCLED PAPER.

PLATE 16 Customers got their Back 2 M·A·C postcard stamped for each empty container returned to the counter; customers would receive a free lipstick after returning six empty containers. Image courtesy of M·A·C Cosmetics. Frank Toskan personal collection.

PLATE 17 Kim Myers-Robertson, pictured here c. 1991, was the manager of M·A·C's first American stand-alone store at the corner of Christopher and Gay streets in New York's Greenwich Village. The store's visual design, a real source of pride for Frank Toskan, included the mirror collage on the wall and ceiling that Toskan created with Donald Robertson. Frank Toskan personal collection.

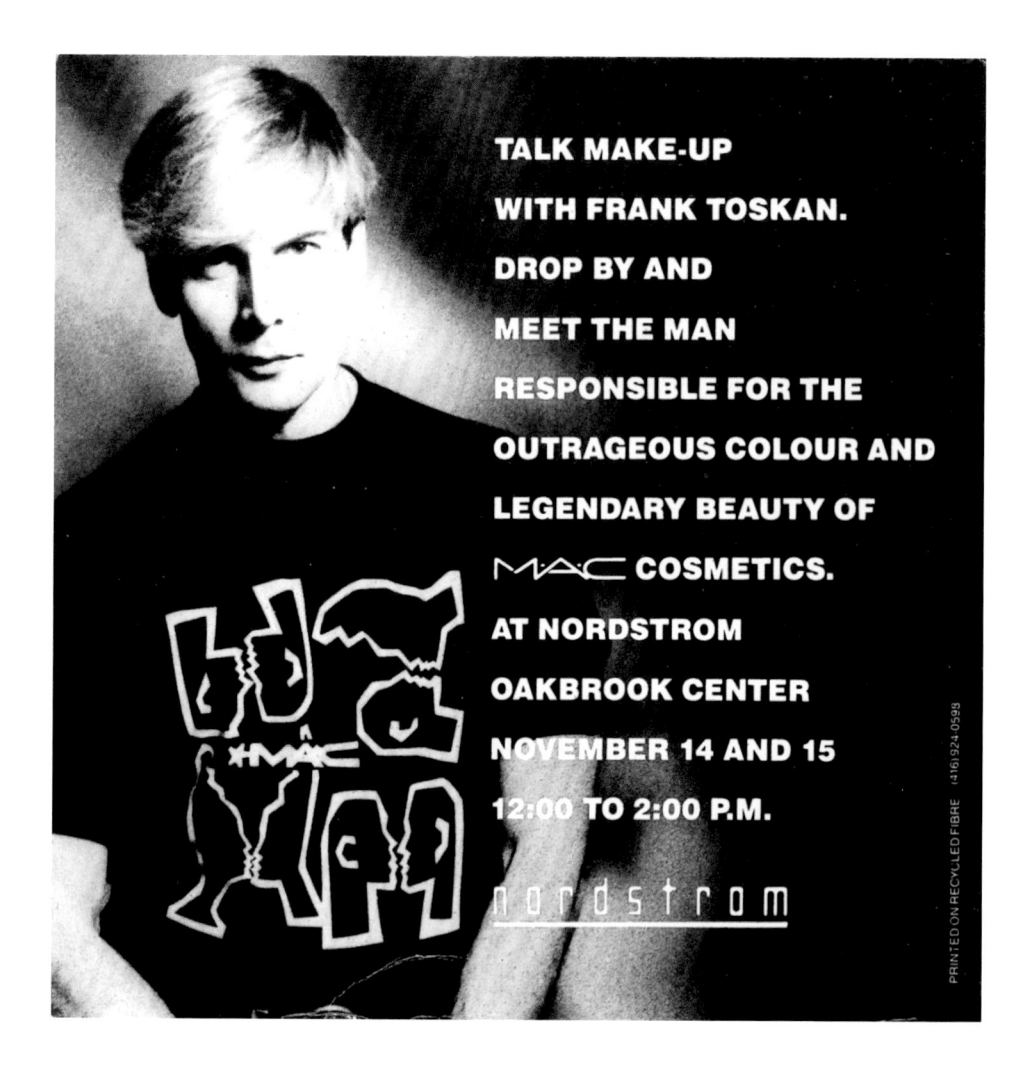

PLATE 18 This postcard, c. 1991, promoted an event for customers to meet Frank Toskan at Nordstrom in the United States. Toskan is wearing the "make up, make out, play safe" T-shirt, signalling how M·A·C was more conspicuously promoting its corporate ethos. T-shirt illustration by Donald Robertson (@drawbertson). Photographed by Floria Sigismondi. Image courtesy of M·A·C Cosmetics. Frank Toskan personal collection.

PLATE 19 The "Put your money where your mouth is" postcard introduced the first VIVA GLAM lipstick in 1992 and its purpose at the M·A·C counter. Interestingly, a production error created a blue lipstick in the image that Toskan ultimately decided to keep. Illustration by Donald Robertson (@drawbertson). Image courtesy of M·A·C Cosmetics. Frank Toskan personal collection.

The crisis is not over!

AIDS continues to rob us of precious friends, lovers and family.

I am proud to introduce M.A.C. VIVA GLAM Lipstick, one of the best matte lip colours I've ever created, and my way of raising millions of dollars to fight AIDS.

Every cent made from the sale of VIVA GLAM will be donated to fund AIDS education, support and prevention.

Please buy, wear and enjoy M.A.C. VIVA GLAM Lipstick, while you help raise AIDS awareness and much needed money.

Thank you. Play Safer.

Frank Toskan

ACTUAL VIVA GLAM COLOUR

M.A.C. location information and phone orders call 1-800-387-6707.

Proceeds to DIFFA, the Canadian AIDS Society and various local AIDS support groups.

M·A·C IS A REGISTERED TRADEMARK OF MAKE-UP ART COSMETICS LIMITED, TORONTO, ONTARIO M5A 2L2. (416) 924-0598. PRINTED IN CANADA ON RECYCLED FIBRE.

PLATE 20 The back of the "Put your money where your mouth is" postcard had a personal message from Frank Toskan to customers, as well as a swatch of the "Actual VIVA GLAM colour." Note Toskan's handwritten instructions to graphic designer Tom Burton to change the size of the font for the next print run of the postcard. Image courtesy of M·A·C Cosmetics. Frank Toskan personal collection.

Every cent of the retail selling price of M·A·C VIVA GLAM lipstick is donated to the fight against AIDS.

PLATE 21 RuPaul for M·A·C VIVA GLAM and the M·A·C AIDS Fund, 1995. This was M·A·C's first ad, photographed by Albert Sanchez and art directed by Frank Toskan and Donald Robertson (@drawbertson). Image courtesy of M·A·C Cosmetics.

PLATE 22 k.d. lang for M·A·C VIVA GLAM II and the M·A·C AIDS Fund, 1997. Frank Toskan created a new lipstick shade specifically for the Canadian singer, who was photographed by David LaChapelle (@david_lachapelle). Image courtesy of M·A·C Cosmetics.

PLATE 23 RuPaul, k.d. lang, and Frank Toskan for M·A·C VIVA GLAM and the M·A·C AIDS Fund, 1997. Toskan generally stayed away from the limelight whenever possible but he enjoyed participating in this promotional postcard, photographed by David LaChapelle (@david_lachapelle). Image courtesy of M·A·C Cosmetics.

Every cent of the
retail selling price of
M·A·C VIVA GLAM
Lipstick
is donated to the fight against
AIDS.
Thanks to our customers and staff, over
5.5 millon dollars has been raised so far.

M·A·C IS A REGISTERED TRADEMARK OF MAKE-UP ART COSMETICS.
PRINTED IN CANADA ON RECYCLED PAPER.

80115-10/96

PLATE 24 Frank Toskan's personal message of thanks for supporting VIVA GLAM and the M·A·C AIDS Fund appeared on the back of the 1997 postcard. Image courtesy of M·A·C Cosmetics.

we stand for ... As a small company, there's more of an opportunity to change things and make more of a statement. We don't have to be so concerned about the masses.[65]

Toskan's personal articulation of M·A·C's small-scale production ethic, despite the Lauder partnership, and his sincere commitment to HIV/AIDS awareness and fundraising likely rendered M·A·C's AIDS advocacy far more believable in the eyes of critics and consumers.

This is not to say there was no pushback. When Valerie MacKenzie began working at M·A·C in 1992, there were three phone lines, often answered by Frank Angelo himself. In 1994, around the time that VIVA GLAM was launched, a 1-800 number was set up to begin properly directing customer service issues and customer orders. One day, there were three hundred calls, and they kept coming. Most were inquiries about purchasing VIVA GLAM, for it could also be purchased over the phone directly from M·A·C's head office on Carlton Street. People ordered over the phone for many reasons; sometimes it had to do with the local unavailability of M·A·C, but often it was because customers were more comfortable with the anonymity the phone offered. Some male customers told MacKenzie they were cross-dressers; other customers were transwomen who preferred to order by phone and were relieved that they could to do so without judgment or discrimination. But MacKenzie did receive numerous complaints about the RuPaul ad, and specifically about the "M" part of the visual. She estimates that she received well over a hundred complaints. Her practice was to acknowledge the customer's feelings and listen to the complaint – the essence of good customer service. Like the artists at the counter, MacKenzie would then attempt to educate the customer about AIDS and what the VIVA GLAM initiative was all about, explaining how M·A·C's position was to help communities affected by AIDS. The goal was to decrease the stigma surrounding AIDS and bring visibility to those who needed this support, she told them. MacKenzie says that RuPaul's shock value was definitely a key factor in attracting attention to M·A·C but was ultimately less important to the brand: VIVA GLAM "was more to get the message out there; of individuality and acceptance.

It really, really was that message: let's just help each other, no matter what our views or what our beliefs are." Sometimes she was successful, and sometimes she was not.

One particularly angry phone call stands out for MacKenzie, more than two decades later. After she went through her usual service routine, the customer asked to speak to the owner of M·A·C. While not an owner, but rather a managing partner, Julie Toskan-Casale was nearby and in a position to take the call, and so MacKenzie passed the customer over to her. The customer was still not satisfied, and again asked to speak to the owner. Since Frank Toskan just happened to be in the office at that moment, MacKenzie put him on the line. Toskan picked up the phone and quietly and intently listened to the woman's complaint. When she was finished, he simply said, "Well, you can just fuck off and buy another brand." Toskan said to MacKenzie, "I don't want a customer like that, who feels that way about the gay community." MacKenzie remembers, as many M·A·C employees do, that Toskan and Angelo were completely comfortable about the prospect of losing business, whether from one individual customer or an entire department store, over issues they believed in. Toskan was not afraid to stand up to these people.[66] Other companies would apologize for offending a customer, but not the Franks.

The fashion field occupies an intermediary position between art and commerce, a characteristic that helps mitigate this sharp distinction between these seemingly distinct poles, and Toskan continued his creative practices in several important ways that alleviated some of the inconsistencies the Lauder deal initially presented. First, Toskan maintained the "art" in "Make-up Art Cosmetics" by continually emphasizing his intention to create an artistic product that had its origins in fashion, not commerce, even though M·A·C was, of course, well on the way to becoming a globally successful commercial enterprise. Toskan also remained firm about M·A·C's creative objectives and reaffirmed the brand's cultural authority in this regard within the field: "We're not sitting at a boardroom table and evaluating what colors are hot. We know what's hot because we're out on the photo shoot."[67] More importantly, the Franks' altruistic, not marketing, goals were publicly and repeatedly attached to the M·A·C brand, thus emphasizing the non-commercial ethos at the centre of M·A·C's corporate philanthropy. These goals or values were evident in the ways that Toskan promoted AIDS advocacy with VIVA GLAM, which were, of course, historically related to M·A·C's founding values and practices of diversity, acceptance, and inclusivity and to the creative forms of activism intrinsic to the Toronto fashion scene. These actions, over time, had built and sustained a public trustworthiness, and it was this belief in the brand that largely protected M·A·C from accusations that it had "sold out" with the Lauder deal.

Moving On

On 12 January 1997, the M·A·C family suffered a huge shock: Frank Angelo passed away unexpectedly, at the age of forty-nine, due to complications from routine surgery in a Miami hospital. He had suffered a heart attack during the procedure. Rumours quickly circulated that Angelo had been undergoing cosmetic surgery, but this was denied. At times this gossip overshadowed the tributes to Angelo's life. There was no mention in any of Angelo's obituaries of Toskan or his M·A·C family – only of his mother, Cecilia Notarangelo, sister, Carmen Kent, both of Montreal, and brother, Nick Notarangelo of Toronto.[68] Angelo had never come out as gay, and his family thought everything at M·A·C belonged to him. They entered the Franks' house and took Angelo's possessions, and Toskan, respecting the family, stepped back and let them do what they wanted. To complicate matters even more, Angelo had nothing in place in terms of a will, so even though the Franks had been together for twenty-five years, Toskan had no input into the management of Angelo's financial matters or personal effects after his death. The family decided that Frank Angelo would be cremated and buried in Montreal. Toskan realized then how important it was for same-sex couples to be clear about the things they wanted to happen.

Later that year, in September, a devastating article about M·A·C appeared in *Elm Street*, a new Toronto magazine marketed to women. For this piece, which piled more hurt on the grieving

M·A·C family, author Robert Collison had interviewed Frank Toskan, and now he revealed some surprising and even salacious personal details about the Franks' intimate life in the final years of their relationship. Perhaps in an effort to create some hype around this new magazine, especially for the all-important September issue, the author made his account tabloid-worthy. The article was one of the very few negative media treatments of "Canada's M.A.C.nificent make-up company" – deliberately negative, it would seem – and it only added to the pain and sadness for a family that was still deep in mourning.[69] Furthermore, the article noted how Frank Toskan had courted more rare personal controversy in the spring of 1997. The previous December, Toskan had opened a clothing shop called Koolhaus in the exclusive Holt Renfrew Centre on Bloor Street in Toronto. The boutique showcased fine art by Canadian artists in a revolving gallery exhibition but seemingly did not sell very much in the way of Canadian fashion designers.[70] In March, the doors were shut. A number of creditors, still owed money and tired of not having had their bills paid by Koolhaus, came up with a unique way of pressuring Toskan and Julie Toskan-Casale to settle accounts: six creditors promised to donate half of their outstanding bills to the upcoming Fashion Cares – the combined amount would have totalled more than $18,000. Julie Toskan-Casale was deeply unimpressed, and it did not happen.[71]

Despite Angelo's death, M·A·C's business showed no signs of slowing down. By March 1997, there were rumours that Lauder was preparing for the second stage of its M·A·C purchase. Gayle MacDonald, covering the story in the *Globe and Mail*, reported that Lauder was ready to buy another 19 per cent, which it subsequently did, bringing Lauder's total stake in M·A·C to 70 per cent. M·A·C's business was now vast: in 1996, retail sales had been $250 million, and it employed two thousand people. Exports to the United States, Britain, France, Singapore, and Hong Kong accounted for 75 per cent of M·A·C's revenue; the Canadian market was relatively small, though still important.[72] VIVA GLAM II, the new colour that had been created especially for k.d. lang, had raised $1 million in its first seven weeks, bringing the cumulative total raised for the M·A·C AIDS Fund to $6 million in 1997.[73] M·A·C's sales were expected to reach a staggering $380 million in 1997.[74]

M·A·C VIVA GLAM Fashion Cares Photo Ball in 1997 was dedicated to Frank Angelo.[75] RuPaul offered a humorous but touching tribute, best appreciated in full:

> Now, I want to talk a little bit about Frank Angelo. Now, we lost Frank in January of this year, and his presence is really missed at this one. I want to tell you a little bit about Frank. I don't know how many of you guys know this guy, but he was a real dreamer, a real maverick; the kind of person who – if you wanted something he'd get it for you. He was my M·A·C daddy, honey. Now M·A·C – Frank Angelo, of course, was Italian, so when he laughed, he laughed out loud, and when he cried, he cried hard. And I just want to say, he's missed but his spirit lives on here at this event. It's events like this, his spirit – I mean, it's about the perpetuation of life and of the dreamer. I think all of you are dreamers here. You're all lovers of life. I'd like everybody right now to think about Frank Angelo for a minute as we say "love" out loud. Everybody say, "love." Everybody say, "love!" And that's for Frank Angelo.[76]

In his own speech, Frank Toskan reiterated the mutual commitment he and Angelo had made personally and professionally to AIDS awareness and fundraising:

> When M·A·C first became involved with Fashion Cares back in 1986 we were aware that it was in support of a worthwhile and moving cause. We also saw it as our responsibility to give back to a community and people that had inspired and supported us. In the past few years, many other corporate sponsors have also come forward and committed to this grand and most generous event. And tonight, with your help, we will probably raise more than half a million dollars for AIDS – and I couldn't be more proud. Our customers, our staff, and our retail partners have contributed so much. And M·A·C continues to be so enriched by its involvement here. It has brought us together with a common purpose and has allowed us to affirm our company values. For all of these reasons, M·A·C will remain committed.

Toskan continued with his own tribute to Angelo:

> Twenty-five years ago, I was very fortunate to have met a wonderful and extraordinary person, Frank Angelo, who became my friend and partner and who wouldn't have missed this show tonight for anything, so he's here with us tonight. Eleven years ago, we started M·A·C. We both shared a commitment to the fight against AIDS. We also inspired each other to become part of, and supporters of, this event. Frank unfortunately passed away in January of a sudden heart attack. But the strong intention he and I had for supporting this event will live on in our entire M·A·C family.[77]

Frank Toskan's demeanour the following year at M·A·C VIVA GLAM Fashion Cares Beautiful World was subdued, and given the events going on behind the scenes, it is not difficult to surmise why. As he spoke, Toskan was identified in *FashionTelevision*'s credits as M·A·C's "Creative Director," after years of being distinguished as M·A·C's "Co-founder." When asked by Sook-Yin Lee, host of a one-hour *MuchMusic* broadcast of the show, about M·A·C's involvement with Fashion Cares, Toskan again emphasized his intentions regarding the brand's association with AIDS: "We really care. We care about our community here and in our involvement, and it certainly, as a company, has brought a lot back to us, a lot of goodwill, and as a company it brings us together and our people with a common goal so we can enjoy other things, other than just selling make-up. We can enjoy doing events like this."[78] Toskan's emotional distance from M·A·C at Fashion Cares in 1998 was justified: just three months earlier, in February 1998, Estée Lauder had exercised its option to buy the remaining shares of M·A·C for $60 million from Frank Toskan and managing partners Julie Toskan-Casale and Victor Casale.

The event program featured an unusual set of VIVA GLAM "ads." Following the k.d. lang VIVA GLAM II ad and a short biography of the singer, the first image comprised a full-page illustration of the first VIVA GLAM lipstick in deep red tones, with this message: "M·A·C VIVA GLAM / Every cent raised from the selling price of VIVA GLAM and VIVA GLAM II helps bring love and healing to those in your community living with HIV and AIDS." The second full-page image, opposite the first, showed another illustration, this time of VIVA GLAM II. It read, "M·A·C VIVA GLAM II / By buying VIVA GLAM lipsticks, you have helped raise over 13 million dollars so far, which M·A·C gives to AIDS organizations worldwide, to support their ongoing commitment and efforts. / Thank you. F. Toskan," and was followed by Toskan's signature, consistent with the way he had signed his name to various M·A·C communications since the beginning. Like the signatures on the original Fashion Cares T-shirt, Toskan's marked the sign of the creator. As Pierre Bourdieu states, "The creator's signature is a mark that changes not the material nature but the social nature of the object. But this mark is a proper name – and at once the problem of succession arises, because you can only inherit common names or common functions, but not proper names."[79] Denoted by the authentic sign of the artist, Frank Toskan finally released M·A·C Cosmetics in full to Estée Lauder, and its succession was complete.

CHAPTER 6

Dragging Theory into Practice

The two VIVA GLAM campaigns featuring RuPaul and k.d. lang are classic advertising campaigns as much for their function as for being M·A·C's first and (at the time) only advertisements, as well as for the ways they can now be seen as having encapsulated and represented M·A·C's philanthropic practices. In this final chapter, a closer look at the VIVA GLAM campaigns will further dispel accusations that M·A·C had "sold out." These ads did not appear out of thin air; rather, they were the culmination of more than a decade of developing a corporate ethos that nurtured creativity, art, fashion, and acceptance of difference, and they represented a proud local (and later Canadian) identity as well as a tradition of AIDS fundraising existing deep within organizational practices. If, for some, the VIVA GLAM ads seemed to come out of left field, for M·A·C they made perfect sense. Certainly, M·A·C's artistic intersection with the drag scene and queer culture had been apparent in its business operations for years, going as far back as Toskan's photo shoots with drag queens at his laundromat in the early 1980s. The store's retail counters had always drawn drag queens and gender-fluid make-up artists. Since the drag queens had been among M·A·C's first customers, they had accepted the VIVA GLAM campaign and imbued it with energy from the start. And M·A·C and RuPaul had already worked together, back when RuPaul and Lady Bunny were M·A·C's official store greeters in New York. Even at that time, Toskan had remarked, "[o]ur approach is to say that we are for all sexes, all races, all ages ... I would be happy to use an image of a man in make-up; 10 years ago, we tried to get [British pop singer] Boy George."[1] As fashion journalist David Livingstone astutely noted in his column in the *Globe and Mail* on 18 May 1995, M·A·C's RuPaul ad was "dragging theory into practice" in a number of significant and relevant ways.[2]

Setting aside the obvious assessment that he wore make-up to great effect, thus demonstrating the creative and transformative practices of drag culture, RuPaul was a natural brand spokesperson for VIVA GLAM and chairperson for the M·A·C AIDS Fund because he and M·A·C promoted the same values of acceptance, diversity, and glamour. RuPaul had emerged from a field of cultural production even smaller than fashion: drag. Rising from the New York drag and club scenes of the 1980s, where he had been a star for years, RuPaul represented the authentic and "real" underground drag performers, including his friend Lady Bunny. His 1992 hit song, "Supermodel (You Better Work)," came straight from the street, gaining popularity within the New York dance club scene and support from dance specialty shops, DJs, and the drag community, and hitting the *Billboard* charts in 1992 even though mainstream music retailers were reluctant to display and promote the single in-store.[3] "Supermodel (You Better Work)" was RuPaul's send-up of the fashion industry, even while he unabashedly expressed his admiration for it. RuPaul referenced fashion's "supermodels," a new term for the models who had attained such unprecedented celebrity status in the 1990s that first names were enough: "Linda" (Evangelista), "Christy" (Turlington), "Cindy" (Crawford), "Naomi" (Campbell), "Claudia" (Schiffer), and "Niki" (Taylor). The lyrics of "Supermodel" focused on the beauty "work," or practices, of clothes, make-up, and attitude required in order to achieve the glamorous representations of female beauty the supermodels embodied. Such work suggested that the highly idealized version of femininity exemplified by these supermodels and seen in fashion magazines and beauty ads was a calculated performance. In the "Supermodel" video, RuPaul inserts himself into this model group, posing on the runway and in photo shoots, but with the tongue-in-cheek knowledge, shared with the audience, that this supermodel is a man and therefore must "work" extra hard at performing femininity. The video ends with RuPaul's overglamorized "breakdown" in a Joan Crawford-style parody that references the classic drag performance of the Hollywood femme fatale. Yet RuPaul's commentary on the performance of femininity, exemplified by the supermodel, and celebrated within celebrity culture, was not simply parody.

Drag has a fashionable quality that further enhanced RuPaul's "Supermodel" persona. English literature scholar Marjorie Garber notes in *Vested Interests: Cross-Dressing and Cultural Anxiety* that much of the visual identity of drag and cross-dressing is about the signs of gender and the signs of sexuality that also exist within fashion.[4] Fashion itself is a system of signs, a "vestimentary" code, one that is open to decoding, as the French literary theorist Roland Barthes described in *The Fashion System*.[5] The supermodel's "work" is an exaggerated and celebrated form of the work, or practices, that many women routinely perform every day. Drag style involves similar acts and gestures, including the use of lipstick to create a stylized, often fashionable, femininity, downplaying what is often thought to be an "essential" gender identity, a notion that is also contested. RuPaul was certainly aware of these tensions, saying, "I dress like our cultural made-up version of what femininity is, which isn't real."[6] The VIVA GLAM ad explicitly relied on drag's fashionable aura to celebrate the diversity and individuality that stood as M·A·C's core brand ideals, now realized in practice on an entirely new level. Furthermore, while the ad implicitly drew upon drag history and style, it also capitalized on a cultural moment in the early 1990s when androgyny and queer culture were acquiring a new relevancy, evidenced in mainstream media and popular culture.[7]

Many representations of drag emerged in the 1990s, both preceding and coinciding with M·A·C's RuPaul ad. One of the best-known forms of drag in the 1990s, from which the RuPaul ad implicitly drew inspiration, and which had an obvious link to fashion, was "voguing." Voguing was a dance phenomenon that arose from deep within New York's African American and Latino American gay communities in 1980s Harlem. Jennie Livingston's 1990 documentary *Paris Is Burning* captured this late-1980s subcultural scene. The film's participants ranged from part-time drag queens to transsexuals to transgendered women, all of whom belonged to "houses" such as the "House of Xtravaganza," reminiscent of the great

Parisian haute couture houses. Performers performed at "balls" – competitive spaces with categories such as "Executive" or "School Girl" – where they could engage in fantasies of being rich, famous, and, most importantly, socially accepted as women. The participants discussed how they emulated the supermodels (like those seen in fashion bible *Vogue*) rather than the past stars of movies, balls, and drag shows. Performances involved sophisticated make-up, clothes, and the "shante" of strutting down the runway, which RuPaul later directly incorporated into the lyrics of "Supermodel." In the film, prolific voguer Willi Ninja's dance style included performing the practices of applying make-up and endless variations of the model pose for an imaginary photographer. The ultimate goal of a performance's "realness" was to pass as the straight counterpart of the person being emulated, without satire or parody. The film shows this Harlem drag community performing at the "Love Ball" for the Design Industries Foundation Fighting AIDS (DIFFA) in 1989, raising $400,000 for homeless people affected by HIV/AIDS. Madonna appropriated voguing in her 1990 music video "Vogue," focusing on its fashionable and celebrity qualities and bringing this art form to a much more mainstream level of recognition.

Toronto itself was certainly a hotbed of drag performance. The 1991 Fashion Cares Red Hot & Blue fashion show explored these new representations of gender-bending and androgyny. The *Toronto Star*'s Bernadette Morra observed at the time, perhaps naively, that some men had modelled women's fashions as part of "the growing trend to cross-dressing which the gay community is using to make their own particular fashion statement."[8] Model and singer Miles Roberts wore a dress designed by Toronto designer Susan Dicks, marking a Fashion Cares first. Roberts recalled: "At the time, voguing was just about to come up in North America. That whole energy of voguing that I had seen and had been a part of in New York was presented onstage that night. It was a new identity, a different time in fashion in Toronto that culminated in the performance."[9] Rosie Levine commented in *NOW* on the sense of "whimsy and androgyny" that permeated the fashion show's looks.[10] Drag was also explored in art, photography, and film. Antoine Tempé's Midnight Divas photography exhibit, which travelled to Toronto in the summer of 1993, was one illustration of this moment. These photos documented Manhattan's drag scene and included a pre-M·A·C RuPaul. Tempé noted that "until not so long ago, cross-dressers belonged only to the gay culture and remained confined to the underground cabarets. But during the nightclub frenzy of the early 80s they started coming out of the closet ... [and] the fashion and entertainment world started noticing them."[11] David Livingstone recognized that this photo exhibit articulated the connection between fashion and drag, saying that "transvestitism has been for a few years already also a matter of fashionability," noting in particular the creative make-up worn by the male subjects, even while conflating drag performance with cross-dressing, which are not the same phenomena.[12] The show opening for Midnight Divas was co-hosted by the designers of Toronto men's fashion label Hoax Couture, of the infamous clear derrière trousers from the 1987 Fashion Cares. The following year, Toronto-based photographer MaryAnn Camilleri released a new photography book on drag called *Ladies, Please!* Her five-year project chronicled the drag scenes in Toronto and New York, noting that drag was "a celebration of energy and life. It's in your face in a very light way and I think that's why people like it."[13]

David Livingstone also commented on how drag had recently emerged in film, on television, and in literature. The Canadian film *Outrageous* (1977) and its sequel *Too Outrageous* (1987), about a drag performer and his roommate, were based on the real life of the late Toronto actor Craig Russell. Now, the 1990s ushered in an entire genre of films featuring drag queens, female impersonators, and cross-dressers, including *The Crying Game* (1992) and *Orlando* (1992). By the time the M·A·C RuPaul ad was released in 1995, other films had joined this group, notably *The Adventures of Priscilla, Queen of the Desert* (1994), *Ed Wood* (1994), and *To Wong Foo, Thanks for Everything! Julie Newmar* (1995); in the latter, RuPaul had a small role.[14] These films questioned gender norms and compulsory heterosexuality in ways that some earlier gender-bending films such as *Some Like It Hot* (1959), *Tootsie* (1982), *Victor/Victoria* (1982), and *Mrs. Doubtfire* (1993) – what philosopher and gender theorist Judith Butler calls "high het entertainment" – had not, since they were not subversive in the ways that they maintained hegemonic gender categories and associated sexualities.[15]

On 13 May at the Moss Park Armoury in Toronto, two months after VIVA GLAM's "Who is the M·A·C Girl?" party at Henri Bendel in New York, M·A·C VIVA GLAM Fashion Cares Salute to Suburbia An Evening of Pure Polyester was held. This fashion show was worlds away from Paris haute couture. "We always verge on camp," said Fashion Cares producer Phillip Ing, "but I thought, let's take camp and put a capital C on it."[16] A living room scene at the bottom of the runway provided the dramatic "suburban" set. The show opened with RuPaul descending a long, winding staircase flanked by two human-sized red lipsticks. Strutting down the runway to his own song "House of Love" and wearing his signature red bustier and red thigh-high stiletto boots, sporting a long blonde wig, RuPaul coyly surveyed his audience before announcing, "My name is RuPaul, the first face of M·A·C Cosmetics." The fashion show then paraded a number of campy fashion vignettes ranging from "favourite products," to the National Ballet of Canada's prima ballerina Karen Kain interpreting *Married ... with Children*'s Peg Bundy, to Rex Harrington in ballet drag, swathed in a tutu, make-up, and wig, portraying a less-than-classic black swan from the ballet "Swan Lake."[17] RuPaul had made an appearance at The Bay on Queen Street earlier that day. Audience member John McCracken, who attended both events, remembers that RuPaul sat at a long table on the main floor of The Bay's cosmetics department, and there was a "huge line-up of people waiting to get a signature on some M·A·C ads." RuPaul "exuded a really happy upbeat energy. She really made each person she talked to feel important."[18]

For M·A·C, using a drag performer in its first ad spoke to deep cultural convictions about sexuality, since the AIDS epidemic drew attention not only to male bodies and the more technical aspects of men who had sex with men, but also to homosexual desire and the politics within the many gay male communities. In one of the few scholarly inquiries into the VIVA GLAM campaigns, Angeline Lucinda Weiss's semiotic analysis of the ads offers a useful entry point for considering potential consumer meaning-making on these issues. Weiss argues that many contradictions are expressed in the M·A·C RuPaul ad. She discusses how the ad intends to highlight gay pride even while continuing to signify heterosexual desire; she also points out that the seriousness of AIDS may be undermined by the ad's playful imagery – an accusation that had also been levelled at Fashion Cares at various times through the years. RuPaul's facial expressions, red bustier, and blonde hair solidified the classic bombshell image. Weiss notes how the ad played on heterosexual male desire, instigated by gazing upon the beautiful "female" in a cosmetics ad: "She [RuPaul] works as something men desire for their women, and for women to dream about becoming for their men. She is both the fantasy of what to buy and what to be."[19] The desire instigated here is enhanced by cosmetics, and in this sense the ad is consistent with other aspirational cosmetics ads that feature beautiful women. However, Weiss notes, this male desire/female aspiration creates tension for the moment when the viewer becomes aware of RuPaul's sexual identity, throwing the binaries of male/female, heterosexuality/homosexuality into largely humorous chaos, although with the potential to devolve into violence.

Weiss further argues that the ad challenges dominant discourses about AIDS by attempting to normalize them through the medium of beauty advertising, even though the RuPaul ad explicitly subverts cosmetics advertising conventions. Weiss first states that the image and the copy are incongruent: "the subject matter of the serious copy and the playful, sexual imagery are in opposition to each other, and the disjunction between the copy and the image produce dichotomies of normal/deviant, and flamboyant/repressed within the relationship of the image and the copy."[20] However, Weiss then suggests that the ad's copy "anchors" the image, since it describes how every cent from the sale of VIVA GLAM goes to the M·A·C AIDS Fund. By guiding meaning, the copy discursively legitimizes the image and how AIDS is contextualized by placing both within the relatively "normal" space of the beauty ad. There is some merit to Weiss's claim; AIDS had been rendered invisible by the silence surrounding it since the epidemic's early days, including in the first Fashion Cares poster in 1987. However, Weiss considers the M·A·C RuPaul ad discretely without considering how other ads in circulation at the same time, such as Benetton's 1992 David Kirby ad, might also have "normalized" or disrupted meanings about AIDS.

Weiss's reading of the RuPaul ad is supported by gender theory, although she does not explicitly deploy any in her own work. In *Gender Trouble: Feminism and the Subversion of Identity*, Judith Butler famously argues that gender is "performative." Gender identity is constituted by symbolic acts and discursive constructions that challenge the notion of an inner or original reality about gender identity: "acts and gestures, articulated and enacted desires create the illusion of an interior and organizing gender core, an illusion discursively maintained for the purposes of the regulation of sexuality within the obligatory frame of reproductive heterosexuality," Butler states.[21] Gender confusion is "often parodied within the cultural practices of drag, cross-dressing, and the sexual stylization of butch/femme identities," resulting in a double performance in which the original is seen to be parodied. However, she asserts, this feat is impossible because no such original exists – it is "an imitation without an origin."[22] Based on Lacanian theory, this performance of gender, and specifically of femininity, also calls to mind the "masquerade" of femininity.[23] As parody, drag deprives the hegemonic culture of its claim to heteronormativity by calling attention to gender's social construction. Butler states that one of the problems with drag performance is that it can, paradoxically, work to solidify hegemonic heterosexuality, a point Weiss similarly makes about the RuPaul ad when she notes that RuPaul plays with stereotypically aspirational signs of female beauty, such as blonde hair, large breasts, and long legs. The stylized manner in which gender norms are performed in drag serves to situate them more strongly *as* norms, often undermining drag's subversive potential. Butler argues throughout *Gender Trouble* that gender and sex are arbitrarily linked through language and discourse and are loaded with power relations that support compulsory heterosexuality.

However, the relationship between the image and the copy in the RuPaul ad is much more complex than this. RuPaul spells each of the V-I-V-A G-L-A-M letters with his body, literally objectifying the product name and becoming the ad copy himself. Image and copy are united. Butler argues that performativity is "that aspect of discourse that has the capacity to produce what it names."[24] If gender performativity is discursively constructed, such performativity is extended in this ad to the product itself. RuPaul in drag also performs and produces a brand identity within and through the discursive space of the ad. Furthermore, the most shocking letter – the M – is noteworthy for the way RuPaul's sprawl exposes his genital area but actually conceals any suggestion of his male genitals.[25] As Butler points out, one's sex does not directly correspond to a gender identity existing as an innate quality; both are discursive. The ad's "reveal" is evidence of RuPaul's successful "tuck" of his genitals but also discursively reinscribes RuPaul's sex back onto his body with the "M," which could also represent "Male." Yet RuPaul presents as female in the ad, simultaneously negating this discursive gender identity altogether.

There are other seemingly contradictory aspects to the ad, including the playfulness and humour that contrasts with its serious cause (an issue that had arisen with regard to Fashion Cares in the past). Cultural anthropologist Esther Newton claims that humour is essential to a successful drag performance. Newton's classic 1972 ethnography of the drag scene, *Mother Camp: Female Impersonators in America*, identifies "humour," along with "incongruity" and "theatricality," as integral to the drag performance.[26] "Incongruity" refers to the juxtaposition of different things, including the masculine/feminine contrast, but it also includes mixing high art and low art, and youth and old age. The drag performance relies on a certain tension between these contrasts. In M·A·C's RuPaul ad, the use of a male "model" in a cosmetics ad targeted to women is the most obvious and immediate disjuncture. As noted, RuPaul is both "passing" and "performing" as a beautiful woman/supermodel, another incongruous mix. "Theatricality" refers first to style – how something looks and how it is done – and also to dramatic form, meaning there is a performer, an audience, and a role being played. Drag is not "high" art, even though drag was founded in musical theatre and has a long history there.[27] RuPaul honoured drag's long-standing tradition of credible stage performances and glamorous impersonations of well-known female entertainers. However, he was distinctive because he wrote and sang his own songs rather than lip-synching drag classics.[28] Furthermore, RuPaul's humorous and campy drag performances resonated more with contemporary fashion and popular culture instead of directly referencing old Hollywood glamour. His impersonation of the contemporary fashion "supermodel" and the glamorous side of celebrity culture can thus be regarded as both classic and very modern, while still being quite humorous.

Drag draws attention to the complexities of gender presentation, gender identity, and the object of sexual desire, but the RuPaul ad also spoke implicitly to gay male desire, a germane but often deeply troubling aspect of the AIDS epidemic in the ways that it drew out violent homophobia. While there is no causal link between being gay and performing drag, representations of drag have long had strong connotations of a gay subculture and identity. Esther Newton observes that "drag and camp are the most representative and widely used symbols of homosexuality in the English speaking world."[29] For the RuPaul ad to be effective on this level, it had to, at the very least, call upon an assumed link between drag, gay men, and gay male sex and desire. This connection between cross-dressing, drag culture, homosexuality, and gay identity is, however, one that is historically contingent, as explained by Marjorie Garber, who traces cross-dressing historically through a number of cultural forms including theatre, literature, film, television, and music. She asserts that a firm link between cross-dressing and gay identity has not been historically or geographically fixed, citing the Renaissance as one example, and changing meanings of drag in the East and the West as another. Cross-dressing and gay identity have only more recently become signs for each other. Yet as Steven P. Schacht and Lisa Underwood's ethnography of the drag scene confirms, the overwhelming majority of drag artists do identify as gay.[30] However indirect or implicit the link between drag and gay men may be, the RuPaul image relied on this connotation to function as an AIDS ad. To be an effective fundraising mechanism for AIDS, a disease with a high gay male frequency that has homophobia firmly attached to it, the RuPaul ad banked on inspiring this meaning-making in consumers. However, the performative aspects of drag also allowed M·A·C to continue to challenge cultural convictions about sexuality, bodies, desire, and life, subvert them, make them acceptable (through humour, incongruity), and, importantly, inspire real action and a different type of "work" around AIDS fundraising. When Toskan turned M·A·C into a platform for discussing social issues, he underestimated the cultural work the RuPaul ad could accomplish.

Writer Debra Goldman had suggested in *Adweek*: "It's probably only a matter of time before RuPaul signs his first celebrity endorsement contract. Frankly, I'm surprised no agency has thought of it yet. Pop culture's latest cross-dressing phenom is the perfect commercial hero(ine) for the times." Goldman's comment highlighted how, by 1994, cross-dressing was seemingly becoming conventional, even within advertising. Other contemporary ads that featured cross-dressers, she noted, included those for Bud Light and Wavy Lays potato chips. Goldman said, "[i]f cross-dressing weren't already in vogue, advertising would have to invent it."[31] Roland White, writing in the *Sunday Times* (London), observed that in the UK, drag was already common. A Levi's ad had used the New York drag queen Zaldy to advertise jeans, and RuPaul had already promoted Baileys Irish Cream there.[32] While RuPaul's recent career success appeared to represent, in part, the mainstreaming of drag, there was seemingly no precedent in the cosmetics industry for a man fronting an advertising campaign. Contracts with prestige cosmetics brands were traditionally reserved for top models – the "supermodels" – and, increasingly, celebrities. When *FashionTelevision*'s Jeanne Beker interviewed Frank Toskan at the 1995 Fashion Cares show, she asked: "Choosing a supermodel to represent all races, all ages, all sexes: now, that is quite a task. Why did you think it was important to have someone who was that far-reaching?" Toskan replied it was because RuPaul "represents and shares a lot of the things M·A·C stands for; our philosophies."[33] And, since 1992, M·A·C had quietly been a corporate sponsor of Wigstock, the outdoor drag festival held yearly in New York City, where Robertson and Toskan had first seen RuPaul perform. For his part, RuPaul called the Franks "mavericks. They're not ordinary people and I'm not an ordinary person either. So it's a match made in heaven."[34]

Indeed, many in the fashion and cosmetics industries perceived the partnership between M·A·C and RuPaul as positive. One Canadian news story suggested that "[w]hile MAC's decision to contract a six-foot-four black drag queen as its spokesperson is a marketing move that shatters the myth of Canadian business's innate conservatism, RuPaul's flamboyant stage personae takes drag out of gay nightclubs and pushes it into the mainstream. Along the way, it shatters a few myths."[35] Christian Arthur Bain, writing in the *Advocate*, noted that "the most astonishing aspect of the campaign's success has been the widespread acceptance of a gender-bending openly gay man in a role previously reserved for the world's most beautiful and glamorous women." Of course, RuPaul was only *performing* the role of supermodel in the ad – a persona he had already established in his music video, even if his own style of supermodel was different from, say, Cindy Crawford's. Bain postulated that naming RuPaul "Chairperson" of the M·A·C AIDS Fund was brilliant but that it may have also been designed to "overcome any objections to the campaign on the part of retailers or consumers" about its connections of AIDS and gay sexuality.[36] The potential objections to RuPaul were thus mitigated somewhat by the semantics of the official title of "Chairperson," rather than just "model."

In other press, reaction was mixed. Journalist Cyndee Miller seemed dubious, asking outright in *Marketing News*, "Would you buy lipstick from this man?"[37] Miller was referring to RuPaul, not Frank Toskan. Bain reported that American *Vogue* received both angry and supportive letters from readers after running the VIVA GLAM ad.[38] *New York Daily News* gossip columnists A.J. Benza and Michael Lewittes asserted in 1996 that RuPaul signified "an advertising world gone completely haywire."[39] Literary scholar and cultural critic Phillip Brian Harper noted that the criticism that met RuPaul as the M·A·C spokesperson reflected deeper concerns not just around disrupted gender normativity but also about race relations: "So the offense the writers [Benza and Lewittes] see RuPaul as embodying is not just the affront of the drag queen to generic femininity, but the assault of the black man on white womanhood – that ages-old threat with a postmodern twist."[40] Sociologist Zine Magubane suggests that the M·A·C RuPaul ad may have instigated fears about black strength and hypermasculinity while calling on a white supremacy that has historically dominated and exploited the black body, inducing (white) guilt and shame.[41] This aspect seems to have resonated with consumers. At M·A·C's head office, Valerie MacKenzie remembers that a substantial number of the complaints she received about the RuPaul ad came from self-identified straight black women. These women felt that M·A·C was exploiting the black man's sexuality, although to be fair, many other straight black women called the M·A·C office to share precisely the opposite sentiment. Later, in 1997, when the VIVA GLAM ads ran in Italy to coincide with the first M·A·C store opening there, Bishop Alessandro Maggiolini from Como described the ads as "sick" and "repulsive": "I'm not interested in what they say or what it's for. I just judge the phenomenon," and as such, the ad "goes toward perversion."[42] The RuPaul ad reignited some of these issues and did not easily resolve them.

Judith Butler describes how the drag performances in *Paris Is Burning* frequently normalized, regulated, and self-reproduced the oppressive practices and routines of gender and race as well as class. The film's performances celebrated drag's gender play, but their subversive intentions regarding race were often more ambiguous. As Butler argues, this ambiguity was particularly evident with Venus Xtravaganza, a Latina transwoman who relied on "passing" as white in hopes that a man would remove her to a conventional (i.e., heteronormative) suburban housewife existence.[43] Film scholar Ragan Rhyne observes that white drag queens often reinscribe white supremacy onto their performances of whiteness, renegotiating the boundaries of each.[44] Drag performances routinely perform depictions of race that are inextricably bound to class issues, demonstrating that subverting race through drag is more complex than subverting gender. As literature scholar Sara Salih notes, Butler does not conceptualize race as performative as neatly as she does with gender. Butler does appear to prioritize gender, and she encounters problems with race, since race is already "written" on the body.[45] M·A·C's credo, "all ages, all races, all sexes," attempts to elide race and gender categories (with "all ages" defying the youthful beauty ideal of the traditional cosmetics ad). In the VIVA GLAM ad, RuPaul's appearance as a black man is likewise accorded a secondary role to that of his gender performance. As well, the fact that the ad is for a lipstick – a product that can, cautiously, be viewed primarily as a "feminine" commodity – prioritizes gender performativity over race within the ad.

"A Girl Who Looks Like a Boy"

The RuPaul ad focused on the male-to-female presentation in drag. This was reversed when M·A·C announced at a press conference in March 1996 that Canadian singer, animal rights activist, and out lesbian k.d. lang would be joining RuPaul in representing the M·A·C AIDS Fund.[46] M·A·C had been sponsoring lang's eighty-five-city concert tour in 1996, during which she promoted the M·A·C AIDS Fund. lang was not paid to appear in the VIVA GLAM campaign (the Franks paid only for her travel); she had chosen to participate strictly because she wanted to do so. A pale-pink version of VIVA GLAM was created especially for lang (who only wore make-up for television and performances), thus establishing the VIVA GLAM franchise. lang had previously worked with M·A·C in 1992 on the PETA "Fur Is a Drag" fashion show. At that show, lang wore the same female "drag" as in her 1992 "Miss Chatelaine" music video, where she had "appeared in make-up, jewelry and a hyperfeminine flowing gown and loved every minute of it. For a tomboy who used to perform in spiky hair and a wedding dress, to appear as an echt [authentic] woman is as much an example of drag as anything RuPaul could do."[47] lang also released a new cover album of songs about smoking in 1997 titled *Drag*. These *double entendres* of drag, in its various forms, reinforced lang's own play on drag's cultural practices. For this new VIVA GLAM lipstick, M·A·C released another unconventional advertising image in March 1997 featuring lang. It was important to the Franks that k.d. lang was Canadian, since being Canadian was a fact that M·A·C had always highlighted (for example, by spelling "colour" with a "u" on its packaging). Toskan recalls: "It kind of bothered me that he [RuPaul] wasn't Canadian. That was the other thing: we had to find a Canadian person. There wasn't really anybody else that we gravitated to. I just felt a very natural draw to k.d. lang and the message, her life message, her story, her mission in life. It was very parallel to what we were doing. It was just natural."[48]

The VIVA GLAM II ad was photographed by David LaChapelle in Los Angeles. Prior to this, Toronto designer and filmmaker Lisa Mann had done a test shoot with lang in Toronto. Mann brought in pails of lipstick, and they put it on the walls and also had lang lounge in it. The result was quite beautiful, Toskan remembered, but they decided not to use it because, in the end, it looked like "a blood-smeared mess" – not exactly the intended message for an ad about AIDS. Nonetheless, for the artists involved that day, the process had been "amazing," remembers Toskan, in that it offered a creative outlet and an artistic "high" for everyone involved. The fact that the image was ultimately not used did not seem to matter to them. The image that Toskan finally selected portrayed lang styled as a sailor, sporting an Elvis Presley-esque quiff and a lipstick print on her cheek – presumably planted by a female VIVA GLAM II wearer. This lipstick print was consciously engineered, Toskan recollects: "We wanted to put the lipstick colour, which was hers – that VIVA GLAM colour which was a very soft colour, very neutral – we wanted to put it on [lang] somehow. Her lips didn't necessarily 'read.' We wanted it to read as a lipstick colour. And we wanted it to read as if it [the lipstick print] was obviously coming from a woman ... Not everyone would have picked up on it." They later added the flowers framing her portrait to add "freshness" to the image. The signature on the ad was lang's, not Frank Toskan's, as it usually was on M·A·C's communications, and it represented her own personal message.[49]

k.d. lang once cheekily stated, "I never thought I'd be a lipstick lesbian," alluding to the more conventionally feminine-appearing lesbians who were seemingly trendy at the time.[50] The term "lipstick lesbian" also discursively reinstates codes of femininity and heterosexuality, although lang was also gently ridiculing it. As well, this image seemed to nod to the August 1993 *Vanity Fair* cover that had featured lang and supermodel Cindy Crawford. In that image, Crawford was giving lang a "shave," with lang blissfully enjoying the high-heeled, bathing suit-wearing supermodel's full attention, evidence of yet another convergence of M·A·C with popular culture. Weiss argues that the k.d. lang ad perpetuated a heterosexual "code of desire," but without the ambiguity and trickery inherent in the RuPaul ad. She suggests that its image propelled connotations of the "bad boy" James Dean type, eliciting heterosexual female desire, even though the ad made it visually indisputable that lang was a woman, with her feminine bust line clearly evident. Weiss suggests that the ad "does not seek to appeal to lesbians who look like kd lang, whereas RuPaul could appeal to women wishing to look like her."[51] There may be some veracity to this claim; after all, lang did say she never expected to be a "lipstick" lesbian. However, lang's comment is a clever *double entendre* as well as self-mockery. Long before her VIVA GLAM ad, lang had a history of subverting gender norms in her early country cowgirl-punk presentation and especially in her send-up of traditional femininity in "Miss Chatelaine." Gendered beauty ideals, infused with heterosexuality and hyperfemininity, have traditionally been the norm in cosmetics ads, and clearly lang was not, and was not intended to be, part of that tradition.

Yet in this M·A·C ad, lang appears both *as* a girl and as desirable *to* a girl. Despite the "masculine" hairstyle, lang's breasts are clearly outlined in the image, denoting a woman's body. The kiss print is a sign, an index of lesbian desire, albeit of one who is also apparently a "lipstick lesbian." Weiss's assertion that the RuPaul ad appealed to women wishing to look like him while the k.d. lang ad did not inspire the same aspirational desire in women cannot be substantiated in any way other than by assuming that a conventional, hegemonic beauty code, one also perpetuated by the cosmetics industry among other institutional forces, prescribes the only acceptable and desirable feminine appearance, lesbian or otherwise. Given Toskan's long-standing disdain for the cosmetic advertising, with its narrow representations of female beauty, as well as M·A·C's own endorsement of individual expression from day one, this argument rings hollow; in fact, the opposite is much more likely. The lang ad does not comment on or critique the dominant beauty and sexuality codes in quite the same ways that the RuPaul ad does, but it does similarly call into question the dimensions of gender and sex by adding a new representation of female sexuality. As Butler notes, "performing excessive lesbian sexuality and iconography that effectively counters the desexualization of the lesbian" constitutes the political potential of drag performance; M·A·C's challenge to this "desexualization" is clearly signified in the k.d. lang ad and by the VIVA GLAM lipstick print on her cheek.[52]

M·A·C thus continued to exploit the gender ambiguity that drag represented, with lang's rejection of a conventional feminine appearance, especially for a female singer. Following in RuPaul's (high) heels, lang solidified M·A·C's stance on challenging beauty norms: "I think it's very courageous of such a large company to have two queer people as spokesmodels ... Between us, RuPaul and I break every concept of the beauty myth – the race thing, the gender thing, everything."[53] The RuPaul and lang VIVA GLAM ads critiqued a feminine beauty ideology perpetuated by the cosmetics industry and the mass media. lang said of M·A·C that "they've broken the stereotyping most cosmetic companies practise with their advertising," emphasizing that M·A·C's cultural and creative practices were indeed different because of how they aligned with its own brand of philanthropy.[54] Later that year, Toskan produced a third VIVA GLAM postcard, also photographed by David LaChapelle, that harkened back to the RuPaul ad, except that RuPaul was now joined by lang in spelling out VIVA GLAM, with the "M" reimagined into a less provocative statement. Toskan made a rare promotional appearance in this ad, as the letter "I" (PLATE 23). The back of the postcard offered Toskan's thanks to customers and staff for their contributions to the M·A·C AIDS Fund, which now totalled $5.5 million (PLATE 24).

Toronto's "Forgotten Queens"

The VIVA GLAM ads also borrowed, unconsciously albeit perhaps intuitively, from drag culture in another significant way. Drag, as a field with its own traditions of (sub)cultural production and practices, has historically been at the forefront of AIDS awareness and fundraising within gay communities across North America. In Toronto in particular there had always been a strong historical and cultural precedent for the alliance between AIDS fundraising and drag. Drag, as a cultural form, has, like fashion, its own specific communities, performance sites, audiences, and styles – its own field – and this field's response to AIDS has historically also been strong and motivated. Drag exhibits many forms of expression and purpose. Schacht and Underwood note that "dependent on the observer, drag queens and female impersonators in our society are seen as representing an array of disparate, often contradictory cultural values, limitations and possibilities."[55] They list the many different motivations and goals that drag queens exhibit, including being proponents of queer politics, being street fighters, gender benders, protesters, and provocateurs, and sometimes being misogynists. Drag interrogates identity categories of race, nationalism, religion, and class, as well as concepts such as power, status, authenticity, and patriarchy. There are varying degrees to which drag can be humorous, campy, and subversive. The ways that drag can both challenge and maintain ideological divisions between people are largely determined by the interplay between the drag queen and her audience. Schacht and Underwood note that the critical possibilities for drag depend most specifically on the performer's motivations or intentions: "quite simply, drag performances that question and make light of the dominant structures of society, such as sexism, homophobia, racism, and classism, and the practices of oppression in society, such as exploitation, marginalization, cultural imperialism, powerlessness, and violence" can be seen as subversive.[56] The Stonewall riots of June 1969, during which police attacked drag queens inside the Stonewall Inn in New York City's Greenwich Village, marked the beginning of the gay liberation movement in North America. This event is often viewed as a turning point for the gay rights movement and is now commemorated by annual Pride celebrations worldwide in the month of June. Since the late 1960s, drag has become more than entertainment; it is also a form of politics that challenges dominant power structures.

In Toronto, drag took on a new prominence in the 1970s and came to the forefront in the 1980s, in the underground gay clubs but also on the more popular entertainment scene in Toronto, arguably even becoming mainstream. Its response to AIDS, however, originated in what Bryan Greenwood, a prominent performer in the drag community in the 1980s, called Toronto's "forgotten queens." These were the club kids who, seeking acceptance, community, and purpose, came into their own in the late 1980s and 1990s with the D.Q. – the "Drag Queen" fundraiser for Toronto's new AIDS hospice, Casey House. Alongside more established (by Toronto standards) celebrity queens, a united drag community rallied to take care of its own through drag shows large and small around the city. They raised money for people who needed it for food, for housing, for experimental drugs, and eventually for funerals.[57]

In 1985, Canadian journalist and activist June Callwood had approached the AIDS Committee of Toronto with the idea for an AIDS hospice to be called Casey House (after her late son, who had died in an accident), which would offer palliative care for people with AIDS. Eric Turner, a Toronto interior designer (and drag legend Sacha MacKenzie), suggested a novel idea to Callwood: he offered to do a "D.Q." – a "drag queen" show – as a fundraiser to help the fledgling AIDS hospice get off the ground. Callwood famously asked how they were going to raise money with ice cream, referring to the restaurant Dairy Queen that went by the moniker "DQ." This anecdote about D.Q.'s origins became legendary, repeated in show programs and media pieces for years. Callwood suggested that Turner approach talent agent Michael Oscars, who handled the Canadian comedians Andrea Martin, John Candy, and Martin Short, to ask for assistance, and D.Q. was born. The idea was to make the show "light, [and] keep it silly," said Oscars, with musical numbers, skits, and comedy all performed by local drag entertainers, both professional and amateur.[58]

There was, however, some initial trepidation among Casey House organizers about D.Q.'s viability and success. Turner said: "When they [the Casey House Steering Committee] found out it was drag queens, they kept us at arm's length. We were too freaky to associate with the cause."[59] D.Q. director Michael Oscars remembered that "[d]rag in the 80s was not cool, it was only in bars."[60] The D.Q. collective was not formally involved in other Toronto AIDS activist politics, although it is likely that many individuals participated in various activist groups and events in Toronto. The shows avoided overt political references and instead aimed to make audiences laugh. AIDS had exhausted a community tired of death, mourning, and fear, and it needed some levity – exactly what drag offered. "We were under attack, we were in a war," said Oscars. "Not just from the disease itself, but also from the ignorance around the disease, the stigmatization. It was awful. There were years when the Proud Lives [memorial] section in *Xtra* was pages long. And we knew everyone in there."[61] "We'd do bar shows ahead in order to promote," said David Clark, one of the performers. "Woody's [a popular bar] would give us three or four hundred dollars, and it all went to pay for costumes, including the tips. Every night of the run a different bar would host a party with great food, cocktails and a social experience."[62]

In 1987, three months before the fashion industry assembled to produce the first Fashion Cares at the Diamond Club, the first D.Q. event was held. The event drew a large crowd; four to five hundred people paid $20 a ticket to attend five sold-out shows at the Bathurst Street Theatre in downtown Toronto over the weekend of 7 March.[63] Bryan Greenwood attended the event and had friends in many of the performances. The whole theatre had a feeling of community, and "the laughter was over the top." But he also characterized this response as "manic":

> It was like fiddling while Rome burned ... because we were all here in the room for this very serious cause. And inside we were all weeping ... we were weeping. We were sad. We were scared. How many people in that room were actually dying from AIDS? How many people in that room were HIV positive, knowing that their time was limited? They had nowhere to go. There was no money; there was no funding; there were no drugs. And these queens were on the stage making us howl. This is what I mean; it was manic.[64]

"We raised $38,000," said organizer Eric Turner, "which we mailed to the house. Unknown to us there was a bridge financing problem to the tune of $30,000. Literally, if it wasn't extended they wouldn't have gotten the house. The cavalry rode in in the form of drag queens and Canada Post."[65] The D.Q. money bridged a major funding gap at the exact moment when it was needed the most, allowing the Casey House Steering Committee to close on the property on Huntley Street that soon became Casey House. This story about D.Q. providing the necessary funds for the property also became part of the legend for both D.Q. and Casey House. It was repeated in press releases and programs, by Callwood herself, and indeed even in subsequent scholarly work on Casey House.[66]

A fundraising success, the event returned on 8 to 17 April 1988 at the Bathurst Street Theatre in Toronto as "D.Q. The Sequin." Drag performer Morgan Holliday performed a spoof of the Marilyn Monroe classic, "Diamonds Are a Girl's Best Friend," substituting "diamonds" with "condoms" as a humorous take on the safe sex message. After a four-year gap, D.Q. was revived in 1992. These shows were held from 29 February to 7 March 1992 at the Bathurst Street Theatre. They were devised and created by Michael Oscars, with direction by Maria Armstrong, and the associate director and choreographer was Les Porter. A press release urged would-be audience members to order tickets immediately because "[o]perators are standing by ... and their heels are killing them!!!"[67] D.Q. had by now drawn the interest of noted figures in the Canadian arts scene who were no longer "uncomfortable" being associated with "freaky" drag queens.[68] This could be attributed to the increasing representations of drag in popular culture and to the lessening discomfort with the topic of AIDS overall. Honorary patrons that year included actor Jackie Burroughs, author Timothy Findley, opera singer Maureen Forrester, *Globe and Mail* film critic Jay Scott, and the charmingly named Judy Garland Memorial Bowling League. At the time of the show's 1995 run, Michael Oscars observed: "D.Q.'s only 'anomaly' is that it is a drag show and even drag now has become 'mainstream.'"[69] That year, drag queen Rusty Ryan performed an impression of Mrs. Doubtfire. Another act spoofed the drag queen film *The Adventures of Priscilla, Queen of the Desert*, Canadian-style. It featured Priscilla's northern relatives, beauty queens who, to an aria from Delibes's *Lakmé*, made their way across Canada (instead of the film's Australia). One queen's headpiece displayed the CN Tower, another, moose ears, and the last, the schooner *Bluenose*.[70] The AIDS Committee of Toronto acknowledged the strong local link between AIDS fundraising and awareness and the drag community in a tribute to D.Q. in the D.Q.'95 program:

> Since the very beginnings of the community push to establish a free-standing hospice for people with AIDS, the Drag Community has been there. Dedicated individuals took the beginnings of an idea for the first DQ and transformed it into an organizing force to be respected.

The Drag Community has constantly raised funds – and awareness – when other sources fell through or disappeared. Your unique sense of pride and style has produced wonderful events that reach out to the outrageous in all of us.

ACT would like to thank the Drag Community for their ongoing leadership and support in the fight against AIDS and against mediocre entertainment everywhere![71]

The AIDS Committee of Toronto was certainly well attuned to the political and creative spectrum of AIDS activism in Toronto.

Another, less well-known AIDS fundraising initiative also appeared that year. In the D.Q. '95 program, a list of "D.Q. '95 Fundraisers" revealed that Dino Dilio, a Toronto make-up artist, had created a "D.Q. Red Lipstick" as part of a fundraising project. On the back cover of the program was an ad for the lipstick. Advertised as "Morgan Holliday presents D.Q. Red Lipstick," it was "the glamourous lipstick that takes you from the street to the stage." Available from a number of local clubs and retailers, all proceeds from the $10 lipstick were donated to Casey House.[72] The D.Q. Red Lipstick appears to have been a one-off effort, and it was not widely distributed, nor is there any mention of this product in subsequent programs. Morgan Holliday was a make-up artist for drag queens and female impersonators and wrote a monthly column in an independent Toronto-based publication called the *Transie Times*. Her first column detailed the problems that transvestites, "transies," and female impersonators faced in shopping for cosmetics and obtaining advice and service at the make-up counter, and she included numerous make-up application tips for "transforming a man to a woman." An ad for her book, *The Morgan Mystique: Morgan Holliday's Essential Guide to Living, Loving, and Lip Gloss*, appeared in the *Transie Times* in January 1991. The book sold for $19.95, with 25 per cent of the purchase price donated to the Toronto PWA (People with AIDS) Foundation. Her next column, in February 1991, specifically discussed M·A·C Cosmetics as a professional line well suited for "transies."[73] Fashion journalist David Livingstone promoted the D.Q. Red Lipstick in his *Globe and Mail* "Style Notes" column, tuned in to the fact that the D.Q. Red Lipstick creator Dino Dilio was, in fact, the drag queen Morgan

Holliday.[74] Dilio, by then the creative director at the upscale Mira Linder Spa in Yorkville, was also a member of the fashion community; with his fundraising lipstick, he represented one tangible link between these two fields of cultural production in Toronto.

Frank Toskan, who attended all of the D.Q. events, thought the fundraising red lipstick was a really touching gesture. He was less cognizant at the time of any conscious appropriation of drag politics into M·A·C's visual storytelling but has since realized that such subcultural traditions and practices surely must have informed his and M·A·C's ethos. There is no evidence that D.Q. crossed paths with M·A·C during that time, except for Toskan's attendance at the shows, though it seems that some performers participated in both Fashion Cares and D.Q. But the cultural connection between them, established at the grassroots level early in the AIDS epidemic in Toronto, is undeniable. As the later event programs show, by the 2000s, D.Q. had become a legitimate, corporate-sponsored event that, much like Fashion Cares, had substantial clout on the Toronto fundraising scene. In 2003, following in the footsteps of Fashion Cares, the M·A·C AIDS Fund became the official title sponsor of D.Q., formalizing yet another convergence between M·A·C, AIDS, philanthropic practices, and fields of cultural production. The M·A·C AIDS Fund remained D.Q.'s title sponsor until its final show in 2007.

Drag as Politics

As essayist Jeffrey Hilbert discusses, a number of drag queens performed at ACT UP rallies in the 1980s, for example, Atlanta's Lurleen and Los Angeles performer Vaginal Creme Davis, an indication of how drag strategically straddles the line between entertainment and politics. Hilbert's interviews with drag queens demonstrate the various ways that such "activist" efforts can combine with entertainment. "The way to reach people is to make them laugh and, at the same time, make them think more about serious issues," says performer Glennda Orgasm. "The people I see at our shows are not the people I see at ACT UP or Queer Nation meetings, but they do listen to what we're talking about because we are entertaining." The Stonewall riots may have been a defining moment for gay and drag politics, but, as Hilbert observes, "it was not until the late eighties and the acceleration of the AIDS crisis that drag again embraced a political message."[75] Butler similarly points out in *Bodies That Matter: On the Discursive Limits of Sex* that the activist potential of a drag performance can have strong critical import depending on its context, especially if it is directed towards AIDS activism. As she outlines in *Gender Trouble*, a gender *performance* is different from gender *performativity*, the latter occurring when the discursive norms that "cite" gender into existence produce a binary gender identity long before any subjective choice or agency does so. Drag performances, however, can often (although not always) resist the hegemonic, heteronormative, heterosexist power structures that produce and reproduce the systems in which this performativity occurs and makes sense. Depending on the context, such performances offer a potential site for challenge, critique, and action.

For instance, Butler notes that drag performances that highlight the rejection of the gay male body and AIDS usually emphasize the latter's deathly aspect. Her observation is worth quoting in full:

> [T]he hyperbolic "performance" of death in the practice of "die-ins" and the theatrical "outness" by which queer activism has disrupted the closeting distinction between public and private space have proliferated sites of politicization and AIDS awareness throughout the public realm. Indeed, an important set of histories might be told in which the increasing politicization *of* theatricality for queers is at stake.

Continuing this line of thinking, Butler notes that these intentional performances of gender have great political import when they converge around AIDS and sexuality. Such a history would include

> cross-dressing, drag balls, street walking, butch-femme spectacles, the sliding between the "march" (New York City) and the parade (San Francisco); die-ins by ACT UP, kiss-ins by Queer Nation, drag performance benefits for AIDS (by which I would include both Lypsinka's and Liza Minnelli's in which she, finally, does Judy); the convergence of theatrical work with theatrical activism, performing excessive lesbian

sexuality and iconography that effectively counters the desexualization of the lesbian; tactical interruptions of public forums by lesbian and gay activists in favor of drawing public attention to the failure of government funding of AIDS research and outreach.[76]

Butler does not consider the commercial sphere when she catalogues these ways that gender performance can be subversive, but certainly the advertising space, especially in light of the Benetton David Kirby ad, could be added to this list of seemingly inappropriate contexts. Drag artist Lypsinka, who had appeared in a Gap ad in 1992 and also performed at AIDS fundraisers, did not consider herself to be overtly "political."[77] RuPaul was also in this camp – he self-identified as an entertainer who advocated for AIDS awareness but in a non-political way. When asked if he felt pressure to do AIDS benefits, RuPaul said he did, but added that his job was really about setting an example and showing "love for myself, and love for life."[78] Yet RuPaul's performance of femininity (and celebrity, and fashion, and beauty) was framed within the highly "incongruent" advertising space. Political potential *might* be diffused by its commercial implications as an ad, but such political import could also be considerably heightened by its (inappropriate) context within a public, commercial space, as confirmed by the ad's critics and others who were uncomfortable with the RuPaul image.

Although the VIVA GLAM ads challenged hegemonic gender, sex, and race categories, and raised millions for AIDS charities through the M·A·C AIDS Fund while doing so, such fundraising campaigns were far from unproblematic for many, and not just from the perspective of the legitimacy of corporate philanthropy and cause marketing. For marginalized communities, a total destruction of dominant and seemingly oppressive power structures of gender, race, class, and sexuality was not, ironically, always absolutely desirable. There were some less positive outcomes resulting from the commodification of AIDS and the mainstreaming of gay culture, of which the VIVA GLAM ads were just a small part. The need to remain subcultural, to speak authentically from a marginal place, and to maintain a collective identity were, paradoxically, often threatened by the mainstream visibility and commercial success of AIDS awareness. As Daniel Harris points out, the association of AIDS with fashion and commerce (as seen with "AIDS kitsch") sometimes simplified and destabilized the seriousness of AIDS, for its commodification weakened the political impact of many gay communities' actions and activism. Harris notes that drag "helped push the selling of the subculture up the economic food chain," due to the realization that gay people were also consumers, and sympathy and affect around AIDS could be commodified and targeted to the gay community. In this process, a way for gay culture to be more acceptable to the mainstream took shape. Yet, Harris observes, "AIDS has perversely legitimized the gay community as a group of consumers, making us an object of pity that can be openly addressed through advertising and thus welcomed into the fold of conventional shoppers."[79] Much to Harris's dismay, mainstream success also indicated an irretrievable loss of much of drag and gay culture's subcultural ethos, with, simultaneously, its acceptance by society. The commodification that Harris describes was undoubtedly part of VIVA GLAM's goals; it had to be, since it was a fundraising venture. But that is not all it was.

RuPaul's call to love everyone and to live life glamorously also posed a substantial challenge to the AIDS activist movement's focus on death. The M·A·C RuPaul ad did not use drag to call attention to the more abject aspects of the gay male body and the physical and deathly qualities of AIDS that Butler identifies. Instead, it offered a new presentation of AIDS that emphasized the life, glamour, and love that had also propelled the "creative activism" that was simultaneously driving Fashion Cares, a function that Toskan had always recognized. The M·A·C RuPaul ad could thus be read as, on one hand, skimming the surface of the issues to which it referred, making light of them by virtue of its humorous and entertaining presentation, and as a result reinforcing hegemonic categories of gender, race, and sexuality. Yet on the other hand, the M·A·C RuPaul ad also critically challenged and subverted these categories as it called attention to the AIDS crisis. While never a planned or conscious marketing strategy, but rather an organic convergence of popular culture, intuition, opportunity, historical conditions, and risk-taking – and, importantly, knowing the rules of the game – the VIVA GLAM ads were embedded in, and embodied, lasting ideological and political power. Reflecting on when M·A·C reran the RuPaul ad in 2013, now as "The Original," Toskan reveals: "I was glad that they did ... I guess they must have felt a need to return to the roots."

EPILOGUE

The Brightest Jewel in Our Crown

John Demsey joined M·A·C in July 1998 as its new president, moving to Toronto from Lauder's corporate headquarters in New York. Frank Toskan stayed on as creative director and chairman of the M·A·C AIDS Fund and worked on new projects. Michelle Feeney, the new vice-president of global communications for M·A·C, was also implanted in M·A·C's Toronto office from New York in September 1998 and was charged with raising M·A·C's global profile. One of Feeney's first goals was "to really get MAC's credo out there; MAC is a cult, it's for all races, sexes and ages," and to promote VIVA GLAM, because "[n]obody knows about it, and raising awareness of VivaGlam [sic] will also serve to support MAC's message." Feeney's comments appear unusual, since by 1998, the total funds raised for the M·A·C AIDS Fund amounted to $16 million.[1] Yet the commercial imperative was unmistakable: M·A·C and the M·A·C AIDS Fund were now considered mutually reinforcing entities that unavoidably served M·A·C's brand value.

Julie Toskan-Casale resigned as head of M·A·C's public relations in October 1998. Frank Toskan resigned as creative director in December 1998 but remained as chairman of the M·A·C AIDS Fund and pursued new philanthropic projects with his sister. Victor Casale continued to oversee M·A·C's production in Markham, Ontario, and stayed very involved with innovation at M·A·C until 2000.[2] Upon his resignation in December 1998, Frank Toskan said: "At this point in my life I think I've brought a lot to the company and there are many other things I want to [do] ... I think

I need time away from all the routine business stuff and to focus on my creative energies and certainly focus on the MAC AIDS Fund, which is really still very much part of the personality and the core of what makes MAC ... My heart, my soul, and my interests will always remain at MAC."[3] Full ownership of M·A·C by Lauder was effective in March 1999, ushering in a new era for M·A·C, VIVA GLAM, and the M·A·C AIDS Fund.

When the Lauder deal had been struck back in 1994, it did not seem to the Franks that a complete buyout was inevitable. Frank Toskan thought he would be with his company and Lauder for years. But after Frank Angelo died, this perspective changed. Toskan wanted to keep doing what he had always done – create and innovate – and not visit the Lauder offices or talk about business strategies. Frank Angelo had always buffered Toskan from Lauder and all the business aspects, which he had loved, but now that Toskan was alone and in a different position with respect to Lauder, he was no longer interested. Once Toskan left M·A·C, there was a seven-year non-compete agreement in place, but there was no non-disclosure agreement, nor was there any other clear agreement with Lauder on other matters. For some time after the final sale, Toskan was invited to store openings and events, but he ultimately realized that he needed a very clean break with M·A·C and its staff. Toskan could not even go into a M·A·C store because the change was still too fresh. The staff still wanted to tell him their problems, but they eventually realized that the chain of command was different and they needed to learn who "the new family" was at Lauder. Toskan focused his energy on raising his own family in Toronto: three sons and a daughter with his partner Darren Zakreski, a well-known Toronto hairstylist. Toskan was assured that M·A·C was in good hands, remembering Leonard Lauder's promise that M·A·C would always remain "the brightest jewel" in Lauder's "crown," a promise seemingly honoured with VIVA GLAM's continuing contributions to the M·A·C AIDS Fund.

More than twenty years after Frank Toskan created VIVA GLAM and he and Frank Angelo formed the M·A·C AIDS Fund, Toskan's work in AIDS fundraising and his "creative activism" were acknowledged and celebrated by his own local community at Toronto's DX Intersection "Rise Up" gala in 2014. Asked now if he regards the M·A·C AIDS Fund's work as a type of activism, Toskan responds in the affirmative:

> Yes, I see it more so now. In the moment, it just was a response to – what was supposed to be. I didn't really think about it in that way. We were just responding. Today, I guess I look at it in a very different way. We went out there and took big risks and we brought a lot of people on board. Yeah, it was activism. I didn't see it as that then, but today, yes, I can look back and say we were pretty active in making change and creating around something that was such a horrible subject to most people.[4]

And there is no question that M·A·C's remarkable VIVA GLAM ads featuring RuPaul and k.d. lang figured prominently in Toskan's own type of "creative activism."

As Mara Einstein demonstrates in *Compassion, Inc.*, true corporate social innovation is rare, and much corporate philanthropy reduces social change to consumerism, even though, as she states emphatically, "shopping is not philanthropy. Period."[5] Statements such as these are valid critiques and illustrate the considerable uneasiness about the ways that consumerism has become framed as the solution to all sorts of social ills. Yet cultural studies and media studies scholarship on cause marketing does not usually consider a brand's historical relationship with its chosen social cause. There is no question that this can be painstaking work; analysing a diverse array of historical and archival materials, including newspaper and magazine articles, films, T-shirts, video footage, posters, and programs, and interviewing key members of Toronto's fashion community, was necessary for this cultural and business history of M·A·C. Bourdieu similarly notes that "[o]ne of the major difficulties of the social history of philosophy, art or literature is that it has to reconstruct these spaces of original possibilities which, because they were part of the self-evident givens of the situation, remained unremarked and are therefore unlikely to be mentioned in contemporary accounts, chronicles or memoirs."[6] This book, in examining and re-creating the historical dimensions of a brand's association with a social cause within its "spaces of original possibilities" – these "self-evident givens" of M·A·C, Toronto fashion, and the AIDS epidemic – offers a deeper assessment of M·A·C's cultural work and its philanthropic practices as a unique form of "creative activism." Historical work on other brands' charitable efforts, similarly incorporating cultural theory, may also yield worthwhile cultural and business histories and go some way towards alleviating the scepticism that corporate philanthropy can often present to outsiders.

M·A·C's form of cause marketing and its unusual philanthropic practices would be difficult, if not impossible, to replicate or consciously engineer; in this regard, the company is, admittedly, an anomaly. The cultural history of M·A·C presented in *Viva M·A·C* does not, and certainly does not seek to, offer a formula or set of guidelines for successful cause marketing, nor does it offer "rules" for negotiating or navigating a perfect brand/cause fit. However, even while failing to offer a strategy in any instrumental or rational manner, this history of M·A·C's philanthropic practices suggests that long-term success is achieved precisely *because* the brand/cause fit cannot be strategized and that an authentic connection arises from the internal dynamics generated by personal and professional practices. The practices of those who work within, and for, a brand or corporation within a field – like Toskan, Angelo, their staff, and the other voices seen and heard throughout this book – can contribute more meaningful and significant value to corporate philanthropy than a marketing or advertising-driven communications initiative. M·A·C Cosmetics demonstrates that when the social is composed of routine acts and practices that *over time* become embedded and embodied, and coalesce into a brand's identity, corporate philanthropy may be more likely to withstand critique to become a viable channel for social innovation. Ultimately, M·A·C's historical relationship to AIDS has been both the cause *and* the outcome of these creative organizational practices, making M·A·C's philanthropic practices stand out as so distinctive and long-lasting, as something different, something more than the conventional marketing and advertising strategies and processes that have come to define many contemporary cause marketing initiatives.

Notes

Prologue: Rise Up

1 Jeanne Beker, interview with author, 7 July 2015.
2 Two of the numerous examples of early media messages about AIDS include, in Canada, Ornstein, *AIDS in Canada*; and in the United States, Kinsella, *Covering the Plague*. For a different take on the discourse (and silence) surrounding AIDS and the effects of this in the United States, see Myrick, *AIDS, Communication, and Empowerment*.
3 John Demsey, interview with author, 7 July 2016.
4 While this self-deprecating comment sounds like something a Canadian might say, it was actually observed by Mo White; see White, "MAC Daddy."
5 For work on Estée Lauder, see Koehn, "Estée Lauder"; and Lauder's autobiography, *Estée: A Success Story*. For work on Max Factor, see Basten, *Max Factor*. For Charles Revson, founder of Revlon, see Tobias, *Fire and Ice*. For Madam C.J. Walker, see Lommel, *Madam C.J. Walker*; and Lowry, *Her Dream of Dreams*. On Elizabeth Arden, see Shuker, *Elizabeth Arden*. For Helena Rubinstein and L'Oréal founder Eugène Schueller, see Brandon, *Ugly Beauty*. For the competition between Rubinstein and her rival Elizabeth Arden, see Woodhead, *War Paint*. For a history of the Avon brand, see Klepacki, *Avon*.
6 See Ragas and Kozlowski, *Read My Lips*; Pallingston, *Lipstick*; and Corson, *Fashions in Makeup from Ancient to Modern Times*.
7 See Jones, *Beauty Imagined*; Willett, ed., *The American Beauty Industry Encyclopedia*; Gavenas, *Color Stories*; Malkan, *Not Just a Pretty Face*; and Tungate, *Branded Beauty*, 105–7.
8 Kerner and Pressman with Essex, *Chasing Cool*; Ross and Holland, *100 Great Businesses and the Minds Behind Them*, 345–8. See also Haig, *Brand Success*, 154–6; and Morgan, *Eating the Big Fish*.

9 The M·A·C Cosmetics website contained a thorough archive of press releases and media articles from the early 1990s up to 2012. In 2013 it suddenly disappeared and a new interface appeared. I had fortuitously printed out every piece of communication shortly before everything disappeared. These pieces later became available again by searching archive.org.
10 Susie Sheffman, interview with author, 6 August 2016.
11 Arvidsson, *Brands*; Lury, *Brands*; and Moor, *The Rise of Brands*.
12 Zwick and Cayla, Introduction to *Inside Marketing*, 3–19; and Holt, *How Brands Become Icons*.

Introduction: The Rules of Make-up Art Cosmetics

1 Although frequently called "cause-related marketing" (CRM), I prefer "cause marketing" and use it throughout.
2 Van de Ven, "An Ethical Framework for the Marketing of Corporate Social Responsibility"; Brønn and Vrioni, "Corporate Social Responsibility and Cause-Related Marketing."
3 For instance, see discussion by Stole, "Philanthropy as Public Relations."
4 Selleck, "Pretty in Pink." See also Bruce Burtch, "Bruce Burtch – the Cause Marketing Catalyst" (n.d.), http://www.bruceburtch.com/about.htm. See Marriott's 1976 "Great America" ad here: https://www.youtube.com/watch?time_continue=2&v=0xb-boQU4B4.
5 King, *Pink Ribbons, Inc.*
6 Ibid, xxvi.
7 Ibid, xxvii.
8 Information on Yoplait can be found on its website: http://153.13.148.213/yoplait-in-action/friends-in-the-fight.
9 Information on Dove can be found on its website: https://www.dove.com/ca/en/home.html.
10 Susie Orbach, Nancy Etcoff, et al., "The Real Truth about Beauty: A Global Report: Findings of the Global Study on Women, Beauty, and Well-Being" (2004). While this paper no longer appears on the Dove website, it has been archived in a number of places, including http://www.clubofamsterdam.com/contentarticles/52%20Beauty/dove_white_paper_final.pdf.
11 See Sarah Banet-Weiser, "'Free Self-Esteem Tools'? Brand Culture, Gender, and the Dove Real Beauty Campaign," in Mukherjee and Banet-Weiser, eds., *Commodity Activism*, 39–56; see also Banet-Weiser, *Authentic*™.
12 Johnston and Taylor, "Feminist Consumerism and Fat Activists."
13 For early critique, encompassing popular and industry perspectives, see Cohen, "Selling Soap"; Flavelle, "T.O.-Made 'Evolution' Ad Part of Online Revolution"; Pozner, "Dove's 'Real Beauty' Backlash"; Postrel,

"The Truth about Beauty"; Gardner, *The 30 Second Seduction*; and Wentz, "Real Beauty Gets Global Breakout Via Evolution."
14. For additional scholarly analysis, see Millard, "Performing Beauty"; Scott and Cloud, "Reaffirming the Ideal," n.p.; Lachover and Brandes, "A Beautiful Campaign?"; Bissell and Rask, "Real Women on Real Beauty"; Murray, "Branding 'Real' Social Change in Dove's Campaign for Real Beauty"; and Taylor, Johnston, and Whitehead, "A Corporation in Feminist Clothing?"
15. The relatively large body of scholarly work on (RED) cuts across many disciplines, including international development, branding, medicine, and race studies. See Kuehn, "Compassionate Consumption"; Ponte, Richey, and Baab, "Bono's Product (RED) Initiative"; Stole, "Philanthropy as Public Relations"; Banet-Weiser and Lapsansky, "RED Is the New Black"; Michelle Amazeen, "Gap (RED)"; O'Manique and Labonte, "Rethinking (Product) RED"; Richey and Ponte, "Better (Red)™ Than Dead?"; Jungar and Salo, "Shop and Do Good?"; and Sarna-Wojcicki, "Refigu(red)."
16. Information on (RED) can be found on its website: https://red.org.
17. Kuehn, "Compassionate Consumption"; Banet-Weiser and Lapsansky, "RED Is the New Black"; Littler, *Radical Consumption*.
18. Stole, "Philanthropy as Public Relations," 31.
19. Richey and Ponte, *Brand Aid*.
20. Anderson, "Fighting AIDS."
21. Mahon, "The Business Case for Giving Away Lipstick."
22. Karen Buglisi Weiler, interview with author, 7 July 2016.
23. Pringle and Thompson, *Brand Spirit*, 4.
24. A very small cross-section from the business literature includes a variety of studies such as Trimble and Holmes, "New Thinking on Antecedents to Successful CRM Campaigns"; Nan and Heo, "Consumer Responses to Corporate Social Responsibility (CSR) Initiatives"; and Gupta and Pirsch, "The Company-Cause-Consumer Fit Decision in Cause-Related Marketing."
25. Einstein, *Compassion, Inc.*, 157–8.
26. John Demsey, interview with author, 7 July 2016.
27. Hansen, "Business History." See also see Chandra, "From Fictional Capital to Capital as Fiction," in which Chandra also observes that in the contemporary global context, business disciplines and the humanities have each necessarily adopted the theoretical tenets of the other.
28. Hansen, "Business History," 693.
29. Lipartito, "Connecting the Cultural and the Material in Business History." This observation also appeared in his earlier work, "Culture and the Practice of Business History."

30 Lipartito, "Connecting the Cultural and the Material in Business History," 694.
31 Ibid., 687.
32 Friedman and Jones, "Creative Industries in History," 240.
33 Like most social or cultural theories, Bourdieu's concepts help bring social phenomena to light, but they are not perfect, and there are blind spots. One of the most relevant critiques is that Bourdieu is unable to recognize the legitimacy of "mass" culture and mass media, as well as the increasing influence of fashion from subcultural origins that developed in his lifetime. Such discussions are offered by, for instance, Hesmondhalgh, "Bourdieu, the Media and Cultural Production"; and McRobbie, *British Fashion Design*. For a specific critique of Bourdieu and fashion, see Rocamora, "Fields of Fashion."
34 Lipartito, "Connecting the Cultural and the Material in Business History," 702.
35 Bourdieu, "Haute Couture and Haute Culture."
36 Bourdieu and Delsaut, "Le couturier et sa griffe."
37 Bourdieu, "Haute Couture and Haute Culture," 132.
38 Bourdieu, "Some Properties of Fields."
39 All by Bourdieu: *Outline of a Theory of Practice*; *The Rules of Art*; *Distinction*; "The Field of Cultural Production"; *The Logic of Practice*; "But Who Created the 'Creators'?"
40 Bourdieu, "Haute Couture and Haute Culture," 134–5.
41 The date of this debate is not noted in Bourdieu, "Haute Couture and Haute Culture," 133–4.
42 Bourdieu, "The Field of Cultural Production," 50–1.

1. The Kitchen Sink

1 Cordileone, "Helping Others Is His Style."
2 For a monumental history of the hippie "scene" in Toronto's Yorkville district in the 1960s, see Henderson, *Making the Scene*.
3 Frank Toskan, interview with author, 6 May 2015.
4 See Arvidsson and Malossi, "Customer Co-production from Social Factory to Brand." Additionally, Arvidsson offers a history of twentieth-century Italy in *Marketing Modernity*, in which he discusses how Italy developed from an economy based on agriculture, especially in the north (where Toskan's family hailed), to an American-influenced consumer society after the Second World War. Arvidsson's work with Malossi on the Italian fashion industry (following from that earlier study) looks at the co-production of brand value for the Fiorucci brand by artists, designers, and consumers within what they call the Milan "social factory."

5 Simpsons was purchased by the Hudson's Bay Company ("The Bay") in 1978, and the Queen Street store operated under The Bay banner beginning in 1991. This explains M·A·C's relatively easy expansion into The Bay stores across Canada in the 1980s and 1990s.
6 Toskan's new business was incorporated on 2 February 1981 under the name Make-up Art (Cosmetics) Limited (Ontario corporation 469257); it included Il-Makiage, effective 22 April 1981. Corporate profile information throughout has been acquired from Corporate Profile Reports, Ministry of Government Services, Province of Ontario.
7 Freed, "A Casual Approach at New Unisex Salon." For early examples of advice articles and profiles of local personalities featuring M·A·C, see Bot, "Anchor Favors 'Adventurous' Fashions"; Morra, "Summer Beauty"; Bot, "TV Host Builds Wardrobe around Blazers"; Bot, "Television Personality Nerene Virgin Has a Frugal Approach to Fashion"; and Morra, "Personal Best Hair and Makeup Artists."
8 Interview with Rod Ulmer by Diane Buckner, *Venture*, CBC Television, Toronto, ON, 3 March 1996.
9 Another of the Franks' side businesses (and perhaps a story of its own) was a record label they owned called Broken Records, and they had worked with Knight professionally in this capacity.
10 Victor Casale, interview with author, 21 June 2016.
11 Ibid.
12 In personal conversations with the author, both Toskan and Casale emphasized how much they disliked wasting resources, and they repurposed any number of prototypes, often saving them for years.
13 Frances Hathaway, interview with author, 17 June 2016.
14 Victor Casale, interview with author, 21 June 2016.
15 Carter, "MAC: From a Toronto Kitchen to a $20-Million Cosmetics Business in Six Years."
16 Jones, *Beauty Imagined*, 157.
17 Jones, *Beauty Imagined*, 119, 156; and Peiss, *Hope in a Jar*. See also Peiss, "On Beauty ... and the History of Business," for more on the histories of female entrepreneurs in the beauty industry.
18 See McGovern, "Creams Rise to Top."
19 Delean, "Entrepreneur Took On Makeup Industry Giants"; McGovern, "Family-Run Cosmetic Firms Join Forces."
20 Frank Toskan, interview with author, 27 April 2015.
21 See also Jones, "Globalization and Beauty."
22 Peiss, *Hope in a Jar*, 262.
23 Linda Scott discusses this topic extensively in *Fresh Lipstick*, 281–309.
24 Jones, "Globalization and Beauty."

25 See Malkan, *Not Just a Pretty Face*.
26 Jones, *Beauty Imagined*.
27 Suzanne Boyd, interview with author, 25 May 2015.
28 See, for example, Kilbourne, *Can't Buy My Love*, and Wolf, *The Beauty Myth*, for contemporaneous commentary on this topic.
29 Suzanne Boyd, interview with author, 25 May 2015.
30 Frank Toskan, interview with author, 6 May 2015.
31 Jane McKay, interview with author, 23 June 2016.
32 Frank Toskan, interview with author, 6 May 2015.
33 Frances Hathaway, interview with author, 17 June 2016.
34 Frank Toskan, interview with author, 6 May 2015.
35 Pierre Bourdieu's classic observation: "Taste classifies, and classifies the classifier." *Distinction*, 6.
36 Frank Toskan, interview with author, 6 May 2015.
37 Spears, "Cosmetics Company Soars by Making Its Own Rules."
38 Frank Toskan, interview with author, 6 May 2015.
39 Craik, *Fashion*, 42–7.
40 Frances Hathaway, interview with author, 17 June 2016.
41 Reckwitz, "Toward a Theory of Social Practices."
42 Ibid., 250.
43 Ibid., 255.
44 Frances Hathaway, interview with author, 17 June 2016.
45 Jane McKay, interview with author, 23 June 2016.
46 Frank Toskan, interview with author, 6 May 2015.
47 Frank Toskan, interview with author, 27 April 2015.
48 Tant, "Makeup Curtain-Raiser."
49 Currie, "Tubes of Plenty," 33.
50 Frank Toskan, interview with author, 6 May 2015.

2. Fashion Capital

1 Suzanne Boyd, interview with author, 25 May 2015.
2 Benson and Berman, *Then and Now*.
3 Suzanne Boyd, interview with author, 25 May 2015.
4 Rick Mugford, interview with author, 8 August 2016.
5 Suzanne Boyd, interview with author, 265 May 2015.
6 Frances Hathaway, interview with author, 17 June 2016; Currie, "Tubes of Plenty," 32.
7 Susie Sheffman, interview with author, 6 August 2016.
8 Matteson, "Future's Bright for Young Fashion Illustrator."
9 Frances Hathaway, interview with author, 17 June 2016.

Notes to pages 71–86

10 Donald Robertson, interview with author, 29 October 2015.
11 Frank Toskan, interview with author, 6 May 2015.
12 Donald Robertson, interview with author, 29 October 2015.
13 Suzanne Boyd, interview with author, 25 May 2015.
14 Frank Toskan, interview with author, 6 May 2015.
15 Monahan, "How Cover Girl's Fantasy Face Was Created by Makeup Artist."
16 Hastings, "Bring on the Night."
17 Morra, "Soft Focus Fall Beauty."
18 Tant, "Makeup Curtain-Raiser."
19 Aarsteinsen, "MAC Is Staying Small for Very Big Success."
20 Morra, "Soft Focus Fall Beauty."
21 Tant, "Polishing Up Your Lips and Eyes with Shades of Summer."
22 Tant, "Makeup Curtain-Raiser."
23 Jane McKay, interview with author, 23 June 2016.
24 Gilbert, "Urban Outfitting," 16. See also Rocamora, *Fashioning the City*, for a discussion of Paris as a fashion centre.
25 Rantisi, "The Ascendance of New York Fashion," 103.
26 See, for instance, Ewen, *Captains of Consciousness*.
27 Merlo and Polese, "Turning Fashion into Business."
28 Ibid., 418.
29 Ibid., 421–2.
30 Ibid., 432.
31 Phillip Ing, interview with author, 17 June 2015.
32 Palmer, *Fashion*.
33 Steven Levy, interview with author, 24 March 2015.
34 Jeanne Beker, interview with author, 7 July 2015.
35 David Livingstone, "Reflections on Canadian Fashion," in Robertson and Hastings, *Canadian Fashion Annual 1989*, 18.
36 Fulsang, "That Was Then, This Is Now," 34, 38.
37 Steven Levy, interview with author, 24 March 2015.
38 Bernadette Morra, interview with author, 27 July 2015.
39 For the full interview with Joe Mimran about the fashion industry in Toronto in the 1980s, see Bernstein, "All Dressed Up, No Place to Go."
40 Alfred Sung, quoted in Robertson and Hastings, *Canadian Fashion Annual 1989*, 34.
41 See Carstairs, "Roots Nationalism."
42 Susie Sheffman, interview with author, 6 August 2016.
43 Bernadette Morra, interview with author, 27 July 2015.
44 Jeanne Beker, interview with author, 7 July 2015.
45 Suzanne Boyd, interview with author, 25 May 2015.

46 Steven Levy, interview with author, 24 March 2015.
47 "Industry Festival 'First of Its Kind.'"
48 Susie Sheffman, interview with author, 6 August 2016.
49 Ibid.
50 Hastings, "Festival of Canadian Fashion Offers Jam-Packed Schedule."
51 Sturdza, "Festival Winners."
52 Aarsteinsen, "M·A·C Is Staying Small for Very Big Success."
53 Aarsteinsen, "Fashion Party Gives Industry Higher Profile."
54 Entwistle and Rocamora, "The Field of Fashion Materialized."
55 Sturdza, "MAC Cosmetics Achieves a Remarkable Success."
56 Frank Toskan, interview with author, 27 April 2015.
57 Susie Sheffman, interview with author, 6 August 2016.
58 Donald Robertson, interview with author, 29 October 2015.
59 For a detailed history, see Fulsang, "The Fashion of Writing, 1985–2000."
60 Hastings, "Fashion Section Begins Tuesday."
61 David Livingstone, in Robertson and Hastings, *Canadian Fashion Annual 1989*, 17.
62 Marina Sturdza promoted the book, which was released the second week of September 1988. Sturdza, "New Book Is a Tribute to Canadian Fashion."
63 Robertson and Hastings, *Canadian Fashion Annual 1989*, 113.
64 Rocamora, *Fashioning the City*, 55.
65 French, "No Liposomes, No Microcells, No Collagen-Elastin Embryo Extracts." Hathaway and others confirmed this point in interviews with the author.
66 Donald Robertson, interview with author, 29 October 2015.
67 Suzanne Boyd, interview with author, 25 May 2015.
68 Jeanne Beker, interview with author, 7 July 2015.
69 One version of the complex debate about who identified HIV first is chronicled in Farber, *Serious Adverse Events*, and looks at the politics of AIDS research within the American medical industrial complex.
70 See King, "The Politics of the Body and the Body Politic."
71 See Gamson, "Silence, Death, and the Invisible Enemy."
72 It is important to note that women were often excluded from early discourses of AIDS, safer sex, and sexual identity politics. This gap is addressed in Goldstein and Marlow, eds., *The Gender Politics of HIV/AIDS in Women*.
73 Best-known are Treichler, *How to Have Theory in an Epidemic*; and Sontag, *Illness as Metaphor and AIDS and Its Metaphors*. See also Shilts, *And the Band Played On*; Gamson, "Silence, Death, and the Invisible Enemy"; and Clarke, "Homophobia Out of the Closet," 323.

74 These data about HIV/AIDS in Toronto and Ontario from the 1980s are found in Remis and Liu, "HIV/AIDS in Ontario," Table 2.14, p. 108; Table 4.1, p. 128. Data about the early days of the epidemic are difficult to locate, given the inaccurate reporting of the time.
75 Phillip Ing, interview with author, 17 June 2016. See also Goddard, "AIDS Is Reshaping Show Business." The first year that AIDS deaths were recorded in Ontario was 1987.
76 AIDS Committee of Toronto, *Twenty Years of Fashion Cares 1987–2006*, 12. This artefact can be found at the Royal Ontario Museum Library and Archives.
77 Bernadette Morra, interview with author, 27 July 2015.
78 Susie Sheffman, interview with author, 6 August 2015.
79 "New York Fashion Designers Cautious." See also Klemesrud, "Dr Mathilde Krim."
80 Sheinman, "AIDS: It's Everyone's Business," 1. Written in the relatively early stages of the epidemic, the article does contain some misinformation that also reflects some of the biases against those who had HIV and developed complications from AIDS. Friedman-Kien had also been quoted in the first mainstream newspaper article on the "cancer" affecting "homosexuals," in Altman's piece in the *New York Times*, "Rare Cancer Seen in 41 Homosexuals."
81 Hymowitz, "AIDS Is Decimating the Fashion Business."
82 Ibid.
83 Susie Sheffman, interview with author, 6 August 2015.
84 Frank Toskan, interview with author, 6 May 2015.

3. Caring Is Never Out of Fashion

1 Rayside and Lindquist, "AIDS Activism and the State in Canada," 41.
2 Along with Rayside and Lindquist, for work on AIDS activism in Canada, see, for instance, Gillett, "The Challenges of Institutionalization for AIDS Media Activism"; idem, *A Grassroots History of the HIV/AIDS Epidemic in North America*; and Kinsman, "Managing AIDS Organizing." A more personal and detailed account of the local activist scene can be found in Silversides, *AIDS Activist*.
3 Rayside and Lindquist, "AIDS Activism and the State in Canada," 45.
4 Maguire, Hardy, and Lawrence, "Institutional Entrepreneurship in Emerging Fields," 661.
5 Rayside and Lindquist, "AIDS Activism and the State in Canada," 49.
6 Alan Sears discusses how AIDS service organizations challenged the tenets of public health in "AIDS and the Health of Nations."

7 Robertson, "An Annotated Chronology," 319. Robertson's chronology is based on media accounts of AIDS in Toronto in the city's major newspapers – the *Toronto Star*, the *Globe and Mail*, the *Toronto Sun* – and in the independent gay community publication *The Body Politic*. Silversides describes this press conference in great detail in *AIDS Activist*, 54–5, since Michael Lynch was one of its founding members.
8 The Casey House announcement was covered by the local mainstream newspapers (*Star*, *Globe and Mail*) through early 1986, as documented by Robertson, "An Annotated Chronology," 341.
9 Chiotti and Joseph, "Casey House," 137.
10 Notice of AAN! Meeting for Wednesday, 5 October 1988, at 7:30 p.m. at the 519 Community Centre, Church Street, Toronto. Vertical Files "CAN 16 AAN 1988, AAN!," Canadian Lesbian and Gay Archives, 34 Isabella Street, Toronto, ON, indicated throughout as "CLGA." Other CLGA locations are identified where relevant.
11 Rayside and Lindquist, "AIDS Activism and the State in Canada," 53.
12 Ibid., 64.
13 It should also be noted that arts activism around AIDS was substantial, although its politicized and disruptive goals were quite different from what I am discussing here. See, for instance, Crimp, with Rolston, "Aids Activist Graphics"; and Crimp, "AIDS: Cultural Analysis/Cultural Activism." Gamson discusses ACT UP's reappropriation of symbols, including the pink triangle, language, and blood, in "Silence, Death, and the Invisible Enemy,'" 361. See also Crimp, "How to Have Promiscuity in an Epidemic"; and Sember and Gere, "'Let the Record Show ...'" For discussion on the Canadian AIDS activist art collective General Idea, see Bordowitz, *General Idea*.
14 Livingstone, "Fund-Raising with Fashion."
15 Lannon, "Fashion, Cosmetic Industries Join Forces at AIDS Benefit."
16 Syd Beder, interview with author, 19 July 2016.
17 See Hastings, "'Fashion Cares' T-Shirt Project Raising Funds for ACT Relief."
18 Interview with Syd Beder, in *M·A·C VIVA GLAM Fashion Cares Future Perfect 1996*, produced by Rogers Cable 10. Video, ACT 0903, Sound and Moving Image Library, York University (hereafter SMIL).
19 Steven Levy, interview with author, 24 March 2015.
20 Silversides, *AIDS Activist*; Rayside and Lindquist, "AIDS Activism and the State in Canada," 52.
21 Hastings, "'Fashion Cares' T-Shirt Project Raising Funds for ACT Relief," D4.
22 *NOW* 6, no. 34, 7–13 May 1987, 44.

23 Chin and Warkentin, "Preparing Fashion's Caring, Outfitting at the Outback." The ad appears on page 6.
24 ACT Newsletter, 5–14 June 1987. Vertical Files "ACT 1987," CLGA.
25 See Livingstone, "T-Shirt Shows that Fashion Really Cares"; Hastings, "Fashion Cares Shirts Launched"; Livingstone, "For Minimalist Chic in Klein Collection."
26 *NOW* 6, no. 39, 4–10, June 1987, 32.
27 David Clark, quoted in Kaplan, ed., *Fashion Cares*.
28 Suzanne Boyd, interview with author, 25 May 2015.
29 Phillip Ing, interview with author, 17 June 2016.
30 Livingstone, "An Entertaining Showcase."
31 Németh, "Pride Opulence."
32 Syd Beder, interview with author, 19 July 2016.
33 Rick Mugford, quoted in AIDS Committee of Toronto, *Twenty Years of Fashion Cares*, 14.
34 Hastings, "Fashion Cares AIDS Benefit Raises Eyebrows – and Funds."
35 Rick Mugford, quoted in AIDS Committee of Toronto, *Twenty Years of Fashion Cares*, 14.
36 Bernadette Morra, interview with author, 27 July 2015.
37 Frank Toskan, interview with author, 6 May 2015.
38 Entwistle and Rocamora, "The Field of Fashion Materialized," 740.
39 The thirty-seven signatures on the T-shirt were: Linda Lundström, Comrags, Emily Zarb, Wayne Clark, Roger Edwards, Yes & No, Urbain Vain, Clotheslines Inc., Hoax Couture, Alexander Reda, Loucas, Pluche, Steven Schact, Roots, Anne Seally, Vila Lobos, Zapata, Mekito, Vivian Shyu, Dean/Dan, Babel, Pat McDonagh, Bent Boys, Marilyn Brooks, Price Roman, Selina, Winston, Robin Kay, Debora Kuchmé, Dominic Bellissimo, Jim Pope, Michael Tong, Mariola Mayer, Wesley and Winsa, Lana Lowon, Times II, Antonucci, and Keith Richardson. When referenced against the Fashion Cares 1987 program, the signatures of some of the designers who contributed to the fashion show are missing from the T-shirt; likewise, there are designers' signatures on the T-shirt that indicate support, but who did not actually participate in the June fashion show. There are also some well-known Canadian designers who neither participated in the show nor offered a signature for the T-shirt.
40 Phillip Ing, interview with author, 17 June 2016.
41 Suzanne Boyd, interview with author, 25 May 2015.
42 Fashion SCares poster. Box ACT 92-175/08, "F/R – Fashion Scares," CLGA.
43 Hastings, "AIDS Benefit Show Draws Small Crowd."
44 Livingstone, "Designer Has Color Clout."

45 It appears that Matteson retired from fashion writing in the late 1980s to become more involved in fashion business ventures, such as becoming Vice-President of Marketing for Town & Country, a women's clothing chain, in 1991. See Leeming, "Town and Country Targets Higher Market."
46 Press release from Sandra Matteson, 22 April 1988. "Publicity – Fashion Blooms," Accession ACT 1988-048/10, CLGA.
47 Press release from Sandra Matteson, 23 March 1988, "Publicity – Fashion Blooms," Accession ACT 1988-048/10, CLGA.
48 Memo from Carrie Sager, ACT, to Stephen Manning, Executive Director, ACT, 27 April 1988. "Correspondence from Sandra – Fashion Blooms," Accession ACT 1988-048/10, CLGA.
49 A copy of the poster is housed in the AIDS Education Posters Collection at the University of Rochester, Rochester, NY, and can be viewed at http://aep.lib.rochester.edu/node/41131.
50 Press release from Sandra Matteson, 22 April 1988. "Publicity – Fashion Blooms," Accession ACT 1988-048/10, CLGA.
51 Ibid.
52 Invitation and poster for Fashion Blooms. "Publicity – Fashion Blooms," Accession ACT 1988-048/10, CLGA.
53 Letter from Lorraine Manley, Development Co-ordinator, ACT, to Ms Travis, 7 April 7, 1987. "Sponsors, Supporters, Patrons – Fashion Blooms," Accession ACT 1988-048/10, CLGA.
54 Letter from Lorraine Manley, Development Co-ordinator, ACT, to Michael Walton, Promotions Manager, *Toronto Star*, 21 March 1988. "Publicity – Fashion Blooms," Accession ACT 1988/048/10, CLGA.
55 Ibid.
56 Letter from Sandra Matteson to Bonnie Bickell, VP B.B. Bargoon's, 9 March 1988. "Correspondence from Sandra – Fashion Blooms," Accession ACT 1988/048/10, CLGA.
57 Letter from Lorraine Manley, Development Co-ordinator, ACT, to Ms Tavis, 7 April 1988. "Sponsors, Supporters, Patrons – Fashion Blooms," Accession ACT 1988/048/10, CLGA.
58 *Inside Fashion: The People, Places and Events Inside the Fashion Business* 2, no. 6 (8 February 1988), 6. "Publicity – Fashion Blooms," Accession ACT 1988-048/10, CLGA.
59 *Inside Fashion: The People, Places and Events Inside the Fashion Business* 2, no. 16 (2 May 1988), 5. "Publicity – Fashion Blooms," Accession ACT 1988-048/10, CLGA.
60 Hastings, "Fashion Expected to 'Bloom' at AIDS Fundraising Gala."
61 Letter from Lorraine Manley, Development Co-ordinator, ACT, to the Honourable Elinor Caplan, Minister of Health, 17 March 1988.

"Sponsors, Supporters, Patrons – Fashion Blooms," Accession ACT 1988-048/10, CLGA.
62 Letter from Sandra Matteson to Alderman Dale Martin, Ward 6, Toronto, 10 May 1988. "Correspondence from Sandra – Fashion Blooms," Accession ACT 1988-048/10, CLGA.
63 Sandra Matteson, quoted in AIDS Committee of Toronto, *Twenty Years of Fashion Cares*, 18.
64 The fashion show can be viewed in ACT's video recording of the event: "Fashion Cares – Fashion Blooms," produced by the Fashion Cares Group of the AIDS Committee of Toronto. Video, ACT 0918, SMIL.
65 Livingstone, "Style Notes: Fund-Raising Party Blooms."
66 See also Entwistle, *The Fashioned Body*, 50, for how cultural capital aids one's ability to discern the differences in fabrication quality.
67 Morra, "AIDS Fundraiser a Blooming Success."
68 Donald Robertson, interview with author, 29 October 2015.
69 Robertson, "An Annotated Chronology," n4, 351. See also Robertson's histories of AIDS activism in Toronto, as well as AIDS coverage in the gay publication *The Body Politic*, which predate *Fashion Cares*, noting only when the AIDS Committee of Toronto was founded. Robertson, "AIDS Coverage in *The Body Politic*, 1981–1987."
70 Silversides, *AIDS Activist*, 118.
71 Susie Sheffman, interview with author, 6 August 2015.
72 Phillip Ing, interview with author, 17 June 2017.
73 Jeanne Beker, interview with author, 7 July 2015.
74 Syd Beder, interview with author, 19 July 2016.

4. Put Your Money Where Your Mouth Is

1 Harris, "AIDS and the Fashion Industry."
2 Hochswender, "AIDS and the Fashion World."
3 Schneider, Connock, and Nolan, "Fashion – An Industry Dressed in Mourning."
4 Shelley Wickabrod, quoted in Livingstone, "Fashion with a Cause."
5 Hastings, "Festival Show Depended on Special Effects."
6 Livingstone, "A Nineties Mod Revival"; Tant, "Cosmetics Take a Leaf from Nature"; Morra, "The Mod Squad"; Tant, "Mod Squad Stages a Comeback Worthy of Emma Peel, Twiggy."
7 Brenner, "MAC Attack."
8 Mussett, "Anti-Aging Creams a 'Scam,' Author Says."
9 Donald Robertson, interview with author, 29 October 2015.
10 D. Brady, "The M·A·C Attack."

11 See Aucoin's influential books *Face Forward*; *Making Faces*; and *The Art of Makeup*. Aucoin died in 2003.
12 O'Hagan, "At Face Value."
13 Carter, "MAC."
14 Gayle, "Brushing Up on Cosmetics."
15 Valerie MacKenzie, interview with author, 28 June 28.
16 Brady, "The M·A·C Attack," 44.
17 Reguly, "Toronto Firm Catches the Eye of U.S. Glamor Set"; MacDonald, "Facing Up to the M·A·C Attack," 62.
18 Conversations with Toskan and Casale about this issue can be found in several contemporaneous articles, such as Bot, "Cosmetics Chief Is Comfortable"; Mussett, "Pin to Support AIDS Research"; Tant, "Back to Basics Meets High Tech"; and Currie, "Tubes of Plenty," 32–4.
19 Graff would go on to co-found CoverFX, a cosmetics line devoted entirely to skin tone and complexion needs, with Victor Casale at the helm of product innovation as chief innovation officer.
20 Victor Casale, interview with author, 21 June 2016.
21 Phillip Ing, interview with author, 17 June 2016.
22 Fashion Cares An Evening of Sheer Drama was held on 9 May 1989 at the Terrace Roller Rink on Mutual Street in downtown Toronto, a venue also known simply as "The Terrace." The event poster can be viewed at http://aep.lib.rochester.edu/node/42990.
23 Ronnie Richman, quoted in Livingstone, "Sheer Drama Raises Funds for AIDS."
24 *Fashion Cares: An Evening of Sheer Drama*, 1989 program. Vertical Files, "Fashion Cares 1989," CLGA.
25 *Fashion Cares: The Crystal Ball*, 1990 program. Vertical Files, "Fashion Cares 1990," CLGA.
26 Livingstone, "Show an Astrological Parade."
27 *Fashion Cares: Red Hot & Blue*, 1991 program. Vertical Files, "Fashion Cares 1991," CLGA.
28 Interviews with Jane McKay and Bill Angst, "Fashion Cares Red Hot + Blue," Rogers Community 10, directed by David Bailey, produced by Silvia Wineland, 24 April 1991. Video, ACT 0882, SMIL.
29 See Bourdieu, *The Rules of Art*, 142; idem, "The Field of Cultural Production," 53.
30 Kaplan, *Fashion Cares*, 2013.
31 *Fashion Cares: Red Hot & Blue*, 1991 program. Vertical Files, "Fashion Cares 1991," CLGA.
32 Jeanne Beker, interview with author, 7 July 2015.
33 Carter, "MAC."

34 Frank Toskan, interview with author, 6 May 2015.
35 Helen Jefferson Lenskyj discusses how public health campaigns about HIV and AIDS existed in the mid-1980s in Toronto and were well-established by the 1990s. Lenskyj, "Clinically Correct?"
36 Frank Toskan, interview with author, 6 May 2015.
37 Not until 1996 were highly active (or effective) antiretroviral therapies (HAART) developed that significantly delayed HIV progression. That is when AIDS-related deaths started to dramatically decrease. For mortality trends, see Schanzer, "Trends in HIV/AIDS Mortality in Canada, 1987–1998."
38 Frank Toskan, interview with author, 6 May 2015.
39 Ibid.
40 Ibid.
41 Interview with Frank Toskan by Anastasia MacLean, "M·A·C VIVA GLAM Fashion Cares Wings of Life 1994," Rogers Community 10, produced by Joan Finnighan, directed by Michael McNamara, hosted and narrated by Anastasia MacLean. Video, ACT 0902, SMIL.
42 French, "No Liposomes, No Microcells."
43 Frank Toskan, interview with author, 6 May 2015.
44 See the 1992 video here: http://www.youtube.com/watch?v=VlxJi9tm1BI.
45 Livingstone, "Style Notes: Animal."
46 "Charitable Event Sponsorship" application form. Vertical Files "Fashion Cares 1992," CLGA.
47 Ann Kaplan, *Fashion Cares*, n.p.
48 Fillion, "Overshadowing the AIDS Message."
49 Morra, "AIDS Gala Scores Hits and Misses."
50 Bernadette Morra noted this fact in her mostly negative review of the event in "AIDS Gala Scores Hits and Misses." Sebastian's sponsorship is prominent on the poster, which can be viewed at http://aep.lib.rochester.edu/node/42991.
51 "Fashion Cares Arcouture," Rogers Community 10, produced and directed by David Bailey. Video, ACT 0901, SMIL.
52 Phillip Ing, interview with author, 17 June 2016.
53 *M·A·C VIVA GLAM Fashion Cares Wings of Life* 1994, Rogers Community 10, produced by Joan Finnighan, directed by Michael McNamara, hosted and narrated by Anastasia MacLean. Vídeo, ACT 0902, SMIL.
54 Thanks to Susan Knabe for pointing out this connection.
55 Kaplan, *Fashion,* n.p.
56 See letter of thanks to Farley Chatto, dated August 3, 1994, which reiterated this amount. Reproduced in Kaplan, *Fashion Cares*, no page.

57 The M·A·C AIDS Fund was incorporated as a registered Canadian charity on 30 September 1994. BN Registration number 891111650RR0001.
58 Frank Toskan, interview with author, 6 May 2015.
59 According to the Spring 1995 "M·A·C Mag," an internal magazine Toskan created for his employees, the full list of recipients included, in Canada: Toronto People with AIDS; Canadian AIDS Society, The Teresa Group, ACT, Anglican Houses Street Outreach Services (S)S); in the United States: Tanya's Children, DIFFA (Design Industries Foundation Fighting AIDS), God's Love We Deliver, AIDS Project L.A., Children's Diagnostic and Treatment Center of South Florida, Tuesday's Child, Caring for Babies with AIDS, Dimock Community Health Center–Boston Pediatric AIDS Project, Cook County Hospital, Bronx-Lebanon Hospital Center, Friends in Needs, AIDS Dance-A-Thon, The Center; in the UK: Children with AIDS Charity at St Mary's Hospital, AIDS Crisis Trust. From Frank Toskan's personal collection.
60 Frank Toskan, interview with author, 6 May 2015.
61 Although convention and etiquette dictate that drag queens take the female pronoun while performing, according to both their gender portrayal and their drag name, RuPaul is referred to throughout by the male pronoun. RuPaul is also his given name, and he self-identifies as RuPaul whether he is in drag or not. Additionally, RuPaul is most often (but not always) referred to as "he" or "him" in interviews and articles.
62 "Hot Dance Breakouts," *Billboard*. See also Flick, "RuPaul."
63 Morra, "Drag Queen Crowned the New Face of MAC."

5. Selling Out

1 French, "On the Wane."
2 Moore, "How About a Little Rouge, Sir?"
3 Frank Toskan, interview with author, 6 May 2015; Victor Casale, interview with author, 21 June 2015.
4 Moore, "Restricted."
5 Formula K was folded into the M·A·C business in 1993. Knight Hair Care Inc. (Ontario corporation 847286) was amalgamated with M·A·C, now known as Make-up Art Cosmetics Limited (brackets around "Cosmetics" removed) on 31 December 1993 (Ontario corporation 969448).
6 Frank Toskan, interview with author, 6 May 2015.
7 Lowe, "Will Success Spoil MAC?"
8 The fact that this "secret" was the Franks' idea is also discussed in the television interview by Diane Buckner, "MAC Cosmetics," *Venture*, CBC Television, 3 March 1996.

9 See Strom, "Lauder in Distribution Venture with Rival." The deal was also noted in cosmetics industry trade journals. See "Lauder Markets MAC Outside Canada," *Cosmetics*.
10 Miller, "Would You Buy Lipstick from This Man?"
11 Lowe, "Will Success Spoil MAC?," 43–5; interview by Diane Buckner, "MAC Cosmetics," *Venture*, CBC Television, 3 March 1996.
12 Jane McKay, interview with author, 23 June 2016.
13 Valerie MacKenzie, interview with author, 27 June 2016.
14 Siklos, "Staid Lauder Owns Rad M.A.C." Siklos states that Lauder raised $458 million in its IPO.
15 William Lauder, quoted in television interview by Diane Buckner, "MAC Cosmetics," *Venture*, CBC Television, 3 March 1996.
16 MacDonald, "Facing Up to the M·A·C Attack," 62.
17 Valerie MacKenzie, interview with author, 27 June 2016.
18 Interview with Frank Angelo by Deirdre McMurdy, "Canada AM," hosted by Leslie Jones, CTV Television, Toronto, 22 April 1996.
19 "In Your Face," *Canadian Business*.
20 Victor Casale, interview with author, 21 June 2016.
21 Spears, "Cosmetics Company Soars by Making Its Own Rules," C1.
22 See "Looking Good!," *Materials Management and Distribution*.
23 For instance, M·A·C's sales were $4 million at Henri Bendel alone, twice that of any other cosmetic line there. See Strom, "Lauder in Distribution Venture with Rival." M·A·C was sold in 110 outlets or "doors" worldwide, with a small number of stand-alone stores (including one on Toronto's Bloor Street), even though it only started turning a profit in 1991.
24 "That Old MAC Magic," *Marketing*.
25 Brady, "Putting a New Face on Asia."
26 Victor Casale, interview with author, 21 June 2016.
27 Stephen P. Manning, Executive Director of ACT, keynote to the Annual General Meeting of the Canadian AIDS Association Annual General Meeting, 12 May 1990, Winnipeg, Manitoba. Vertical Files "ACT 1993," CLGA.
28 The history of Cole's AIDS philanthropy, including this image, can be found on the company's website: https://www.kennethcole.com/lgfg-making-aids-history.html.
29 This story is described in the documentary *Pink Ribbons, Inc.* (dir. Léa Pool, 2011), based on Samantha King's 2006 book of the same name.
30 Miller, "Tapping into Women's Issues Is Potent Way to Reach Market."
31 Bracuk, "The Style Samaritans."
32 Jennings and Andersen, "The Importance of Social and Political Context"; see also Sturken, *Tangled Memories*.

Notes to pages 173–9

33 Margolies and the NAMES Project, *Always Remember*.
34 Kraft, "In the Name of Charity."
35 Harris, "Making Kitsch from AIDS." This article subsequently appeared (edited) as "The Kitschification of AIDS," in Harris's anthology *The Rise and Fall of Gay Culture*, 219–38, and hereafter this text is cited.
36 Harris, "The Kitschification of AIDS," 223.
37 To see the original photo, and for the history of Frare's photographs, see http://time.com/3503000/behind-the-picture-the-photo-that-changed-the-face-of-aids; and for video: https://www.youtube.com/watch?v=jxaCvvPr98E
38 Scalvini, "Glamorizing Sick Bodies."
39 On this point, also see Tinic, "United Colors and Untied Meanings."
40 Sturken, *Tangled Memories*, 170–2.
41 Rutherford, *Endless Propaganda*, 156–64.
42 For a discussion of these issues in relation to Benetton's advertising, also see Giroux, "Consuming Social Change.'"
43 Giese, "To Die For!"
44 "ACT Proposed ACT Policy on Outside Fundraising Events," 7 August 1994. "Fundraising Policy:" Box 1999-026/01 ACT R.0.3, CLGA offsite location.
45 "That Old MAC Magic," 1, 11.
46 "M·A·C VIVA GLAM Fashion Cares Salute to Suburbia: An Evening of Pure Polyester 1995," *FashionTelevision*, CityTV, produced, written, directed, and hosted by Jeanne Beker, May 1995. Video, ACT 0900, SMIL.
47 Brian Gluckstein, quoted in AIDS Committee of Toronto, *Twenty Years of Fashion Cares*, 32.
48 Beker, *Jeanne Unbottled*, 176.
49 All of the other corporate sponsors can be viewed on the poster *M·A·C VIVA GLAM Fashion Cares Salute to Suburbia* 1995, available at http://aep.lib.rochester.edu/node/46117.
50 "Thanks 2 You," *The Province* (Vancouver).
51 French, "No Liposomes, No Microcells, No Collagen-Elastin Embryo Extracts," 75.
52 Eikenberry, "The Hidden Costs of Cause Marketing." A more detailed version is offered in Nickel and Eikenberry, "A Critique of the Discourse of Marketized Philanthropy."
53 This discussion is found in Miller, "Would You Buy Lipstick from This Man?"
54 Bain, "Truth in Advertising."
55 Loxley, "k.d. Joins M.A.C."
56 French, "Beauty Queens."

Notes to pages 180–9

57 Jim Hicks, interviewed in Lowe, "Will Success Spoil MAC?," 43–5.
58 Interview with Frank Toskan by Jeanne Beker, "Fashion Cares 10th Anniversary Special: Future Perfect," *FT – FashionTelevision*, CityTV, May 1996, produced and written by Jeanne Beker and Michael Proudfoot. Video, ACT 0883, SMIL.
59 Morra, "Fashion Dares."
60 *M·A·C VIVA GLAM Fashion Cares Future Perfect* program 1996. Vertical Files CAN 2435, "Fashion Cares 1996," CLGA.
61 "Fashion Cares 10th Anniversary Special: Future Perfect," *FT-FashionTelevision*, CityTV, May 1996, produced and written by Jeanne Beker and Michael Proudfoot. Video, ACT 0883, SMIL.
62 Delap, "Buzz."
63 Tant, "Unconventional Models Puts Cosmetics Firm in Spotlight."
64 Phillip Ing, interview with author, 17 June 2016.
65 Miller, "Would You Buy Lipstick from This Man?"
66 Valerie MacKenzie, interview with author, 28 June 2016.
67 Miller, "Would You Buy Lipstick from This Man?"
68 See Morra, "300 Pay Tribute to Cosmetics Master"; idem, "MAC Fashions Fine Funeral in Wake of Angelo's Death"; Schiro, "Frank Angelo, 49, Cosmetics Innovator, Dies"; MacKinnon, "Frank Angelo Ran Cosmetics Firm"; Delap, "M·A·C Co-founder Was Cosmetic's Firm's Marketing Mind."
69 Collison, "Profit & Loss."
70 Delap, "Can Con in the House?"
71 Harris, "Koolhaus Creditors Issue Challenge."
72 MacDonald, "Managing Strategy."
73 Leeming, "Lang Boosts M·A·C AIDS Fund." One of the local beneficiaries of the Fund was the BC First Nations AIDS Society.
74 MacDonald, "Managing Strategy," B9.
75 The event was held on 10 May 1997 at the Moss Park Armoury.
76 "M·A·C VIVA GLAM Fashion Cares Photo Ball 1997." Video, ACT 0919, SMIL.
77 Ibid. Toskan is incorrect about the year of the first *Fashion Cares*; it was 1987, not 1986. Likewise, M·A·C was founded much earlier than "eleven years ago," i.e., in 1986. The year 1984 is given as M·A·C's official founding, but of course the company actually began its operations much earlier than this.
78 "M·A·C VIVA GLAM Fashion Cares Beautiful World 1998," hosted by Sook-Yin Lee, MuchMusic, CityTV/MuchMusic. Video, ACT 0904, SMIL.
79 Bourdieu, "Haute Couture and Haute Culture," 137.

6. Dragging Theory into Practice

1. Tuck, "Andrew Tuck Considers Makeup for Men."
2. Livingstone, "RuPaul: Dragging Theory into Practice."
3. Flick, "RuPaul: Changing the Makeup of Pop Music," 1.
4. Garber, *Vested Interests*.
5. Barthes, *The Fashion System*.
6. Harron, "A Hero for Our Times."
7. See, for example, DeCaro, "Being 'Out' Was Very 'In' for Lesbians, Gays in 1993"; Clark, "What a Drag!"; Pugsley, "Queerness Bursts into the Mainstream"; Jones, "'Supermodel' with His Own 'Je Ne Sashay Quoi.'"
8. Morra, "Rags 2 Riches."
9. Miles Roberts, quoted in AIDS Committee of Toronto, *Twenty Years of Fashion Cares*, 26.
10. Levine, "Caring Richness."
11. Hanna, "Antoine Tempé Surveys Drag Scene."
12. Livingstone, "The Camera in Drag."
13. Morra, "Book on Cross-Dressers Not a Drag, Photographer Says."
14. *The Crying Game* (1992, dir. Neil Jordan); *Orlando* (1992, dir. Sally Potter); *The Adventures of Priscilla, Queen of the Desert* (1994, dir. Stephan Elliott); *Ed Wood* (1994, dir. Tim Burton); *To Wong Foo, Thanks for Everything! Julie Newmar* (1995, dir. Beeban Kidron).
15. Butler, *Bodies That Matter*, 85. Here, Butler specifically refers to *Some Like It Hot* (1959, dir. Billy Wilder); *Tootsie* (1982, dir. Sydney Pollack); *Victor/Victoria* (1982, dir. Blake Edwards); and *Mrs. Doubtfire* (1993, dir. Chris Columbus).
16. Interview with Phillip Ing by Jeanne Beker, "M·A·C VIVA GLAM Fashion Cares Salute to Suburbia: An Evening of Pure Polyester 1995," *FashionTelevision*, CityTV, 13 May 1995. Video, ACT 0900, SMIL.
17. "M·A·C VIVA GLAM Fashion Cares Salute to Suburbia: An Evening of Pure Polyester 1995," Rogers Community 10, 13 May 1995. Video, ACT 0692, SMIL.
18. John McCracken, interview with author, 1 November 2018.
19. Weiss, "Desire for Good," 24.
20. Ibid., 25.
21. Butler, *Gender Trouble*, 136.
22. Ibid., 138.
23. From psychologist Joan Riviere's response to Freud, to the performance of femininity as a response to male subjectivity in Hitchcock's 1958 film *Vertigo*, to the 1990s supermodels and RuPaul discussed here, there is

no question that a gendered presentation of femininity involves masquerade. This masquerade is also meaningful when considering the "mask" cosmetics offer, compounded by the drag performance, which also requires a mask as part of its costume. My approach here, however, has been to highlight the aspects of femininity that result from practices, routines, and behaviours, and to rely less on the psychoanalytic, Lacanian foundation that underpins Butler's psychoanalytic approach in *Gender Trouble*, although there is no doubt that considering masquerade more fully alongside these practices would produce a fruitful analysis. See Riviere, "Womanliness as a Masquerade"; and Leonard, "A Fall from Grace."

24 Butler, in Osborne and Segal, "Gender as Performance," 33.
25 RuPaul (correctly!) assumed that many readers would be interested in the details of his "tuck" method, which he describes in *Lettin It All Hang Out*, 8.
26 Newton, *Mother Camp*.
27 See Garber, *Vested Interests*.
28 Harron, "A Hero for Our Times," 4.
29 Newton, *Mother Camp*, 100.
30 Schacht and Underwood, "The Absolutely Fabulous but Flawlessly Customary World of Female Impersonators."
31 Goldman, "Boys Will Be Girls."
32 White, "What a Drag."
33 Interview with Frank Toskan by Jeanne Beker, "M·A·C VIVA GLAM Fashion Cares Salute to Suburbia: An Evening of Pure Polyester," 13 May 1995, Rogers Community 10, produced by Phillip Ing. Video, ACT 0692, SMIL.
34 Interview with RuPaul by Jeanne Beker, "M·A·C VIVA GLAM Fashion Cares Salute to Suburbia: An Evening of Pure Polyester," Rogers Community 10, produced by Phillip Ing, 13 May 1995. Video, ACT 0692, SMIL.
35 Curson, "Ru, Moisturize, Moisturize!"
36 Bain, "Truth in Advertising," 52.
37 Miller, "Would You Buy Lipstick from This Man?," 1.
38 Bain, "Truth in Advertising," 52.
39 A.J. Benza and Michael Lewittes, quoted in Harper, *Are We Not Men?*, 192.
40 Harper, *Are We Not Men?*, 192.
41 Magubane, "Black Skins, Black Masks."
42 Reuters, "Bishop Attacks Use of Drag Queen in Ads."
43 Butler, *Bodies That Matter*, 84–5.
44 Rhyne, "Racializing White Drag."

45 Salih, "On Judith Butler and Performativity."
46 Loxley, "k.d. Joins M.A.C," D8.
47 Clark, "What a Drag!," J1.
48 Frank Toskan, interview with author, 22 June 2015.
49 Ibid.
50 French, "Beauty Queens," 42.
51 Weiss, "Desire for Good," 27.
52 Butler, *Bodies That Matter*, 178.
53 k.d. lang, quoted in Frankel, "Wham, Bam! VIVA GLAM!"
54 Gibson, "Lang New MAC Voice."
55 Schacht and Underwood, "The Absolutely Fabulous but Flawlessly Customary World of Female Impersonators," 3.
56 Ibid, 11.
57 My thanks to Gerry Lavallee for first describing to me how drag shows in Toronto's gay clubs in the 1980s were frequently engaged in AIDS fundraising, often doing condom demonstrations on bananas. I am also indebted to Susan Knabe for directing me specifically to the DQ shows in Toronto.
58 Michael Oscars, interviewed by Rowesome, "25 Years of Casey House," 6. See also Zekas, "Not Your Garden-Variety Show." Zekas covered most of the DQ shows in the *Toronto Star*.
59 Eric Turner, interviewed by Rowesome, "25 Years of Casey House," 6.
60 Zekas, "Boys Will Be Girls."
61 Michael Oscars, quoted in "25 Years of Casey House," 6. The Proud Lives section was a list of obituaries and memorials.
62 David Clark, quoted in Rowesome, "25 Years of Casey House," 6.
63 Wilson, "Use of Condoms Becomes Standard in Gay Bathhouses."
64 Bryan Greenwood, interview with author, 19 October 2014.
65 Eric Turner, quoted in Rowesome, "25 Years of Casey House," 6.
66 Chiotti and Joseph, "Casey House."
67 Press release, 14 January 1992. Vertical Files "DQ 1328," CLGA.
68 "Show Drags in $101,000 For Casey House," *Toronto Star*.
69 Michael Oscars, D.Q. '95 program. Vertical Files "D.Q. 1329" CLGA. The show took place 9 to 18 March 1995 at the Bathurst Street Theatre.
70 "D.Q. '95." Video, ACT 0587, SMIL.
71 D.Q. '95 program. Vertical Files "DQ 1329," CLGA.
72 Ibid.
73 *Transie Times*, January 1991, 18–19. These artefacts can be found at the Pride Library, University of Western Ontario. I am following Holliday's own language within the publication.
74 Livingstone, "Rearing-to-Go."

75 See Hilbert, "The Politics of Drag."
76 Butler, *Bodies That Matter*, 177–8.
77 See Lypsinka's website: http://www.lypsinka.com/press/pressOLD.html.
78 Flick, "RuPaul Recalls a Year of Work, Work, Work."
79 Harris, "The Aesthetic of Drag," 218, in *The Rise and Fall of Gay Culture*.

Epilogue: The Brightest Jewel in Our Crown

1 Bittar, "MAC's Feeney to Spread the Word."
2 "Lauder Acquiring Remaining Interest in MAC," *Cosmetics*.
3 French, "He Changed the Face of Makeup."
4 Frank Toskan, interview with author, 6 May 2016.
5 Einstein, *Compassion, Inc.*, 130. See also, for instance, Banet-Weiser, who articulates a similar position in *Authentic™*.
6 Bourdieu, "The Field of Cultural Production," 31.

Bibliography

Archival Collections

Canadian Lesbian and Gay Archives (CLGA), Toronto, ON.
Pride Library, D.B. Weldon Library, University of Western Ontario, London, ON.
River Campus Libraries Rare Books and Special Collections, University of Rochester, Rochester, NY.
Royal Ontario Museum Library and Archives, University of Toronto, Toronto, ON.
Sound and Moving Image Library, Room 125, Scott Library, York University, Toronto, ON.

Interviews and Correspondence

Syd Beder. Interview with author, 19 July 2016.
Jeanne Beker. Interview with author, 7 July 2015.
Suzanne Boyd. Interview with author, 25 May 2015.
Karen Buglisi Weiler. Interview with author, 7 July 2016.
Victor Casale. Interviews with author, 21 June 2016, 6 July 2016.
John Demsey. Interview with author, 7 July 2016.
Bryan Greenwood. Interview with author, 19 October 2014.
Frances Hathaway. Interview with author, 17 June 2016.
Phillip Ing. Interview with author, 17 June 2016.
Shauna Levy. Interview with author, 24 February 2015.
Steven Levy. Interview with author, 24 March 2015.
David Livingstone. Interview with author, 27 July 2015.
Valerie MacKenzie. Interview with author, 28 June 2016.
John McCracken. Interview with author, 1 November 2018.

Jane McKay. Interview with author, 23 June 2016.
Bernadette Morra. Interview with author, 27 July 2015.
Rick Mugford. Interview with author, 8 August 2016.
Donald Robertson. Interview with author, 29 October 2015.
Susie Sheffman. Interview with author, 6 August 2015.
Frank Toskan. Interviews with author, 17 April 2015, 6 May 2015, 22 June 2015, 10 May 2016, 14 December 2017, 19 September 2018.

Sources

AIDS Committee of Toronto. *Twenty Years of Fashion Cares, 1987–2006*. Toronto, ON: AIDS Committee of Toronto, 2006.
Amazeen, Michelle. "Gap (RED): Social Responsibility or Window Dressing?" *Journal of Business Ethics* 99 (2010): 167–82.
Arvidsson, Adam. *Brands: Meaning and Value in Media Culture*. London: Routledge, 2006.
– *Marketing Modernity: Italian Advertising from Fascism to Postmodernity*. London: Routledge, 2003.
Arvidsson, Adam, and Giannino Malossi. "Customer Co-production from Social Factory to Brand: Learning from Italian Fashion." In *Inside Marketing: Practices, Ideologies, Devices*, edited by Detlev Zwick and Julien Cayla, 212–33. Oxford: Oxford University Press, 2011.
Aucoin, Kevyn. *The Art of Makeup*. New York: HarperCollins, 1994.
– *Face Forward*. Boston: Little, Brown, 2000.
– *Making Faces*. Boston: Little, Brown, 1999.
Banet-Weiser, Sarah. *Authentic:™ The Politics of Ambivalence in a Brand Culture*. New York: NYU Press, 2012.
Banet-Weiser, Sarah, and Charlotte Lapsansky. "RED Is the New Black: Brand Culture, Consumer Citizenship, and Political Possibility." *International Journal of Communication* 2 (2008): 1248–68.
Barthes, Roland. *The Fashion System*. Translated by Matthew Ward and Richard Howard. Berkeley, CA: University of California Press, 1990.
Basten, Fred E. *Max Factor: The Man Who Changed the Faces of the World*. New York: Arcade, 2011.
Beker, Jeanne. *Jeanne Unbottled: Adventures in High Style*. Toronto, ON: Stoddart, 2000.
Benson, Denise, and Stuart Berman. *Then and Now: Toronto Nightlife History*. Toronto, ON: Three O'Clock Press, 2015.
Bissell, Kimberly, and Amy Rask. "Real Women on Real Beauty: Self-Discrepancy, Internalization of the Thin Ideal, and Perceptions of Attractiveness and Thinness in Dove's Campaign for Real Beauty." *International Journal of Advertising* 29, no. 4 (2010): 643–68.

Bordowitz, Gregg. *General Idea: Imagevirus*. London: Afterall Books, 2010.
Bourdieu, Pierre. "But Who Created the 'Creators'?" In *Sociology in Question*. Translated by Richard Nice, 139–48. London: Sage, 1993.
– *Distinction: A Social Critique on the Judgement of Taste*. Translated by Richard Nice. Cambridge, MA: Harvard University Press, 1984.
– "The Field of Cultural Production, or: The Economic World Reversed." In *The Field of Cultural Production*. Edited by Randal Johnson, 9–73. New York: Columbia University Press, 1993.
– "Haute Couture and Haute Culture." In *Sociology in Question*. Translated by Richard Nice, 132–8. London: Sage, 1993.
– *The Logic of Practice*. Translated by Richard Nice. Stanford, CA: Stanford University Press, 1980.
– "The Market of Symbolic Goods." In *The Field of Cultural Production*. Edited by Randal Johnson, 112–41. New York: Columbia University Press, 1993.
– *Outline of a Theory of Practice*. Translated by Richard Nice. Cambridge, UK: Cambridge University Press, 1977.
– *The Rules of Art: Genesis and Structure of the Literary Field*. Translated by Susan Emanuel. Stanford, CA: Stanford University Press, 1992.
– "Some Properties of Fields." In *Sociology in Question*. Translated by Richard Nice, 72–7. London: Sage, 1993.
Bourdieu, Pierre, and Madame Yvette Delsaut. "Le couturier et sa griffe: contribution à une théorie de la magie." *Actes de la recherche en sciences sociale* 1, no. 1 (January 1975): 7–36.
Brandon, Ruth. *Ugly Beauty: Helena Rubinstein, L'Oréal, and the Blemished History of Looking Good*. Toronto, ON: McClelland and Stewart, 2011.
Brønn, Peggy Simcic, and Albana Belliu Vrioni. "Corporate Social Responsibility and Cause-Related Marketing: An Overview." *International Journal of Advertising* 20 (2001): 207–22.
Butler, Judith. *Bodies That Matter: On the Discursive Limits of "Sex."* New York: Routledge, 1993.
– *Gender Trouble: Feminism and the Subversion of Identity*. New York: Routledge, 1990.
Carstairs, Catherine. "Roots Nationalism: Branding English Canada Cool in the 1980s and 1990s." *Social History/Histoire Sociale* 39, no. 77 (2006): 235–55.
Chandra, Sarika. "From Fictional Capital to Capital as Fiction: Globalization and the Intellectual Convergence of Business and the Humanities." *Cultural Critique* 76 (Fall 2010): 49–73.
Chiotti, Quentin P., and Alun P. Joseph. "Casey House: Interpreting the Location of a Toronto AIDS Hospice." *Social Science and Medicine* 41, no. 1 (1995): 131–40.

Clarke, Juanne N. "Homophobia Out of the Closet in the Media Portrayal of HIV/AIDS 1991, 1996, and 2001: Celebrity, Heterosexism and the Silent Victims." *Critical Public Health* 16, no. 4 (December 2006): 317–30.

Corson, Richard. *Fashions in Makeup: From Ancient to Modern Times*. London: Peter Owen, 2003.

Craik, Jennifer. *Fashion: The Key Concepts*. Oxford: Berg, 2009.

Crimp, Douglas. "AIDS: Cultural Analysis/Cultural Activism." *October* 43 (Winter 1987): 3–16.

– "How to Have Promiscuity in an Epidemic." *October* 43 (Winter 1987): 237–71.

Crimp, Douglas, with Adam Rolston. "Aids Activist Graphics: A Demonstration." In *The Subcultures Reader*, edited by Ken Gelder and Sarah Thornton, 359–66. London: Routledge, 1997.

Eikenberry, Angela M. "The Hidden Costs of Cause Marketing." *Stanford Social Innovation Review* (Summer 2009): 51–5.

Einstein, Mara. *Compassion, Inc.: How Corporate America Blurs the Line between What We Buy, Who We Are, and Those Who Help*. Berkeley, CA: University of California Press, 2012.

Entwistle, Joanne. *The Fashioned Body: Fashion, Dress, and Modern Social Theory*. Cambridge, UK: Polity Press.

Entwistle, Joanne, and Agnès Rocamora. "The Field of Fashion Materialized: A Study of London Fashion Week." *Sociology* 40, no. 4 (2006): 735–51.

Ewen, Stuart. *Captains of Consciousness: Advertising and the Social Roots of the Consumer Culture*. New York: Basic Books, 1976.

Farber, Celia. *Serious Adverse Events: An Uncensored History of AIDS*. Hoboken, NJ: Melville House, 2006.

Friedman, Walter A., and Geoffrey Jones. "Creative Industries in History." *Business History Review* 85 (Summer 2011): 237–44.

Fulsang, Deborah. "The Fashion of Writing, 1985–2000: Fashion-Themed Television's Impact on the Canadian Fashion Press." In *Fashion: A Canadian Perspective*, edited by Alexandra Palmer, 315–38. London: Routledge, 2004.

Gamson, Josh. "Silence, Death, and the Invisible Enemy: AIDS Activism and Social Movement 'Newness.'" *Social Problems* 36, no. 4 (October 1989): 351–67.

Garber, Marjorie. *Vested Interests: Cross-Dressing and Cultural Anxiety*. New York: Routledge, 1992.

Gardner, Andrea. *The 30 Second Seduction: How Advertisers Lure Women through Flattery, Flirtation, and Manipulation*. Berkeley, CA: Seal, 2008.

Gavenas, Mary Lisa. *Color Stories: Behind the Scenes of America's Billion-Dollar Beauty Industry*. New York: Simon and Schuster, 2002.

Gilbert, David. "Urban Outfitting: The City and the Spaces of Fashion Culture." In *Fashion Cultures: Theories, Explorations and Analysis*, edited by Stella Bruzzi and Pamela Church Gibson, 7–24. London: Routledge, 2000.

Gillett, James. "The Challenges of Institutionalization for AIDS Media Activism." *Media, Culture, and Society* 25 (2003): 607–24.

– *A Grassroots History of the HIV/AIDS Epidemic in North America*. Milwaukee: Marquette Books, 2010.

Giroux, Henry A. "Consuming Social Change: The 'United Colors of Benetton.'" *Cultural Critique* 26 (Winter 1993–4): 5–39.

Goldstein, Nancy, and Jennifer L. Marlow, eds. *The Gender Politics of HIV/AIDS in Women*. New York: NYU Press, 1997.

Gupta, Shruti, and Julie Pirsch. "The Company-Cause-Consumer Fit Decision in Cause-Related Marketing." *Journal of Consumer Marketing* 23, no. 6 (2006): 314–26.

Haig, Matt. *Brand Success: How the World's Top 100 Brands Thrive and Survive*. London: Kogan Page, 2004.

Hansen, Per H. "Business History: A Cultural and Narrative Approach." *Business History Review* 86 (Winter 2012): 693–717.

Harper, Phillip Brian. *Are We Not Men? Masculine Anxiety and the Problem of African-American Identity*. Oxford: Oxford University Press, 1998.

Harris, Daniel. *The Rise and Fall of Gay Culture*. New York: Hyperion, 1997.

Henderson, Stuart. *Making the Scene: Yorkville and Hip Toronto in the 1960s*. Toronto, ON: University of Toronto Press, 2011.

Hesmondhalgh, David. "Bourdieu, the Media, and Cultural Production." *Media, Culture, and Society* 28, no. 2 (2006): 211–31.

Hilbert, Jeffrey. "The Politics of Drag." In *Out in Culture: Gay, Lesbian, and Queer Essays on Popular Culture*. Edited by Corey K. Creekmur and Alexander Doty, 463–9. Durham, NC: Duke University Press, 1995.

Holt, Douglas B. *How Brands Become Icons: The Principles of Cultural Branding*. Boston, MA: Harvard Business School Press, 2004.

Jennings, M. Kent, and Ellen Ann Andersen. "The Importance of Social and Political Context: The Case of AIDS Activism." *Political Behavior* 25, no. 2 (June 2003): 177–99.

Johnston, Josée, and Judith Taylor. "Feminist Consumerism and Fat Activists: A Comparative Study of Grassroots Activism and the Dove Real Beauty Campaign." *Signs: Journal of Women in Culture and Society* 33, no. 4 (2008): 941–66.

Jones, Geoffrey. *Beauty Imagined: A History of the Global Beauty Industry*. Oxford: Oxford University Press, 2010.

- "Globalization and Beauty: A Historical and Firm Perspective." *EurAmerica* 41, no. 4 (December 2011): 885–916.
Jungar, Katarina, and Elaine Salo. "Shop and Do Good?" *Journal of Pan African Studies* 2, no. 6 (September 2006): 92–101.
Kerner, Noah, and Gene Pressman, with Andrew Essex. *Chasing Cool: Standing Out in Today's Cluttered Marketplace*. New York: Atria, 2007.
Kilbourne, Jean. *Can't Buy My Love: How Advertising Changes the Way We Think and Feel*. New York: Simon and Shuster, 1999.
King, Samantha. *Pink Ribbons, Inc.: Breast Cancer and the Politics of Philanthropy*. Minneapolis, MN: University of Minnesota Press, 2006.
- "The Politics of the Body and the Body Politic: Magic Johnson and the Ideology of AIDS." *Sociology of Sport Journal* 10 (1993): 270–85.
Kinsella, James. *Covering the Plague: AIDS and the American Media*. New Brunswick, NJ: Rutgers University Press, 1989.
Kinsman, Gary. "Managing AIDS Organizing: 'Consultation,' 'Partnerships,' and the National AIDS Strategy." In *Organizing Dissent: Contemporary Social Movements in Theory and Practice*, edited by William Carroll, 215–31. Toronto, ON: Garamond, 1997.
Klepacki, Laura. *Avon: Building the World's Premier Company for Women*. Hoboken, NJ: John Wiley and Sons, 2005.
Koehn, Nancy. "Estée Lauder: Self Definition and the Modern Cosmetics Market." In *Beauty and Business: Commerce, Gender, and Culture in Modern America*, edited by Philip Scranton, 217–51. New York: Routledge, 2001.
Kuehn, Kathleen M. "Compassionate Consumption: Branding Africa through Red." *Democratic Communique: Journal of the Union for Democratic Communications* 23, no. 2 (Fall 2009): 23–40.
Lachover, Einat, and Sigal Barak Brandes. "A Beautiful Campaign? Analysis of Public Discourses in Israel Surrounding the Dove Campaign for Real Beauty." *Feminist Media Studies* 9, no. 3 (2009): 301–16.
Lauder, Estée. *Estée: A Success Story*. New York: Random House, 1985.
Lenskyj, Helen Jefferson. "Clinically Correct? AIDS Education in Ontario in the 1980s and 1990s." *Canadian Bulletin of Medical History/Bulletin canadien d'histoire de la médecine* 24, no. 2 (2007): 403–21.
Leonard, Garry L. "A Fall from Grace: The Fragmentation of Masculine Subjectivity and the Impossibility of Femininity in Hitchcock's *Vertigo*." *American Imago* 47, no. 3 (Fall 1990): 271–91.
Lipartito, Kenneth. "Connecting the Cultural and the Material in Business History." *Enterprise and Society* 14, no. 4 (December 2013): 686–704.
- "Culture and the Practice of Business History." *Business and Economic History* 24, no. 2 (Winter 1995): 1–41.

Littler, Jo. *Radical Consumption: Shopping for Change in Contemporary Culture*. Maidenhead, UK: Open University Press, 2009.

Lommel, Cookie. *Madam C.J. Walker: Entrepreneur*. Los Angeles, CA: Melrose Square, 1993.

"Looking Good! Canadian Cosmetics Company MAC Is Ready to Take On the World, Thanks to a Picking System Make-Over." *Materials Management and Distribution* 40, no. 11 (November 1995): 18–20.

Lowry, Beverly. *Her Dream of Dreams: The Rise and Triumph of Madam C.J. Walker*. New York: Vintage Books, 2003.

Lury, Celia. *Brands: The Logos of the Global Economy*. London: Routledge, 2004.

Magubane, Zine. "Black Skins, Black Masks, or 'The Return of the White Negro': Race, Masculinity, and the Public Personas of Dennis Rodman and RuPaul." *Men and Masculinities* 4, no. 3 (2002): 233–57.

Maguire, Steve, Cynthia Hardy, and Thomas B. Lawrence. "Institutional Entrepreneurship in Emerging Fields: HIV/AIDS Treatment Advocacy in Canada." *Academy of Management Journal* 47, no. 5 (2004): 657–79.

Mahon, Nancy. "The Business Case for Giving Away Lipstick." *Harvard Business Review*, 20 September 2010. http://blogs.hbr.org/2010/09/the-business-case-for-giving-away-lipstick.

Malkan, Stacy. *Not Just a Pretty Face: The Ugly Side of the Beauty Business*. Gabriola Island, BC: New Society, 2007.

Margolies, Paul, and the NAMES Project. *Always Remember: A Selection of Panels Created by and for International Fashion Designers*. New York: Simon and Shuster, 1996.

McRobbie, Angela. *British Fashion Design: Rag Trade or Image Industry?* London: Routledge, 1998.

Merlo, Elisabetta, and Francesca Polese. "Turning Fashion into Business: The Emergence of Milan as an International Fashion Hub." *Business History Review* 80, no. 3 (Autumn 2006): 415–47.

Millard, Jennifer. "Performing Beauty: Dove's "Real Beauty" Campaign." *Symbolic Interaction* 32, no. 2 (2009): 146–68.

Moor, Liz. *The Rise of Brands*. Oxford: Berg, 2007.

Morgan, Adam. *Eating the Big Fish: How Challenger Brands Can Compete against Brand Leaders*. Hoboken, NJ: John Wiley and Sons, 2009.

Mukherjee, Roopali, and Sarah Banet-Weiser, eds. *Commodity Activism: Cultural Resistance in Neoliberal Times*. New York: NYU Press, 2012.

Murray, Dara Persis. "Branding 'Real' Social Change in Dove's Campaign for Real Beauty." *Feminist Media Studies* 13, no. 1 (2013): 83–101.

Myrick, Roger. *AIDS, Communication, and Empowerment: Gay Male Identity and the Politics of Public Health Messages*. New York: Harrington Park Press, 1996.

Nan, Xiaoli, and Kwangjun Heo. "Consumer Responses to Corporate Social Responsibility (CSR) Initiatives: Examining the Role of Brand-Cause Fit in Cause-Related Marketing." *Journal of Advertising* 36, no. 2 (Summer 2007): 63–75.

Newton, Esther. *Mother Camp: Female Impersonators in America*. Chicago, IL: University of Chicago Press, 1972.

Nickel, Patricia Mooney, and Angela M. Eikenberry. "A Critique of the Discourse of Marketized Philanthropy." *American Behavioral Scientist* 52, no. 7 (2009): 974–89.

O'Manique, Colleen, and Ronald Labonte. "Rethinking (Product) RED." *The Lancet* 371 (10 May 2008): 1561–3.

Ornstein, Michael. *AIDS in Canada: Knowledge, Behaviour, and Attitudes of Adults*. Toronto, ON: University of Toronto Press, 1989.

Osborne, Peter, and Lynne Segal. "Gender as Performance: An Interview with Judith Butler." *Radical Philosophy* 67 (Summer 1994): 32–9.

Pallingston, Jessica. *Lipstick: A Celebration of the World's Favorite Cosmetic*. New York: St Martin's Press, 1999.

Palmer, Alexandra, ed. *Fashion: A Canadian Perspective*. Toronto, ON: University of Toronto Press, 2004.

Peiss, Kathy. "On Beauty ... and the History of Business." In *Beauty and Business: Commerce, Gender, and Culture in Modern America*, ed. Philip Scranton, 7–22. New York: Routledge, 2001.

– *Hope in a Jar: The Making of America's Beauty Culture*. New York: Henry Holt, 1998.

Ponte, Stafano, Lisa Ann Richey, and Mike Baab. "Bono's Product (RED) Initiative: Corporate Social Responsibility That Solves the Problems of 'Distant Others.'" *Third World Quarterly* 30, no. 2 (2009): 301–17.

Pringle, Hamish, and Marjorie Thompson. *Brand Spirit: How Cause-Related Marketing Builds Brands*. New York: John Wiley and Sons, 1999.

Ragas, Meg Cohen, and Karen Kozlowski. *Read My Lips: A Cultural History of Lipstick*. San Francisco, CA: Chronicle Books, 1998.

Rantisi, Norma. "The Ascendance of New York Fashion." *International Journal of Urban and Regional Research* 28, no. 1 (March 2004): 86–106.

Rayside, David M., and Evert A. Lindquist. "AIDS Activism and the State in Canada." *Studies in Political Economy* 39 (Autumn 1992): 37–76.

Reckwitz, Andreas. "Toward a Theory of Social Practices: A Development in Culturalist Theorizing." *European Journal of Social Theory* 5, no. 2 (2002): 243–63.

Remis, Robert S., and Juan Liu. "HIV/AIDS in Ontario: Preliminary Report, 2011." Ontario Ministry of Health and Long-Term Care and Dalla Lana School of Public Health, University of Toronto, August 2013. http://www.ohemu.utoronto.ca/doc/PHERO2011_report_preliminary.pdf.

Rhyne, Ragan. "Racializing White Drag." *Journal of Homosexuality* 46, nos. 3–4 (2004): 181–94.

Richey, Lisa Ann, and Stefano Ponte. "Better (Red)™ than Dead? Celebrities, Consumption, and International Aid." *Third World Quarterly* 29, no. 4 (2008): 711–29.

– *Brand Aid: Shopping Well to Save the World*. Minneapolis, MN: University of Minnesota Press, 2011.

Riviere, Joan. "Womanliness as a Masquerade." *International Journal of Psychoanalysis* 10 (1929): 303–13.

Robertson, Donald, and Nancy Jane Hastings. *Canadian Fashion Annual 1989*. Scarborough, ON: Prentice-Hall Canada, 1988.

Robertson, Mark L. "AIDS Coverage in *The Body Politic*, 1981–1987: An Annotated Bibliography." *American Review of Canadian Studies* (Autumn 2001): 415–31.

– "An Annotated Chronology of the History of AIDS in Toronto: The First Five Years, 1981–1986." *Canadian Bulletin of Medical History CBMH/BCHM* 22, no. 2 (2005): 313–51.

Rocamora, Agnès. *Fashioning the City: Paris, Fashion, and the Media*. London: I.B. Tauris, 2009.

– "Fields of Fashion: Critical Insights into Bourdieu's Sociology of Culture." *Journal of Consumer Culture* 2, no. 3 (2002): 341–62.

Ross, Emily, and Angus Holland. *100 Great Businesses and the Minds behind Them*. Naperville, IL: Sourcebook, 2006.

RuPaul. *Lettin It All Hang Out*. New York: Hyperion, 1995.

Rutherford, Paul. *Endless Propaganda: The Advertising of Public Goods*. Toronto, ON: University of Toronto Press, 2000.

Salih, Sara. "On Judith Butler and Performativity." In *Sexualities and Communication in Everyday Life: A Reader*, edited by Karen E. Lovaas and Mercilee M. Jenkins, 55–68. Thousand Oaks, CA: Sage, 2007.

Sarna-Wojcicki, Margaret. "Refigu(red): Talking Africa and AIDS in 'Consumer' Culture." *Journal of Pan African Studies* 2, no. 6 (September 2008): 14–31.

Scalvini, Marco. "Glamorizing Sick Bodies: How Commercial Advertising Has Changed the Representation of HIV/AIDS." *Social Semiotics* 20, no. 3 (June 2010): 219–31.

Schacht, Steven P., and Lisa Underwood. "The Absolutely Fabulous but Flawlessly Customary World of Female Impersonators." *Journal of Homosexuality* 46, nos. 3–4 (2004): 1–17.

Schanzer, Dena L. "Trends in HIV/AIDS Mortality in Canada, 1987–1998." *Canadian Journal of Public Health* 94, no. 2 (March–April 2003): 135–9.

Scott, Julie-Ann, and Nicole E. Cloud. "Reaffirming the Ideal: A Focus Group Analysis of the Campaign for Real Beauty." *Advertising and Society Review* 9, no. 4 (2008): n.p.

Scott, Linda M. *Fresh Lipstick: Redressing Fashion and Feminism*. New York: Palgrave Macmillan, 2005.
Sears, Alan. "AIDS and the Health of Nations: The Contradictions of Public Health." *Critical Sociology* 18, no. 2 (1991): 31–50.
Selleck, Laurie Gilmore. "Pretty in Pink: The Susan G. Komen Network and the Branding of the Breast Cancer Cause." *Nordic Journal of English Studies* 9, no. 3 (2010): 119–38.
Sember, Robert, and David Gere. "'Let the Record Show ...': Art Activism and the AIDS Epidemic." *American Journal of Public Health* 96, no. 6 (2006): 967–9.
Shilts, Randy. *And the Band Played On*. New York: St Martin's Griffin, 1987.
Shuker, Nancy. *Elizabeth Arden: Beauty Empire Builder*. Woodbridge, CT: Blackbirch Press, 2001.
Silversides, Ann. *AIDS Activist: Michael Lynch and the Politics of Community*. Toronto, ON: Between the Lines, 2003.
Sontag, Susan. *Illness as Metaphor and AIDS and Its Metaphors*. New York: Picador, 1988.
Stole, Inger L. "Philanthropy as Public Relations: A Critical Perspective on Cause Marketing." *International Journal of Communication* 2 (2008): 20–40.
Sturken, Marita. *Tangled Memories: The Vietnam War, the AIDS Epidemic, and the Politics of Remembering*. Berkeley, CA: University of California Press, 1997.
Taylor, Judith, Josée Johnston, and Krista Whitehead. "A Corporation in Feminist Clothing? Young Women Discuss the Dove 'Real Beauty' Campaign." *Critical Sociology* 42, no. 1 (2016): 123–44.
Tinic, Serra A. "United Colors and Untied Meanings: Benetton and the Commodification of Social Issues." *Journal of Communication* 47 (Summer 1997): 3–25.
Tobias, Andrew P. *Fire and Ice: The Story of Charles Revson – the Man Who Built the Revlon Empire*. New York: William Morrow, 1976.
Treichler, Paula A. *How to Have Theory in an Epidemic: Cultural Chronicles of AIDS*. Durham, NC: Duke University Press, 1999.
Trimble, Carrie, and Gary Holmes. "New Thinking on Antecedents to Successful CRM Campaigns: Consumer Acceptance on an Alliance." *Journal of Promotion Management* 19 (2013): 352–72.
Tungate, Mark. *Branded Beauty: How Marketing Changed the Way We Look*. London: Kogan Page, 2011.
Van de Ven, Bert. "An Ethical Framework for the Marketing of Corporate Social Responsibility." *Journal of Business Ethics* 82, no. 2 (October 2008): 339–562.
Weiss, Angeline Lucinda. "Desire for Good: The MAC VIVA GLAM Advertising Campaigns." Master's thesis, University of Georgia, Athens, GA, 2010.

Willett, Julie, ed. *The American Beauty Industry Encyclopedia*. Santa Barbara, CA: Greenwood Press, 2010.

Wolf, Naomi. *The Beauty Myth*. Toronto, ON: Vintage Books, 1990.

Woodhead, Lindy. *War Paint: Madame Helena Rubinstein and Miss Elizabeth Arden: Their Lives, Their Times, Their Rivalry*. Hoboken, NJ: John Wiley and Sons, 2003.

Zwick, Detlev, and Julien Cayla, eds. *Inside Marketing: Practices, Ideologies, Devices*. Oxford: Oxford University Press, 2011.

Popular Press Magazines, Newspapers, and Trade Publications

Aarsteinsen, Barbara. "Fashion Party Gives Industry Higher Profile." *Globe and Mail*, 28 April 1987, B1, B4.

– "M.A.C. Is Staying Small for Very Big Business." *Globe and Mail*, 5 April 1988, C3.

Altman, Lawrence K. "Rare Cancer Seen in 41 Homosexuals." *New York Times*, 3 July 1981, A20. http://www.nytimes.com/1981/07/03/us/rare-cancer-seen-in-41-homosexuals.html.

Anderson, Elisabeth. "Fighting AIDS: How an Edgy Ad Campaign Built a Brand and Brought in Bucks." *onPhilanthropy.com*, 5 September 2007. http://onphilanthropy.com/2007/fighting-aids-how-an-edgy-ad-campaign-built-a-brand-and-brought-in-bucks.

Bain, Christian Arthur. "Truth in Advertising: The Man behind M.A.C. Is Pushing More Than His Latest Shade of Lipstick: Try AIDS Awareness, Human Rights, and RuPaul." *Advocate*, 3 October 1995, 51–2.

Bernstein, Sandra. "All Dressed Up, No Place to Go." *Metropolitan Toronto Business Journal* 77 no. 3 (April 1987): 26–7.

Bittar, Christine. "MAC's Feeney to Spread the Word." *Brandweek* 39, no. 36, 28 September 1998, 41.

Bot, Ellen. "Anchor Favors 'Adventurous' Fashions." *Toronto Star*, 11 August 1988, J6.

– "Cosmetics Chief Is Comfortable." *Toronto Star*, 30 November 1989, J5.

– "Television Personality Nerene Virgin Has a Frugal Approach to Fashion," *Toronto Star*, 21 February 1991, J4.

– "TV Host Builds Wardrobe around Blazers." *Toronto Star*, 14 December 1989, J13.

Bracuk, Diane. "The Style Samaritans: Canadian Fashion Is Harnessing Its Creativity to Fight AIDS, Wife Abuse, and Discrimination: But Is Fashion's New Philanthropy Just Another Trend?" *Flare* 15, no. 10 (October 1993): 70, 72.

Brady, Diane. "The M·A·C Attack: A Canadian Firm Takes on the Cosmetics Giants." *Maclean's* 104, no. 34 (26 August 1991), 44.
– "Putting a New Face on Asia: Toronto Cosmetics Company Launches Expansion in Hong Kong." *Globe and Mail*, 22 November 1995, B10.
Brenner, Leslie. "MAC Attack." *New York Magazine*, 3 June 1991, 22.
Carter, Joyce. "MAC: From a Toronto Kitchen to a $20-million Cosmetics Business in Six Years." *Globe and Mail*, 29 August 1991, D1.
Chin, Loretta, and Juliet Warkentin. "Preparing Fashion's Caring, Outfitting at the Outback." *NOW* 6, no. 39 (4–10 June 1987), 100.
Clark, Joe. "What a Drag!" *Toronto Star*, 15 May 1993, J1.
Cohen, Nicole. "Selling Soap." *Shameless*, Summer 2006. http://www.shamelessmag.com/issues/2006/summer/selling-soap.
Collison, Robert. "Profit and Loss." *Elm Street*, September 1997, 26–30.
Cordileone, Elvira. "Helping Others Is His Style: Frank Toskan Shares His Wealth; Family Foundation Urges Teens to Care." *Toronto Star*, 15 June 2006, K4.
Currie, Jo. "Tubes of Plenty: How a Canadian Cosmetics Firm Built a Snazzy, Successful Line on a Firm Foundation of R & D." *Vista* 2, no. 9 (December 1989), 32–4.
Curson, Steven. "Ru, Moisturize, Moisturize!" *Toronto Sun*, Comment/Books, 4 June 1995, C12.
DeCaro, Frank. "Being 'Out' Was Very 'In' for Lesbians, Gays in 1993." *Toronto Star*, 31 December 1993, C1.
Delap, Leanne. "Buzz." *Globe and Mail*, 17 October 1996, D2.
– "Can Con in the House?" *Globe and Mail*, 26 December 1996, C2.
– "M·A·C Co-Founder Was Cosmetic's Firm's Marketing Mind." *Globe and Mail*, 14 January 1997, F11.
Delean, Paul. "Entrepreneur Took on Makeup Industry Giants – and Prospered." *The Gazette* (Montreal), 12 October 1998, F12.
Fillion, Kate. "Overshadowing the AIDS Message." *Globe and Mail*, 13 May 1993, C1.
Flavelle, Dana. "T.O.-Made 'Evolution' Ad part of Online Revolution." *Toronto Star*, 24 October 2006, A9.
Flick, Larry. "RuPaul: Changing the Makeup of Pop Music." *Billboard*, 5 June 1993, 1.
– "RuPaul Recalls a Year of Work, Work, Work." *Billboard*, 25 December 1993, 46.
Forte, Anouska. "Making a Real Difference." *the business*, October–November 2007, 196–9.
Frankel, Susannah. "Wham, Bam! VIVA GLAM! Who's the New MAC Spokesmodel, Sporting the Hippest Lipstick on the Planet?" *The Guardian*, 15 May 1996, T11.

Bibliography

Freed, Dale Anne. "A Casual Approach at New Unisex Salon." *Globe and Mail*, 28 July 1981, F4.

French, Serena. "Beauty Queens: First, MAC Crowned RuPaul, and Now KD as Canada's Maverick Makeup Company Goes Global." *Flare* 18, no. 6 (June 1996), 42.

– "He Changed the Face of Makeup." *National Post*, 8 December 1998, B1.

– "No Liposomes, No Microcells, No Collagen-Elastin Embryo Extracts." *Toronto Life* 19, no. 1 (January 1995), 72–6.

– "On the Wane: Vintage Clothes Come and Go." *Globe and Mail*, 7 November 1991, D4.

Fulsang, Deborah. "That Was Then, This Is Now: Flare's Birth in 1979 Coincided with the Explosion of Fashion in Canada." *Flare* 21, no. 9 (September 1999): 34, 38.

Gayle, Mariana. "Brushing Up on Cosmetics: Making Up Is Hard to Do: The Price of Face Paint." *The Province* (Vancouver), 30 July 1991, 43.

Gibson, Valerie. "Lang New MAC Voice." *Toronto Sun*, 19 March 1996, 43.

Giese, Rachel. "To Die For! From Ribbon-Mania to Ghetto Flavas, the Fashion Industry Is Out to Accessorize Your Dissent." *This Magazine* 28, no. 1 (June 1994): 17–22.

Goddard, Peter. "AIDS Is Reshaping Show Business." *Toronto Star*, 2 May 1987, G1.

Goldman, Debra. "Boys Will Be Girls." *Adweek* 35, no. 6 (7 February 1994), 22.

Hanna, Deirdre. "Antoine Tempé Surveys Drag Scene," *NOW* 13, no. 39 (27 May 1993), 53, 57.

Harris, Christopher. "Koolhaus Creditors Issue Challenge." *Globe and Mail*, 1 May 1997, C21.

Harris, Daniel. "Making Kitsch from AIDS: A Disease with a Gift Shop of Its Own." *Harper's Magazine* 289, no. 1730 (July 1994), 55–6.

Harris, Joyce Saenz. "AIDS and the Fashion Industry – a Deadly Cloud Dims the Light of the Clothing World's Brightest Stars." *Seattle Times*, 17 January 1990, C1. http://community.seattletimes.nwsource.com/archive/?date=19900117&slug=1051179.

Harron, Mary. "A Hero for Our Times; In America, the Cult of the Drag Queen Has Never Been Bigger." *The Independent* (London), 29 January 1995, 4.

Hastings, Nancy. "AIDS Benefit Show Draws Small Crowd." *Toronto Star*, 5 November 1987, J2.

– "Bring on the Night." *Toronto Star*, 10 December 1987, K1.

– "Fashion Cares AIDS Benefit Raises Eyebrows – and Funds." *Toronto Star*, 18 June 1987, B3.

– "Fashion Cares Shirts Launched." *Toronto Star*, 4 June 1987, B8.

– "'Fashion Cares' T-Shirt Project Raising Funds for ACT Relief." *Toronto Star*, 30 April 1987, D4.

- "Fashion Expected to 'Bloom' at AIDS Fundraising Gala." *Toronto Star*, 21 April 1988, L9.
- "Fashion Industry Knew of Deaths but Kept AIDS a Secret until the Spring." *Ottawa Citizen*, 17 July 1986, D6.
- "Fashion Section Begins Tuesday." *Globe and Mail*, 12 April 1980, P1.
- "Festival of Canadian Fashion Offers Jam-Packed Schedule." *Toronto Star*, April 9, 1987, D10.
- "Festival Show Depended on Special Effects," *Toronto Star*, 7 April 1988, J3.

Heller, Steven. "How AIDS Was Branded: Looking Back at ACT UP Design." *The Atlantic*, 12 January 2012. http://www.theatlantic.com/entertainment/archive/2012/01/how-aids-was-branded-looking-back-at-act-up-design/251267.

Hochswender, Woody. "AIDS and the Fashion World: Industry Fears for Its Health." *New York Times*, 11 February 1990, 1, 42. http://www.nytimes.com/1990/02/11/us/aids-and-the-fashion-world-industry-fears-for-its-health.html?pagewanted=all&src=pm.

"Hot Dance Breakouts." *Billboard*, 28 November 1992, 22.

"How Cover Girl's Fantasy Face Was Created by a Makeup Artist." *The Gazette* (Montreal), 16 December 1986, C5.

Hymowitz, Carol. "AIDS Is Decimating the Fashion Business, as It Kills Key People." *Wall Street Journal*, 8 December 1987, 1, 19.

"In Your Face." *Canadian Business* 68, no. 13 (December 1995), 54.

"Industry Festival 'First of Its Kind.'" *Globe and Mail*, 17 July 1984, F2.

Jones, James T. IV. "'Supermodel' with His Own 'Je Ne Sashay Quoi.'" *USA Today*, 30 March 1993, 1D.

Kaplan, Ann, ed. *Fashion Cares*. Toronto: [self-published], 2012.

Klemesrud, Judy. "Dr Mathilde Krim: Focusing Attention on AIDS Research." *New York Times*, 3 November 1984, 48. http://www.nytimes.com/1984/11/03/style/dr-mathilde-krim-focusing-attention-on-aids-research.html.

Kraft, Ronald Mark. "In the Name of Charity." *The Advocate* 635 (10 August 1993): 42–7.

Lannon, Linnea. "Fashion, Cosmetic Industries Join Forces at AIDS Benefit." *Ottawa Citizen*, 8 May 1986, F3.

"Lauder Acquiring Remaining Interest in MAC." *Cosmetics* 26, no. 3 (May 1998), 52.

"Lauder Markets MAC Outside North America." *Cosmetics* 23, no. 3 (May 1995), 38.

Leeming, Virginia. "Lang Boosts M·A·C AIDS Fund." *Vancouver Sun*, 25 March 1997, C2.

- "Town and Country Targets Higher Market," *Vancouver Sun*, 31 October 1991, C4.

Bibliography

Levine, Rosie. "Caring Richness." *NOW* 11, no. 36 (7 May 1992), 68.
Livingstone, David. "The Camera in Drag." *Globe and Mail*, 3 June 1993, D8.
– "Designer Has Color Clout." *Globe and Mail*, 15 September 1987, C9.
– "An Entertaining Showcase." *Globe and Mail*, 16 June 1987, C9.
– "Fashion with a Cause." *Globe and Mail*, 29 March 1990, C1.
– "Fashioned by a Festival." *Globe and Mail*, 28 April 1987, C2.
– "Fund-Raising with Fashion." *Globe and Mail*, 27 August 1985, F12.
– "High Camp for a Worthy Cause." *Globe and Mail*, 18 May 1995, D1.
– "MAC Takes Manhattan Fall/Winter '96." *Globe and Mail*, 4 April 1996, C5.
– "For Minimalist Chic in Klein Collection." *Globe and Mail*, 9 June 1987, C7.
– "A Nineties Mod Revival." *Globe and Mail*, 30 August 1990, C7.
– "Rearing-to-Go." *Globe and Mail*, 9 February 1995, C7.
– "RuPaul: Dragging Theory into Practice." *Globe and Mail*, 18 May 1995, D1.
– "Sheer Drama Raises Funds for AIDS at a Successful Fashion Gala." *Globe and Mail*, 18 May 1989, C4.
– "Show an Astrological Parade." *Globe and Mail*, 10 May 1990, C4.
– "Style Notes: Animal." *Globe and Mail*, 11 February 1993, D8.
– "Style Notes: Fund-Raising Party Blooms." *Globe and Mail*, 24 May 1988, C4.
– "T-Shirt Shows That Fashion Really Cares." *Globe and Mail*, 2 June 1987, C5.
Lowe, Jennifer. "Will Success Spoil MAC?" *Profit* 15, no. 2 (1 April 1996), 43–5.
Loxley, Trisse. "Feminine Mystique: An About-Face for Fall Makeup." *Globe and Mail*, 17 September 1992, D7.
– "k.d. Joins M.A.C." *Globe and Mail*, 21 March 1996, D8.
MacDonald, Gayle. "Facing Up to the M·A·C Attack." *Financial Post Magazine*, September 1993, 60–2.
– "Managing Strategy MAC Makeover Tightens U.S. Giant's Grip." *Globe and Mail*, 14 March 1997, B9.
MacKinnon, Donna Jean. "Frank Angelo Ran Cosmetics Firm: MAC Founder Dies during Routine Surgery." *Toronto Star*, 15 January 1997, A4.
Matteson, Sandra. "Future's Bright for Young Fashion Illustrator." *Globe and Mail*, 29 May 1986, B8.
McGovern, Sheila. "Creams Rise to Top: Marcelle Line of Non-Irritating Beauty Products Is 50 Years Old and Aging Well." *The Gazette* (Montreal), 8 March 1999, F1.
– "Family-Run Cosmetic Firms Join Forces: Professional Pharmaceutical to Blend in Annabelle." *The Gazette* (Montreal), 2 July 1999, F3.
Miller, Cyndee. "Tapping into Women's Issues Is Potent Way to Reach Market." *Marketing News* 27, no. 25 (6 December 1993), 1, 13.

- "Would You Buy Lipstick from This Man?" *Marketing News* 29, no. 19 (11 September 1995), 1.
- Monahan, Iona. "How Cover Girl's Fantasy Face Was Created by Makeup Artist." *The Gazette* (Montreal), 16 December 1986, C5
- Moore, Kerry. "How About a Little Rouge, Sir?" *The Province* (Vancouver), 19 July 1994, B6.
- "Restricted: MAC Puts Limits on Sales of Its Line of Cosmetics." *Vancouver Province*, 22 October 1996, B9.
- Morra, Bernadette. "AIDS Fundraiser a Blooming Success." *Toronto Star*, 26 May 1988, K7.
- "AIDS Gala Scores Hits and Misses." *Toronto Star*, 13 May 1993, FA7.
- "Book on Cross-Dressers Not a Drag, Photographer Says." *Toronto Star*, 1 December 1994, J8.
- "Drag Queen Crowned the New Face of MAC." *Toronto Star*, 2 March 1995, B3.
- "Fashion Dares: Toronto's Most Colorful AIDS Fundraiser Turns 10." *Toronto Star*, 16 May 1996, B1.
- "MAC Fashions Fine Funeral in Wake of Angelo's Death." *Toronto Star*, 23 January 1997, D2.
- "The Mod Squad: Hairstylists Are Brushing Up on the 60s and Adding a Softer Twist for the 90s." *Toronto Star*, 4 October 1990, D1.
- "Personal Best Hair and Makeup Artists Create a Fresh Image for a Teenager, Her Mother and Grandmother." *Toronto Star*, 9 May 1991, J1.
- "Rags 2 Riches: AIDS Is Taking Its Toll on the City's Fashion Industry but They're Fighting Back." *Toronto Star*, 7 May 1992, E1.
- "Soft Focus Fall Beauty." *Toronto Star*, 15 September 1988, J1.
- "Summer Beauty: Four Different Skin Tones Glow with the Natural Look That's Hot in Makeup This Season." *Toronto Star*, 1 June 1989, K1.
- "300 Pay Tribute to Cosmetics Master." *Toronto Star*, 23 January 1997, A8.
- Mussett, Jane. "Anti-Aging Creams a 'Scam,' Author Says." *Toronto Star*, 11 July 1991, D1.
- "Pin to Support AIDS Research." *Toronto Star*, 16 February 1989, J10.
- Németh, Andrea. "Pride Opulence." *Flare* 28, no. 6 (June 2006), 72, 74.
- "New York Fashion Designers Cautious about Publicly Helping AIDS Research." *Ottawa Citizen*, 13 February 1986, F4.
- O'Hagan, Anne. "At Face Value." *Saturday Night* 106, no. 10 (December 1991), 19.
- Ono, Yumiko. "Earth Tones and Attitude Make a Tiny Cosmetics Company Hot." *Wall Street Journal*, 23 February 2005, B1.
- Penner, Degen. "EGOS and IDS: Red Ribbons Are Turning Black and Blue." *New York Times*, 23 May 1993. http://www.nytimes.com/1993/05/23/style/egos-ids-red-ribbons-are-turning-black-and-blue.html.

Postrel, Viriginia. "The Truth about Beauty." *The Atlantic* 299, no. 2 (March 2007). https://www.theatlantic.com/magazine/archive/2007/03/the-truth-about-beauty/305620.

Pozner, Jennifer L. "Dove's 'Real Beauty' Backlash." *Bitch: Feminist Response to Pop Culture* 30 (Fall 2005). http://www.wimnonline.org/articles/dovebacklash.html.

Pugsley, Alex. "Queerness Bursts into the Mainstream." *Toronto Star*, 14 May 1993, A25.

Reguly, Eric. "Toronto Firm Catches the Eye of U.S. Glamor Set." *Financial Post*, 9 October 1992, 11.

Reuters. "Bishop Attacks Use of Drag Queen in Ads." *Saskatoon StarPhoenix*, 5 November 1997, C16.

Rowesome, Drew. "25 Years of Casey House: An *Xtra* Special Supplement." *Xtra* 740 (7 March 2013): 25–35.

Rubin, Sandra. "A Brush with the Wild Side; Sassy Approach Pays Off for Toronto Cosmetics Firm." *The Gazette* (Montreal), 12 September 1995.

Schiro, Anne-Marie. "Frank Angelo, 49, Cosmetics Innovator, Dies." *New York Times*, 17 January 1997, B7.

Schneider, Karen S., Alex Connock, and Cathy Nolan. "Fashion – An Industry Dressed in Mourning." *People* 33, no. 14 (9 April 1990), 96–9. http://www.people.com/people/archive/article/0,,20117312,00.html.

Sheinman, Mort. "AIDS: It's Everyone's Business." *Women's Wear Daily* 149, 28 May 1985, 1.

"Show Drags in $101,000 for Casey House." *Toronto Star*, 11 March 1992, B3.

Siklos, Richard. "Staid Lauder Owns Rad M.A.C: IPO Filing Reveals Cosmetics Giant Bought Unconventional Firm Last Week." *Financial Post*, 2 December 1995, 3.

Spears, John. "Cosmetics Company Soars by Making Its Own Rules." *Toronto Star*, 5 October 1995, C1.

Strom, Stephanie. "Lauder in Distribution Venture with Rival." *New York Times*, 10 February 1995, D3.

Sturdza, Marina. "Festival Winners." *Globe and Mail*, 5 May 1987, C7.

– "MAC Cosmetics Achieves a Remarkable Success." *Globe and Mail*, 9 March 1989, C5.

– "New Book Is a Tribute to Canadian Fashion." *Globe and Mail*, 6 September 1988, C6.

Tant, Lisa. "Back to Basics Meets High Tech in New Decade Makeup Trend." *Vancouver Sun*, 4 January 1990, D3.

– "Cosmetics Take a Leaf from Nature." *Vancouver Sun*, 13 September 1990, D5.

– "Makeup Curtain-Raiser." *Vancouver Sun*, 28 December 1989, C2.

- "Mod Squad Stages a Comeback Worthy of Emma Peel." *Vancouver Sun*, 22 November 1990, C4.
- "Polishing Up Your Lips and Eyes with Shades of Summer." *Vancouver Sun*, 15 June 1989, C4.
- "Unconventional Models Puts Cosmetics Firm in Spotlight." *Vancouver Sun*, 5 November 1996, C3.

"Thanks 2 You." *The Province* (Vancouver), 2 July 1995, A2.

"That Old MAC Magic: Worldwide Acclaim and an Alliance with a US Cosmetics Icon Haven't Diluted MAC's Grassroots Appeal." *Marketing* 101, no. 5 (5 February 1996), 1, 11.

Tuck, Andrew. "Andrew Tuck Considers Makeup for Men: Will It Catch On?" *Globe and Mail*, 14 July 1994, A24.

Wentz, Laurel. "Real Beauty Gets Global Breakout via Evolution." *Advertising Age* 78, no. 2 (8 January 2007): S7.

White, Mo. "MAC Daddy." *Scotland on Sunday*, 15 July 2001, 38.

White, Roland. "What a Drag." *London Sunday Times*, 17 September 1995, 1.

Wilson, Deborah. "Use of Condoms Becomes Standard in Gay Bathhouses." *Globe and Mail*, 16 March 1987, A1.

Zekas, Rita. "Boys Will Be Girls: Now 10 Years Old, Toronto's Acclaimed DQ Revue Celebrates the Arrival of Drag Culture in the Mainstream." *Toronto Star*, 27 February 1997, G3.

- "Not Your Garden-Variety Show; After a Six-Year Hiatus, DQ Is Back in Full Bloom." *Toronto Star*, 24 April 2003, G01.

Television Interview Transcripts

Interview with Frank Angelo, Frank Toskan, RuPaul, and k.d. lang. *Canada AM*, CTV Television, Toronto, ON. Interviewed by Deirdre McMurdy, hosted by Leslie Jones. Aired 22 April 1996.

"MAC Cosmetics." *Venture*, CBC Television, Toronto, ON. Hosted by Diane Buckner. Aired 3 March 1996.

"The Man behind Canada's Cosmetic Invasion in a CTV Biography." *The National*, CTV National News, Toronto, ON. Hosted by Sandie Rinaldo. Aired 27 May 1995.

Index

Please note: Illustrations are identified by plate numbers (e.g., PLATE 1).

ACT UP (AIDS Coalition to Unleash Power), 108, 146, 212, 213
advertising: AIDS crisis and, 170–9, 196, 214–15; by cosmetics industry, 18–20, 49–50, 53–5, 157, 160–1, 178, 196, 205–6; drag culture and, 200–1, 214; by fashion industry, 78–9, 89, 92, 96; M·A·C's long-time rejection of, 6, 8, 10, 26, 33, 46, 48, 71, 95–8, 157, 159, 205. *See also* cause marketing; VIVA GLAM lipstick (1992); VIVA GLAM lipstick (1995); VIVA GLAM lipstick (1997); VIVA GLAM postcard (1997)
AIDS, 98–109; activism against, 105–9, 212–16; in Africa, 20, 21–4; commodification of, 170–9, 214–15; fear/stigma of, 14, 34, 98–114, 127, 142, 147–8, 175, 177, 183, 208; field of fashion and, 32, 98–104, 105, 117, 126–9, 133–4, 153–4, 173–4, 181; history of, 98–100; media coverage of, 98–9, 102, 107, 109–10, 112; moralistic views of, 7, 99–100, 105–6; New York fashion industry and, 101–4, 110, 127, 133–4, 172, 173–4; "ownership" of, 170–9; Toronto fashion industry and, 30, 98–129; women and, 99, 134, 228n72. *See also* deaths, from AIDS
AIDS Action Now! (AAN!), 108–9
AIDS Committee of Toronto (ACT), 11, 107–9, 171; Casey House and, 107–8, 208, 210–11; Fashion Cares and, 7, 112–14, 116, 118–21, 123, 176, 181
AIDS Project Los Angeles, 173–4
Alaïa, Azzedine, 111
Aldo (shoe retailer), 175–6, 177
Alfred Sung (brand), 69, 76, 84. *See also* Sung, Alfred
Altman, Lawrence K., 98–9
American Express (AMEX), 15, 20, 22–3
American Foundation for AIDS Research (amfAR), 172
Angelo, Frank, 5, 6, 37–48, PLATE 2; background of, 37–9; as business half of partnership, 38–9, 45–6, 75, 163, 165, 218; family of, 185; and first meeting with Toskan, 39; Haircutting Place salons of, 39–43, 61, 69, PLATE 4; hairdressing

school of, 43; and Hathaways, 60, 69, 70; and later separation from Toskan, 168; as not openly gay, 149, 185; and reaction to Fashion Blooms, 124–5; sudden death of, 185, 186, 218; tributes to, 187–8. *See also* "Franks, the"
Angst, Bill, 144
animal testing, 55; M·A·C's rejection of, 75, 134, 140–1, 159, PLATES 13–14
Annabelle (cosmetics brand), 51
Arden, Elizabeth, 9, 50, 53, 79. *See also* Elizabeth Arden (company/brand)
Armstrong, Maria, 210
art and commerce, balancing act between: by fashion industry, 28, 89–90, 118–19, 184–5; by M·A·C, 166–7, 168, 180, 184–5
Assoon brothers, 68. *See also* Twilight Zone, The
Atkinson, Stephen, 107
Aucoin, Kevyn, 137, 139, 234n11
autonomous production (Bourdieu), 29, 33–4, 77, 127, 165–6
Aveda (company/brand), 55
Avon (company/brand), 173

Babel (Toronto clothing line), 69, 110
"Back to M·A·C" recycling program, 48, 134, PLATES 15–16
Baker, Caryl, 51, 52, 53
Bailey, Brian, 142
Bailey, David, 70
Bailey, Stephen, 142
Bain, Christian Arthur, 178–9
Balmain, Pierre, 30, 33
Barthes, Roland: *The Fashion System*, 192
Bay, The, 6, 39, 51, 83, 225n5; and Fashion Cares, 154–5; as M·A·C

retailer, 6–7, 65, 75, 167; RuPaul's appearance at, 195
Beder, Syd, 110–14, 116, 117, 118, 120, 129
Beker, Jeanne, 3–4, 120, 122, 145; on fashion and AIDS, 100–1, 129, 177; as *FashionTelevision* host, 6, 92–3, 100–1, 158, 176, 200; interviews with Toskan by, 176, 180, 200; on M·A·C, 6, 97–8; on Toronto fashion scene, 82–3, 85–6
Benetton ads, 4, 146; with Kirby photo, 174–5, 196, 214
Ben Nye (make-up brand), 42
Berman, Debra, 76
Bickell, Bonnie, 122
Blanks, Tim, 93
Blazer, Phil, 51
Bloomingdale's, 103
Body Politic, The (Toronto magazine), 99, 107, 109
Body Shop, The (company/brand), 55, 74, 173, 178
Bono, 20, 21
Bouchard, Denis, hair salon of, 124, 142
Bourdieu, Pierre, 28–34, 78, 93, 144, 219, 224n33; on field of fashion, 29–34, 77; on signature of creator, 189. *See also entry below*
Bourdieu, Pierre, concepts of: autonomous production, 29, 33–4; capital, 29, 32–4; doxa, 32; field, 29–30; habitus, 29, 30–1. *See also specific concepts*
Boyd, Suzanne: on Fashion Cares, 114, 118, 145; as *Flare*'s editor-in-chief, 55–6, 97; on M·A·C company/brand, 67, 72, 86; as M·A·C customer, 55–6, 57; and Toronto fashion scene, 68–9
Breakfast at Tiffany's (film), 60

Index

breast cancer philanthropy, 16–17, 24, 172–3, 177
Brooks, Marilyn, 86
Brown, Bobbi, 139, 160–1; cosmetics brand of, 160
Brubach, Holly, 133
Buglisi Weiler, Karen, 24–5, 27
Bündchen, Gisele, 21, 23
Burtch, Bruce, 15
Burton, Tom, 71; and VIVA GLAM postcard (1992), 151, PLATES 19–20
Butler, Judith, 34; *Bodies That Matter*, 194, 202, 205, 213–14, 215; *Gender Trouble*, 197–8, 213

Callwood, June, 208, 209. *See also* Casey House
Camilleri, Mary Ann: *Ladies, Please!*, 194
Campbell, Naomi, 65, 135, 191
Canadian AIDS Society (CAS), 108, 146, 151, 156
Canadian Fashion Annual 1989, 93–5, 117
Cape, Michael, 51
Cape, Victor, 51
capital (Bourdieu), 29, 32–4; as built by M·A·C, 33, 58–9, 94–5, 98, 135, 137, 152, 158, 160–1, 179, 182; of cities as fashion centres, 76–81; of Toronto as fashion centre, 81–91; of Toronto fashion industry figures, 111–18, 122, 125–9, 133–4. *See also entry below*
capital, specific forms of: cultural, 32, 58–9, 67, 116, 125–6, 133–4; economic, 33, 77, 126–7; "fashion," 34, 117–18, 122, 129, 135, 137, 152, 158, 160, 179, 182; social, 33, 98, 111–12, 114, 116–18, 126; symbolic, 32–4, 67, 76–82, 94–5, 116–18, 125–6

Caplan, Elinor, 123
Caroline Cosmetics Inc., 51
Caryl Baker Visage, 51. *See also* Baker, Caryl
Casale, Victor, 12, 165, 170, 188; and early work with Toskan, 43–8; labs/production facilities overseen by, 45, 139–41, 168–9, 217; safety/ingredient testing by, 140–1
Casey House (Toronto AIDS hospice), 150, 156; ACT and, 107–8, 208, 210–11; "D.Q." fundraiser for, 207–9. *See also* "D.Q." fundraisers
Caten, Dean and Dan, 69, 84, 85, 142; "Rubberize" dress of, 115–16, 146
cause marketing, 14–27; AIDS crisis and, 20–7, 34, 170–9, 214–16; commodification and, 13, 171–5, 214–15; examples of, 15–16; M·A·C's AIDS fundraising, as standing apart from, 24–7, 176–9, 219–20; neoliberalism and, 16–19; scholarly analysis of, 19–26
celebrities, as M·A·C clients, 6, 69–70, 95, 134–5, 136, 138–9
Chalayan, Hussein, 4
Chanel (company/brand), 41, 64, 74
Chanel, Gabrielle "Coco," 60, 79
Chansel, Philippe, 138, 165
Chatelaine, 92, 152
Cher, 135
Chin, Walter: Hathaway ad photographed by, 70, PLATE 8
Civello, Ray, hair salon of, 124, 142
Clark, David, 114, 209
Clark, Petula, 116
Clark, Wayne, 83, 84, 86, 87, 94, 122, 142
Clinique (brand), 41, 56, 74
Club Monaco (brand), 69, 84, 85, 144

Cohen, Morrie, 51
Cole, Kenneth, 172, 177
Collison, Robert, 185–6
Colt's Plastics Company, 47–8
Comrags, 83, 88, 94, 110, 142
Coppen, Jann, 111, 142
Cornish, Judy, 83–4. *See also* Comrags
corporate social responsibility (CSR), 14–15. *See also* cause marketing
cosmetics industry: advertising by, 18–20, 49–50, 53–5, 157, 160–1, 178, 196, 205–6; American pioneers of, 49–50, 53; Canadian pioneers of, 50–3. *See also specific persons and companies*
Council of Fashion Designers of America (CFDA), 79, 134
Council of Fashion Designers of Canada, 120
Courrèges, André, 31
CoverGirl (company/brand), 51, 54, 74
Cox, Patrick, 69
Cox, Scott, 154
Crawford, Cindy, 191, 201, 204
Creative Salon Services, 39–40, 43–4
Cressman, Scott, 69
"Cruelty Free Beauty," 134, 140, 159, PLATES 13–14. *See also* animal testing

Dal Bello, Lisa, 116
Damian, Michael, 43
Dean and Dan. *See* Caten, Dean and Dan
deaths, from AIDS, 100, 101, 105, 209; defiance of, through creativity/glamour, 150, 208, 215; in drag performances, 212–16; in fashion industry, 102–3, 128, 133–4, 153, 181, 234*n*11; images of, 153–4, 174–5, 196, 214; of Toskan's first boyfriend, 147–8
Deee-Lite, 135, 136
De Freitas, Tony, 148
Demsey, John, 9, 26, 27, 217
Design Exchange (DX) fundraising gala (2014), 3–5; Politics of Fashion | Fashion of Politics exhibition at, 3–4, 7; recognition of Toskan at, 5, 8, 218
Design Industries Foundation Fighting AIDS (DIFFA), 146, 151, 156, 193
Desrosiers, Robert, 113; dance theatre of, 88
Diamond Club (Toronto), 85; as venue of first Fashion Cares, 113–14, 115, 119, 120, 209
Diana, Princess, 70, 135
Dicks, Susan, 193
Dilio, Dino, 211–12
Dior (company/brand), 41, 138
Dior, Christian, 30; "New Look" of, 79
Dove Campaign for Real Beauty, 17–20, 24
Dove Self-Esteem Fund, 18–19
doxa (Bourdieu), 32
"D.Q." fundraisers, 207–12; for Casey House (1987), 207–9; fundraising lipstick introduced at (1995), 211–12; M·A·C AIDS Fund's sponsorship of, 212
drag, 190–216; artistic explorations of, 193–4; gay culture and, 192–6, 199–201, 206–8, 213–14; as masquerade, 197, 240*n*23; performance of, 192–3, 197–9; as politics, 212–16; in Toronto, 193–4, 206–12; VIVA GLAM ads

and, 190–1, 195–206; voguing in, 3, 192–3. *See also entry below*; lang, k.d.; RuPaul
drag queens, 206–16; in advertising, 200–1, 214; and AIDS activism, 212–16; cosmetics tips for, 211–12; culture of, 206–7; as depicted in arts, 192–4, 202, 210; documentary on, 192–3, 202; as long-time M·A·C customers, 6, 58, 65, 190; as photographed by Toskan, 40, 42, 44, 61, 190; and Toronto's "D.Q." fundraisers, 207–12

Eaton's, 39, 83, 155
Eggleton, Art, 123
Ehm, Erica, 116
Einstein, Mara: *Compassion, Inc.*, 25–6, 219
Elizabeth Arden (company/brand), 74, 138
Ellis, Perry, 103
Entwistle, Joanne, and Agnès Rocamora, 89–90, 117–18
Epp, Jake, 105
Espinet, Gordon, 138, 165
Estée Lauder (company/brand), 12, 26, 41, 64, 70, 74, 138; pink ribbon campaign of, 16, 172–3. *See also entry below*
Estée Lauder Companies Inc., acquisition of M·A·C by, 9, 24–5, 34, 162–70, 186, 188–9; employee/customer reactions to, 164–8, 185; initial secrecy of, 163–4, 236n8; and M·A·C AIDS Fund, 24–5, 26, 27, 163, 165, 180, 182–3, 217–18; media reactions to, 164, 180; and production/retail expansion, 168–70; and trustworthiness of brand, 179–85

Estefan, Gloria, 139
Evangelista, Linda, 135, 136, 137, 191
eye shadows, M·A·C, 6, 45, 75, 135, PLATE 5

Factor, Max, 9, 49, 76. *See also* Max Factor (company/brand)
Fairchild, John, 79
Fashion Blooms (1988), 119–26, 141–2, 181; ACT and, 120–1; funding of, 122–3; M·A·C's participation in, 121, 124–5; media coverage of, 122–3, 125–6; as run by fashion elite, 120–6; as traditional haute couture show, 124–5
Fashion Cares, 7, 11–12, 30, 32, 34, 134, 141–3, 173; as ACT fundraiser, 176, 181; corporate involvement with, 141–5, 154–5, 176–7, 187; creativity of, 142, 144, 145, 215; criticisms of, 116–17, 152–4, 196, 198; M·A·C's official sponsorship of, 7, 154–7, 172, 176–9, 188, 212; as non-commercial, 145; political support for, 181. *See also entries below; for shows from 1994 to 1998, see* M·A·C VIVA GLAM Fashion Cares *entries*
Fashion Cares (1987), 110–19, 141–2, 200, 209; as ACT fundraiser, 7, 112–14, 116, 118–21, 123; British event as inspiration for, 110–11, 118, 119; and challenge of AIDS crisis, 113–19, 126–9, 175, 177; creativity of, 114–16; as demonstration of social/fashion capital, 111–12, 113, 114, 116–18; M·A·C's participation in, 115, 187; media coverage of, 113, 115, 116–17; as non-commercial, 111–12, 118–19; playfulness/irreverence

of, 115–17, 196, 198; poster of, 113–14, 196; T-shirt of, 112, 114, 116, 118, 142, 189, 231*n*39
Fashion Cares An Evening of Sheer Drama (1989), 142
Fashion Cares Arcouture (1993), 152–4, 175
Fashion Cares Rags 2 Riches (1992), 153
Fashion Cares Red Hot & Blue (1991), 143–4, 193
Fashion Cares The Crystal Ball (1990), 142–3
fashion centres, cities as. *See* London; Milan; New York; Paris; Toronto, fashion industry in
Fashion Designers Association of Canada, 83
Fashion File (CBC), 93
Fashion Group (US), 79
Fashion Group of Toronto, 120
fashion industry: advertising by, 78–9, 89, 92, 96; AIDS deaths in, 102–3, 128, 133–4, 153, 181, 234*n*11; international centres of, 76–81; in Toronto, 30, 81–129. *See also* media coverage, of fashion industry
Fashion Liaison Committee (City of Toronto), 123–4
Fashion SCares (1987), 119, 120, 121
FashionTelevision (CityTV), 6; Beker as host of, 6, 92–3, 100–1, 158, 176, 200; and Fashion Cares, 11, 188, 200
Fashion Vignettes (Diamond Club show), 113, 125
Feeney, Michelle, 217
Festival of Canadian Fashion (1985–90), 86–91; Levy's organization of, 82, 86–9; M·A·C as showcased at/official brand of, 6, 30, 82, 87–90, 93, 152; M·A·C fashion show at, 88–9, 90, PLATES 11–12; and related to Fashion Cares, 110–13, 117, 118–19, 123, 128, 144; suspension/cancellation of, 145
field (Bourdieu): concepts of, 29–34; external forces on, 31–2. *See also entry below*
field of fashion, 29–34, 74, 77, 81–2; and art vs commerce, 28, 184–5; as constructed through media, 30, 91–8, 149; effects of AIDS on, 32, 98–104, 105, 117, 126–9, 133–4, 153–4, 173–4, 181; fashion shows and, 30, 86–91, 117–19, 126–9; haute couture and, 29–30; insiders in, 125–6; "ordinary" consumers in, 160
Fillion, Kate, 153–4, 175
Fiorucci, Elio, 40–1, 224*n*4
Flanagan, Bill, 155
Flare, 6, 83, 87, 88, 92, 173; Boyd as editor-in-chief of, 55–6, 97
Formula K (hair care line), 43–4, 162
foundations, M·A·C, 45, 56, 73, 141
Franklin, Caryn, 111
Franks, Lynne, 111
"Franks, the," 6, 37–48, 65, 69, 86, 115, 129, 134, 147, 225*n*9; business ethics/practices of, 46–8, 59, 95–6, 98, 166–7, 179, 184–5; and Estée Lauder acquisition, 160–70, 218, 236*n*8; personal relationship of, 39, 60, 149, 168, 185–6; professional partners/employees of, 70, 76, 88, 138–9; RuPaul and, 157–9, 200; stand-alone stores of, 60–1, 135–8, 166; and VIVA GLAM lipstick/ M·A·C AIDS Fund, 149–59, 179, 184–5, 203. *See also* Angelo, Frank; Toskan, Frank

Frare, Therese, 174–5
French, Serena, 96, 160
Friedman, Walter A., 28
Friedman-Kien, Alvin, 102, 229*n*80
Fulsang, Deborah, 91, 92

Gage, Robert, hair salon of, 69, 124, 143
Gallo, Robert, 99
Gap, The, 20, 21, 23, 177
Garber, Marjorie: *Vested Interests*, 192, 199
Gaultier, Jean Paul, 4, 111
gay/lesbian community. *See* LGBTQ community; LGBTQ community in Toronto
Gays in Health Care (GHC, Toronto), 107
Giddens, Anthony, 78
Glennda Orgasm, 212–13
Global Fund to Fight AIDS, Tuberculosis and Malaria, The, 20–1, 23
Gluckstein, Brian, 177
Gostlin, Audrey, 122–3
Graff, Lee, 140
Gran Fury (ACT UP art collective), 146
Greenwood, Bryan, 207, 209
Gribetz, Lester, 103
GRID (gay-related immune deficiency), 99. *See also* AIDS
Gunhouse, Joyce, 83–4. *See also* Comrags

habitus (Bourdieu), 29, 30–1; AIDS crisis and, 127; of fashion show, 117; of Toskan and Angelo, 31, 59, 62
Haircutting Place, The, 39–43, 60–1, 69, PLATE 4
Hairdresser's Choice, The (Toskan shampoo), 40–1, 42, 43, 45

Haley, Charlotte, 173
Hall, Barbara, 181
Hall, Jerry, 69
Halston, 133
Hamnett, Katharine, 4
Harrington, Rex, 195
Harris, Daniel, 174, 215
Harris, Joyce Saenz, 133
Harvey Nichols (London), M·A·C counter at, 169–70
Hassle Free Clinic (Toronto), 108
Hastings, Nancy, 73, 88, 97, 134; and *Canadian Fashion Annual 1989*, 93, 94–5; on Fashion Blooms, 119–20, 123; on Fashion Cares, 113, 116–17
Hathaway, Evelyn, 60, 69
Hathaway, Frances, 47, 58, 60, 61, 62, 96, 158, 181; as ambassador for M·A·C, 69–70, 135, PLATE 8
haute couture, 118, 120; Bourdieu on, 29–30, 31, 93; of Paris, 67, 69, 77, 78, 80, 124, 192–3, 195
Hayter, Richard, 153, 181
Henri Bendel, 78; as M·A·C's first US retailer, 7, 64–5, 76, 94, 135, 169; RuPaul's launch party at, 158, 195
Hepburn, Audrey, 60
heteronomous production (Bourdieu), 33, 77, 127
H. Halpern Esq. (men's wear retailer), 143
Hicks, Jim, 180
Hilbert, Jeffrey, 212–13
HIV (human immunodeficiency virus), 12, 20, 21, 25, 99–100, 105–8, 110–11, 156, 235*n*37; education/knowledge about, 110, 146–7, 150–1; identification of, 99; transmission of, 115, 146–8. *See also* AIDS
Hoax Couture, 69, 116, 194

Holliday, Morgan, 210, 211–12
Holt Renfrew, 86, 143, 144, 155
homophobia, 105–6, 108, 142, 146–9, 184, 199
Hudson, Rock, 105
Hudson's Bay Company. *See* Bay, The
Hunter, Bruce, 156

i.d. (magazine), 110–11
Il-Makiage (make-up brand), 40–4, 51; as sold at Simpsons, 41–4, PLATES 3–4
Ing, Phillip, 82, 84, 88, 100, 158; on Fashion Blooms, 124–5, 126, 141–2; and Fashion Cares, 111, 113, 114–15, 118, 128, 141–2, 154–5, 195; as joining M·A·C, 155, 165; on M·A·C's philanthropy, 182
ingredients, 55; in early M·A·C products, 43, 45, 46–7; education in use of, 140–1; for global markets, 161, 164, 170; listing of, 47, 75; medical uses of, 140; testing of, 140, 161

Jackson, Ed, 107
Jackson, Janet, 136
Jackson, Michael, 136
James, Blair, 39
Jean Macdonald Beautyworks (Toronto), 52–3
Johns Hopkins University Institute for Alternative Testing Methods, 134
Jones, Geoffrey, 28; *Beauty Imagined*, 9, 50, 53
Judy Welch (Toronto modelling agency), 68

Kain, Karen, 195
Kaposi's sarcoma, 99, 101–2
Kato, Alayne, 121, 125

Kawakubo, Rei, 4
Kenneth Cole (company), 172, 177
Kent, Carmen (Frank Angelo's sister), 185
"Kids Helping Kids" (AIDS fundraiser), 156
King, Samantha: *Pink Ribbons, Inc.*, 16–17
Kirby, David, 174–5, 196, 214
Klein, Calvin, 80, 110, 173–4
Knight, Gladys, 43–4, 55, 162
Koolhaus (Toskan clothing shop), 186
Korpan, Cynthia, 109
Kramer, Larry: *The Normal Heart* (play), 108
Kruger, Barbara, 4
Kushner, Tony: *Angels in America* (play), 155

Lady Bunny, 136, 158, 190, 191
Lady Miss Kier (Deee-Lite), 136
LaChapelle, David: VIVA GLAM postcard (1997) photographed by, 206, PLATE 23; VIVA GLAM II ad (1997) photographed by, 203, PLATE 22
Lagerfeld, Karl, 111
Laing, Jeremy, 3–4
Lancôme (company/brand), 53, 74
Landriault, Pauline, 69
Larouche, Vincent, 133
lang, k.d. (VIVA GLAM spokesperson, 1997), 179–80, 203–6; ad featuring, 8, 12, 26, 34, 180, 188–9, 190, 203–6, 219, PLATE 22; at M·A·C's PETA show, 152; "Miss Chatelaine" video by, 152, 203, 205; at opening of M·A·C's Paris store, 181–2; and *Vanity Fair* cover with Crawford, 204; VIVA

GLAM II lipstick created for, 8, 180, 186–7, 203, 204. *See also* VIVA GLAM lipstick (1997), k.d. lang ad for
Lauder, Estée, 9, 49, 50. *See also* Estée Lauder (company/brand); Estée Lauder Companies Inc., acquisition of M·A·C by
Lauder, Evelyn, 172–3
Lauder, Leonard, 162–3, 218
Lauder, William, 165
Laurence, Peter, 121, 125
Layton, Jack, 109
Lee, Sook-Yin, 188
Leibmann, Wendy, 178
Leibovitz, Annie, 172
Levy, Steven, 82, 83, 86–9, 90, 110, 111
Levy-Young, Bryan, 155
LGBTQ community, 8, 58, 66; AIDS crisis in, 98–109, 147–9; and homophobia, 105–6, 108, 142, 146–9, 184, 199; police raids on/violence against, 107, 207, 213; Pride celebrations of, 3, 207. *See also entry below*; AIDS; drag; drag queens
LGBTQ community in Toronto, 58, 99, 100–4, 128–9, 147–9; activism/organizations of, 106–9; and provincial/city governments, 109, 112, 123–4. *See also* AIDS Committee of Toronto; Casey House; Toronto, drag scene in
Lipartito, Kenneth, 28–9
lipsticks, 50; "D.Q. Red," 211–12; M·A·C, 6, 42, 45–8, 74–5, 135, 138, 169. *See also specific products*
Lise Watier (company/brand), 52, 74. *See also* Watier, Lise
Livingston, Jennie, 192–3
Livingstone, David, 83, 92, 97, 109–10, 152, 191, 194, 211–12; and

Canadian Fashion Annual 1989, 93–5; on Fashion Blooms, 120, 125–6; on Fashion Cares, 113, 115, 142, 143
Locke, Michael, 156
London, 67, 77, 84; M·A·C counter and store in, 169–70
L'Oréal (company/brand), 53
Lundström, Linda, 86
Lynch, Michael, 107, 109, 127–8
Lypsinka, 213, 214

M·A·C (company): acronym of, 43; and art vs commerce, 166, 168, 180, 184–5; business ethics of, 46–8; as Canadian, 8–9, 51–3, 82, 90–1, 94, 159, 203; and cause marketing, 24–7, 176–9, 219–20; counterfeiting of, 161; customer service by, 138–9, 159, 167–8, 183–4; Estée Lauder acquisition of, 9, 24–5, 34, 162–70, 179–85, 186, 188–9, 217–18; "kitchen sink" story of, 6, 45, 49; logo of, 71–2, PLATE 10; long-time rejection of advertising by, 6, 8, 10, 26, 33, 46, 48, 71, 95–8, 157, 159, 205; marketing by, 138–9; media coverage of, 73–5, 88, 90, 91–8, 134, 137–8, 146, 152, 160, 164, 167, 168, 176–9, 180, 185–6, 201; product displays of, 42, 75, PLATE 5; product packaging of, 47–8, 96, 161, 170, 177, 203, PLATE 5; recycling program of, 48, 134, PLATES 15–16; sales of, 65, 66, 139, 160, 169, 186–7; US expansion of, 64–6. *See also entries below*
M·A·C (cosmetics): celebrity clients of, 6, 69–70, 95, 134–5, 136, 138–9; colours/pigmentation of, 6, 41, 42, 44–5, 46, 47, 55–6, 64, 72–5,

135, 137–8, 141, 149–50, 180; as "cosmeceutical," 139; early production of, 43–8; ingredients in, 43, 45, 46–7, 75, 140–1, 161, 164, 170; instructions/tips on applying, 63, PLATES 6–7; matte finish of, 6, 44, 46, 64, 74, 135, 137–8, 151; as not tested on animals, 75, 134, 140–1, 159, PLATES 13–14; price of, 46, 74, 138; as professionals' brand, 6, 44–8, 74, 76, 138, 160–1; and women of colour, 6, 44, 55–6, 64–5, 141

M·A·C AIDS Fund, 5, 8–9, 24–7, 212, 217–19; creation of, 33, 34, 155–6, 236n57; as "creative activism," 5, 10, 29, 33, 159, 215, 218–20; Estée Lauder Co. and, 24–5, 26, 27, 163, 165, 180, 182–3, 217–18; Fashion Cares and, 7, 154–7, 172, 176–9, 188, 212; hands-on approach to, 155–7; k.d. lang and, 201, 206; money raised by, 5, 182, 186–7, 189, 206, 217; recipients of money from, 156–7, 236n59; RuPaul and, 157–8, 191, 201, 203; VIVA GLAM lipstick and, 5, 8–9, 32, 33, 150–2, 155–7. *See also* lang, k.d.; RuPaul; VIVA GLAM lipstick (1992); VIVA GLAM lipstick (1992); VIVA GLAM lipstick (1995); VIVA GLAM lipstick (1997); VIVA GLAM postcard (1997)

"M·A·C Cruelty Free Beauty" T-shirt, 134, 140, 159; postcard of, PLATES 13–14

M·A·C retail counters: at Bendel and Nordstrom, 7, 64–6, 76, 94, 135, 169; in Hong Kong, 170; in London, 169–70; special events at, 146, 158, 195, PLATE 18

M·A·C stand-alone stores, 166; London, 169; New York, 135–7, 158, 190, PLATE 17; Paris, 181–2; Toronto, 6, 60–3, 121, 134, 135

M·A·C store/counter employees, 56–63; all-black clothing of, 59–60; and customers, 61–5; individuality of, 56–7; at New York store, 136–7; at Nordstrom, 65–6; payment of, 59

M·A·C VIVA GLAM Fashion Cares Beautiful World (1998), 188–9

M·A·C VIVA GLAM Fashion Cares Future Perfect (1996), 180–1

M·A·C VIVA GLAM Fashion Cares Photo Ball (1997), 186, 187–8

M·A·C VIVA GLAM Fashion Cares Salute to Suburbia: An Evening of Pure Polyester (1995), 176–7, 195, 200

M·A·C VIVA GLAM Fashion Cares Wings of Life (1994), 155

MacDonald, Gayle, 186

Macdonald, Jean, 52–3

MacKay, John, 91–2

MacKenzie, Sacha, 208, 209

MacKenzie, Valerie, 138–9, 164, 165; customer calls/complaints fielded by, 139, 159, 167–8, 183–4, 201–2

Madonna, 64, 134, 135, 139, 140, 193

Maggiolini, Alessandro, 202

Mahon, Nancy, 24, 27

"Make Up, Make Out, Play Safe" T-shirt, 145–8, 151–2, 159, PLATE 18

make-up application process, 61–3; and instructions/tips for customers, 63, PLATES 6–7; and practice theory, 61–2

Make-up Art Centre (Toskan's original make-up business), 40–9, PLATE 3
Make-up Art Cosmetics, 70, 71; "art" in, 167, 184. *See also* M·A·C (company); M·A·C (cosmetics)
Malone, Annie Turnbo, 50
Manley, Lorraine, 121, 122, 123
Mann, Lisa, 203–4
Manning, Stephen P., 171
Marcelle (cosmetics company), 51
March of Dimes, 15–16
Marriott Hotel Corporation, 15
Marshall Field's, 169
Martin, Dale, 123
Mary Kay (company/brand), 51
Matteson, Sandra, 120–4
Max Factor (company/brand), 49, 138
Maybelline (brand), 51
Mazar, Debi, 64
McCartney, Linda, 69
McCracken, John, 195
McEvoy, Trish, 160
McKay, Jane, 57, 62, 76, 138, 143–4, 164, 165
McLauchlan, Murray, 116
McMurdy, Deirdre, 168
McQueen, Alexander, 4
media coverage: of AIDS crisis, 98–9, 102, 107, 109–10, 112; of M·A·C, 73–5, 88, 90, 91–8, 134, 137–8, 146, 152, 160, 164, 167, 168, 176–9, 180, 185–6, 201; of Toskan, 42–3, 73–5, 90, 149, 185–6. *See also entry below; specific journalists and publications/shows*
media coverage, of fashion industry, 11, 91–8, 120, 201; as AIDS-related, 109–10, 112, 133, 153–4, 173–9; at Fashion Blooms, 122–3, 125–6; at Fashion Cares, 113, 115, 116–17, 153–4, 176, 193; at Festival of Canadian Fashion, 88–90; and M·A·C's decision not to advertise, 95–6, 97–8
Milan, 40, 76, 224*n*4; as fashion centre, 67, 76, 80–1, 82, 84, 89, 92
Miller, Cyndee, 164, 173, 178, 201
Mills, Tracy, 103
Mimran, Joe, 69, 84, 87
Mimran, Saul, 84, 87
Mirabelli, Franco, 110
Miss Chatelaine, 92. *See also Flare*
"Miss Chatelaine" (lang), 152, 203, 205
"Missing" (Everything But The Girl), 181
Miyake, Issey, 4
Montagnier, Luc, 99
Morra, Bernadette, 73, 83, 85, 97, 101, 117, 126, 154, 180, 193
Mugford, Rick, 68, 110; and Fashion Cares, 111–13, 116, 117
Munck, Paula, 113–14
Munro, Lily, 123
Myers-Robertson, Kim, 136–7, PLATE 17
Myles, Alannah, 154

NAMES Project AIDS Memorial Quilt, 173
Nars, François, 160
National Institutes of Health, 110
Ness, Ian, 156
Newton, Esther: *Mother Camp*, 198, 199
New York: as fashion centre, 67, 77–80, 82, 84, 92, 95, 134; and fashion industry's response to AIDS crisis, 101–4, 110, 127, 133–4, 172, 173–4; M·A·C store in, 135–7, 158, 190, PLATE 17; Stonewall riots in, 207, 213; Wigstock drag festival in, 157, 200. *See also* ACT UP

Nickleson, Sara, 3–4
Nordstrom: as M·A·C retailer, 7, 65–6, 76, 94, 169; staff issues at, 65–6; Toskan's appearance at, 146, PLATE 18
North American Free Trade Agreement (NAFTA), 122–3
Notarangelo, Cecilia (Frank Angelo's mother), 185
Notarangelo, Frank. *See* Angelo, Frank
NOW (Toronto newspaper), 113–14, 119, 193

"Obsession" (Animotion), 93
Ogilvy (Montreal department store), 65, 135
Ontario, 52, 181; AIDS cases in, 100; government of, 109, 112, 123
Ontario AIDS Network (OAN), 107, 154
Oscars, Michael, 208–9, 210
Outrageous (film), 194

Palmer, Alexandra (ed.): *Fashion: A Canadian Perspective*, 82
Paris, 29–30, 82, 84, 92, 95; haute couture of, 67, 69, 77, 78–80, 124, 192–3, 195; M·A·C store in, 181–2
Paris Is Burning (documentary), 192–3, 202
Peiss, Kathy: *Hope in a Jar*, 54
PETA (People for the Ethical Treatment of Animals), 4; anti-fur fashion show of, 152, 203
Peter, Bob, 167
Pinney, Nicholas, 144
Politics of Fashion | Fashion of Politics exhibition (Design Exchange, 2014), 3–4, 7
Porter, Les, 210

Ports International (label), 85, 94
Prescriptives (brand), 64, 163
Pride celebrations, 3, 207
Prince, 139
Professional Pharmaceutical Corp., 51

Quant, Mary, 4
Quebec, 83, 85, 109, 181; cosmetics companies in, 51–2

Rabanne, Paco, 30
Radley, Hilary, 83; label of, 94
Rantisi, Norma M., 77–8
Rashid, Karim, 69
Reagan, Ronald, 105
Rechelbacher, Horst, 55
(RED) campaign against HIV/AIDS, 20–4, 27
Revlon (company/brand), 50
Revson, Charles, 9, 50
Richey, Lisa Ann, and Stefano Ponte: *Brand Aid*, 23–4
Richman, Ronnie, 121, 142
Rinascente, La (Milan department store), 81
"Rise Up" (Parachute Club), 3–5, 34, 86, 218
Roberts, Miles, 193
Robertson, Donald, 75, 76, 120; and *Canadian Fashion Annual 1989*, 93; and Fashion Blooms, 121; and Festival of Canadian Fashion program, 88, PLATES 11–12; M·A·C artwork by, 70–1, PLATES 6, 9, 15; "M·A·C Cruelty Free Beauty" T-shirt by, 134, PLATE 13; M·A·C logo by, 71–2, PLATE 10; on M·A·C media coverage, 97; and New York store, 136–7, PLATE 17;

non-commercialism of, 71, 91, 126; "Play Safe" T-shirt by, 145–6, PLATE 18; and RuPaul as first M·A·C spokesperson, 157–8, 200; and RuPaul VIVA GLAM ad, 159, PLATE 21; and VIVA GLAM postcard, 151, PLATE 19
Rocamora, Agnès: *Fashioning the City*, 95; Joanne Entwistle and, 89–90, 117–18
Roddick, Anita, 55. *See also* Body Shop, The (company/brand)
Ronstadt, Linda, 65
Roosevelt, Eleanor, 79
Roots (company/brand), 85, 94, 116, 122
Rosenes, Ron, 181
Rubinstein, Helena, 9, 50, 53, 79
RuPaul (VIVA GLAM spokesperson, 1995), 190–202, 203, 204–5, 236n61; ad featuring, 4–5, 7–8, 12, 26, 34, 157–9, 178–9, 182–4, 190–202, 219, PLATE 21; and AIDS awareness, 214, 215–16; career of, 157–8, 191–2, 194, 198–9, 200; at Fashion Cares events, 181–2, 187, 195; and femininity, 191–2, 197, 201, 202, 206, 214; as first "face" of M·A·C brand, 157–9; as New York store "doorman," 136, 158, 190; in postcard photo with lang and Toskan, 206, PLATE 23; in re-released ad, 8, 216; as "supermodel," 7, 157, 191–2, 193, 198–9; tribute to Angelo by, 187. *See also* VIVA GLAM lipstick (1995), RuPaul ad for
Russell, Craig, 194
"Russian Red" (first M·A·C lipstick), 6, 46, 64, 94, 135, 149

Ryerson Polytechnical Institute (now Ryerson University), 83–4, 107

Saint Laurent, Yves, 30
Saks Fifth Avenue, 169
Sanchez, Albert: VIVA GLAM ad (1995) photographed by, 159, PLATE 21
Schacht, Steven P., and Lisa Underwood, 199, 206–7
Scherrer, Jean-Louis, 33
Schiffer, Claudia, 191
School of Makeup Art (Toronto), 71
schools/courses: of fashion design, 79, 83–4, 85, 123; hairdressing (Angelo), 43; make-up, 51, 71
Scott, Linda M.: *Fresh Lipstick*, 54
Searle, Jim, 69. *See also* Hoax Couture
Sebastian International (hair care company), 154
Segato, Lorraine, 3. *See also* "Rise Up" (Parachute Club)
Seibu (Hong Kong), M·A·C counter at, 170
7th on Sale (New York AIDS fundraiser), 134
Shaver, Dorothy, 79
Sheffman, Susie, 84, 85; on AIDS crisis, 101, 103; on Fashion Cares, 128; on Festival of Canadian Fashion, 87–8, 90–1; on M·A·C, 12, 70
Sheinman, Mort, 102, 229n80
Shimmerman, Allan, 156
Shriver, Bobby, 20
Sigismondi, Floria: Toskan postcard photographed by, 146, PLATE 18
Silversides, Ann, 112; Lynch biography by, 127–8
Simpsons, 121, 143, 154, 225n5; Haircutting Place at, 39–43, 60–1, 69, PLATE 4; M·A·C's

beginnings at, 41–3, 57, 59, 61, 64, 65; M·A·C's make-up launch at, 135
Smith, Willi, 103
Sontag, Susan: *AIDS and Its Metaphors*, 100
Stanish, Stephen, 151
Stonewall riots (New York, 1969), 207, 213
Studio Fix (M·A·C foundation), 141
Sturdza, Marina, 88, 90, 93–4, 97
Style with Elsa Klensch (CNN), 93
Sung, Alfred, 69, 76, 84–5, 87, 94, 122, 142
"Supermodel (You Better Work)" (RuPaul), 7, 157, 191–2, 193, 199
supermodels, 21, 65, 135, 191–2, 204; drag culture emulation/impersonation of, 3, 7, 157, 191–3, 198–9, 200–1. *See also individual models by name*
Susan G. Komen Foundation, 17

Tant, Lisa, 74–5
Taylor, Elizabeth, 110
Taylor, Niki, 191
Tempé, Antoine: Midnight Divas photo exhibit of, 193–4
Terrence Higgins Trust (UK), 111
Testino, Mario, 68
Tetro, Pier, 148, 181
Tiegs, Cheryl, 54
toll-free (1-800) customer service number, as set up by M·A·C, 159, 167–8, 183–4
Toronto, drag scene in, 193–4, 206–12; "D.Q." fundraisers of, 207–12
Toronto, fashion industry in, 81–91; and AIDS crisis, 30, 98–129; media coverage of, 91–8

Toronto, gay/lesbian community in. *See also* LGBTQ community in Toronto
Toronto Health Board, 109
Toronto Life Fashion, 6, 71, 91–2, 96
Toronto Ontario Designers (TOD), 86
Toronto People with AIDS Foundation, 108
Toscani, Oliviero, 4; and Kirby photo, 174–5, 196, 214
Toskan, Frank, 5, 6, 37–48, PLATE 1; background/family of, 37–8; early laundry business of, 39–40, 43–4; early photography work by, 40, 42, 44, 61, 190; as "face" of M·A·C brand, 75–6, PLATES 7, 12, 18; first boyfriend of, 147–8; and first meeting with Angelo, 39; hair care products developed by, 40–1, 42, 43–4, 45, 162; and instructions/face charts for customers, PLATE 6; "kitchen sink" story of, 6, 45, 49; and later separation from Angelo, 168; Make-up Art Centre of, 40–9, PLATE 3; make-up tutorial video by, 63, PLATE 7; media coverage of, 42–3, 73–5, 90, 149, 185–6; new partner/family of, 168, 218; and "Play Safe" T-shirt, 145–8, 151–2, 159, PLATE 18; and products developed with Casale, 43–8; tributes to, 5, 8, 218. *See also* "Franks, the"
Toskan, Guido (Frank Toskan's father), 38
Toskan, Julie (Frank Toskan's sister; later Toskan-Casale), 38, 40, 43, 45, 165–6, 170, 184, 186, 188, 217

Toskan, Steven (Frank Toskan's brother), 38
Toskan, Sylvia (Frank Toskan's mother), 38, 40
Toskan, Walter (Frank Toskan's brother), 38
Trigère, Pauline, 102
T-shirts, 4, 11, 20, 21, 174; Fashion Blooms, 121; Fashion Cares (Toronto), 112, 114, 116, 118, 142, 189, 231n39; Fashion Cares (UK), 111, 118; "M·A·C Cruelty Free Beauty," 134, 140, 159; "Make Up, Make Out, Play Safe," 145–8, 151–2, 159, PLATE 18
Turkis, Sam, 88, 113
Turlington, Christy, 21, 191
Turner, Eric, 208, 209
Twiggy: M·A·C lipstick named after, 135, 169
Twilight Zone, The (Toronto nightclub), 68, 69, 72
Tyrell, Chris, 69. *See also* Hoax Couture

Ulmer, Rod, 41–2, 59, 154
"underdogs," of M·A·C's community/clientele, 58, 128–9
Ungaro, Emanuel, 30
Unilever, 17, 53

Vanderbilt, Gloria, 80
Vanity Fair, 21, 178–9, 204
Venus Xtravaganza, 202
Vidal Sassoon (hair salon), 68, 115, 124, 142
VIVA GLAM lipstick (1992), 5, 8–9, 32, 33, 150–2, 155–7; and AIDS information campaign, 150–1; postcard for, 151–2, PLATES 19–20. *See also entries below*

VIVA GLAM lipstick (1995), RuPaul ad for, 4–5, 7–8, 12, 26, 34, 157–9, 178–9, 182–4, 190–202, 219, PLATE 21; complaints about/discomfort with, 183–4, 201–2, 214; critical analysis of, 195–200; re-release of (2013), 8, 216; women and, 192, 196, 198, 201–2, 205
VIVA GLAM lipstick (1997), k.d. lang ad for, 8, 12, 26, 34, 180, 188–9, 190, 203–6, 219, PLATE 22; critical analysis of, 204–5
VIVA GLAM postcard (1997), 206, PLATES 23–24
Vogue, 134, 137, 179, 193, 201
"Vogue" (Madonna), 193
voguing, 3, 192–3

Walker, Madam C.J., 9, 50
Walton, Michael, 122
Warhol, Andy, 69
Washington Fashion Group, Scholarship Fund of, 110
Watier, Lise, 51–2, 54. *See also* Lise Watier (company/brand)
Weinberg, Chester, 103
Weiss, Angeline Lucinda, 195–7, 204–5
Westwood, Vivienne, 4, 111
Wigstock (New York drag festival), 157, 200
Willi Ninja, 193
Wilson Phillips, 139
Winfrey, Oprah, 21
women: AIDS and, 99, 134, 228n72; beauty/cosmetics advertising and, 18–20, 49–50, 53–5, 157, 160, 196, 205–6; Bourdieu on, 31; of colour, 6, 9, 44, 50, 53–4, 55–6, 64–5, 141, 201–2; as cosmetics

entrepreneurs, 50, 51–3, 55; fashion industry and, 79; RuPaul VIVA GLAM ad and, 192, 196, 198, 201–2, 205; transgendered, 183, 192–3, 202, 211
Women's Wear Daily (WWD), 79, 84, 102, 133
WOW (Toronto boutique), 68, 110, 121

Yamamoto, Yohji, 4
Yoplait yogurt, 17
Young, Denny, 121

Zakreski, Darren, 218
Zarb, Emily, 94, 110
Zekas, Rita, 93, 242*n*58
Zuckerman, Gabriella, 178